ARCHAEOLOGICAL
ETHICS

Locations Mentioned in the Book

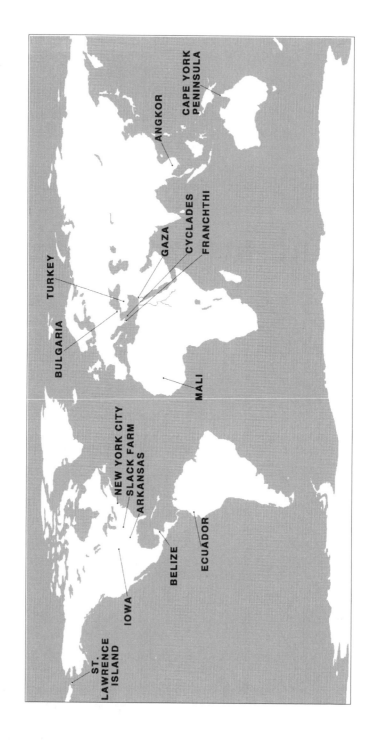

Archaeological Ethics

Edited by
Karen D. Vitelli

Readings from Archaeology *magazine*

ALTAMIRA
PRESS

A Division of Sage Publications, Inc.
Walnut Creek • London • New Delhi

For information address:

AltaMira Press
A Division of Sage Publications, Inc.
1630 North Main Street, Suite 367
Walnut Creek, CA 94596

SAGE Publications Ltd.
6 Bonhill Street
London EC2A 4PU
United Kingdom

SAGE Publications India Pvt. Ltd.
M-32 Market
Greater Kailash I
New Delhi 110 048 India

Printed in the United States of America

Library of Congress Cataloging-in-Publication Data

Vitelli, Karen D.
Archaeological Ethics by Karen D. Vitelli
        p. cm   Includes bibliographical references.
ISBN 0-7619-0530-8 (cloth) ISBN 0-7619-0531-6 (pbk.)
1. Archaeology—Moral and ethical aspects. 2 Antiquities—Collection and preservation—Moral and ethical aspects. I. Vitelli, Karen D.
CC175.A715   1996
930.1—dc20   96-9983
                                                        CIP

96 97 98 99 10 9 8 7 6 5 4 3 2 1

Interior Design and Production by Labrecque Publishing Services
Cover Design by Jack Scott

TABLE OF CONTENTS

6

ABOUT THE EDITOR

Karen D. Vitelli received her Ph.D. in classical archaeology from the University of Pennsylvania in 1974. She has done fieldwork, primarily on prehistoric sites, in Greece, Turkey, and the eastern United States. From 1976 to 1983 she served as editor and columnist for the regular feature "The Antiquities Market" in the *Journal of Field Archaeology*. During that time, she also participated as a delegate from the Archaeological Institute of America in the congressional hearings on implementing the UNESCO Convention. She is active in professional organizations, especially in areas concerned with ethics: she recently completed a term as Vice President for Professional Responsibilities for the Archaeological Institute of America, has been a certified member of the Society of Professional Archaeologists since 1978, and serves on the Ethics Committee of the Society for American Archeology. Her special interests, besides ethics, are in prehistoric ceramics and using experimental ceramic approaches to explore questions about social and economic organization in the Greek Neolithic. She is a professor of anthropology at Indiana University, Bloomington.

PREFACE

For the last several years I have offered a seminar on archaeological ethics, encouraged to do so by Clemency Coggins' enthusiastic accounts of her experience teaching a similar course. Clemency, who had already done so much to bring these issues to the forefront of archaeologists' attention, was right again. My students and I have been profoundly affected by our discussions. We have come from the experience with a desire to share it and to engage others in similar discussions, that they may help find creative solutions to the pressing problems facing the cultural heritage of the world. This collection of articles from *Archaeology* magazine, and the additional materials and suggestions, represent an effort to make it easier for others to engage these issues.

Clemency's class was offered in an art history department. Mine is in an anthropology department. It would be equally at home in a number of other departments. My seminar is available for undergraduate and graduate credit, and the enrollments have been about equally divided. I've had majors from anthropological and classical archaeology, sociocultural and bioanthropology, ancient history, classics, art history, and law. Several students were also recreational sport divers. Some arrived with considerable background in archaeology and a fairly sophisticated and impassioned sense of the issues, others, with little background and only a vague notion of what we would be discussing. A surprising number signed up because of an uncomfortable experience in a field school or classroom, or with a looted site or artifacts, and wanted to explore their own responses.

Regardless of background and initial motivation, every student was quickly caught up in the subject. I've never had to work less to get discussions going; rarely had better, livelier, and more thoughtful papers or more commitment from an entire class. Students seem to respond because, in the context of ethics, archaeology clearly plays a significant role in the larger issues of today's world. It touches our lives and gives each individual a chance to contribute meaningfully, whether as a professional or interested member of the public; it requires grappling with difficult and challenging questions for which the teacher doesn't have the "right" answers (and few answers are absolutely "wrong"); and it gives plenty of room for honest disagreement, lively debate, and new approaches.

Last year, several of the graduate students in the class were teaching their own introductory archaeology classes and decided to see if their students would respond to some of the issues we had been discussing. Without prompting or advice from me, Leslie Bush and Mary Pirkl assigned to their classes an article or two from *Archaeology*. They chose short articles, written in clear, compelling, and accessible language, that raised questions related to points or material the classes had already discussed in other contexts. Both Leslie and Mary were amazed and delighted at the quality of the dialogue the articles prompted. Kevin Glowacki, a colleague in classical studies, had also been assigning articles from *Archaeology* to his Introduction to Classical Archaeology classes, with excellent results. When I mentioned to Mary and Leslie that he had suggested "someone put together a collection of *Archaeology* articles for a reprint edition on ethics," they immediately volunteered to get the project started.

Soon joined by an equally enthusiastic undergraduate, Lori Crittendon, the three scholars combed the 48 volumes of *Archaeology*, reaching back to 1948 (and *Archaeology*'s predecessor, *Art and Archaeology* from 1914 to 1934[1]), extracting everything that had potential value for such a collection. The original stack of photocopies was a good 12 inches high—a formidable pile, and ample testimony to the admirable job *Archaeology* magazine has been doing for nearly half a

---

[1]The issues we are concerned about today are not all new. In 1916, concern over the destruction of monuments during WWI prompted Charles Weller to write an article, "The Destruction of the Parthenon." The same issue also featured "How England Acquired the Elgin Marbles," by William Hyde Appleton.

century in bringing the socially important work and questions of archaeology to a popular audience.

Mary, Leslie, and Lori screened the articles and sorted them into categories, reducing the pile by about half. This provided an excellent guide for my work on the final selection and presentation. Obviously, there are many more good articles in *Archaeology* than we have been able to include in this collection. Mary, especially, and Julie Zimmer— another classmate, now doing dissertation research with the "subsistence diggers" on St. Lawrence Island in Alaska (see the article by Scott, "St. Lawrence: Archaeology of a Bering Sea Island")— have prodded and pushed me to move this project to the top of my agenda. They have provided ongoing assistance, discussion, and enthusiasm, and ensured that Kevin's suggestion became a reality. Patty Gerstenblith and Alice Wickizer provided needed advice on locating legal and government documents. Early in the collecting stage, Peter Young and Phyllis Pollak Katz, editor and publisher of *Archaeology*, provided enthusiastic encouragement. Mitch Allen and Brian Fagan read the initial, much longer draft and gently helped cut it down to a more manageable size. Christina Burke, Mindy Morgan, Caroline Owens, and Ben Stolz served as designated guinea pigs, evaluating the selection of articles and commentary and providing constructive criticism. Kevin Glowacki was generous with his experience and time, as was Ellen Herscher.

We have grouped the articles into broad categories, although nearly every article raises questions that overlap with other categories. We have included a brief summary of each article, to aid in selection of readings, and a list of potential discussion and research questions that follow from each article. Occasionally we've suggested additional reading on a subject to tempt further exploration, but these suggestions are by no means exhaustive. For those wanting to pursue additional research relating to specific articles, we recommend beginning with the suggestions for "Further Reading" that are located in the back of the *Archaeology* issue in which the original publication appeared.

Underwater archaeologists may feel slighted by this collection. Articles on shipwreck archaeology in *Archaeology* magazine have presented positive accounts of archaeological projects, but to date, none that we thought provoked discussion of the many ethical concerns specific to shipwreck archaeology. The popular media are full of publications by treasure salvors; thus their side of the story is widely available. It is more difficult for nonprofessionals to find articulate and compelling presentations of the archaeological side.[2] Perhaps some colleagues will take this observation as a challenge.

Our intent for the present collection was to make available, as quickly as possible, an affordable, lively group of papers that will get discussions started. We wanted to make it easy to begin, but also wanted to leave plenty of room for creative research and new ideas. We hope some professors will choose to use the entire collection as a text for a course on ethics, but each of them is likely to have different areas of interest and focus, and most will want to do additional research and add other topics and readings. Other professors or leaders in student organizations or non-academic groups may want to use just one or two articles for a single discussion session. Individuals may simply want to stimulate their own thinking on the subject.

However you choose to use this collection, we hope it will make you think about the role of archaeology in the modern world. We encourage readers to look at papers that address issues outside their own particular area of expertise and interest. People concerned, for example, primarily with North American reburial issues related to the Native American Graves Protection and Repatriation Act could learn much from the experience of the African-American Cemetery case in New York City (see the article by Harrington, "Bones and Bureaucrats"); from the experiences of archaeologists and Aborigines in Australia (see the article by Gray, "Champion of Aboriginal Art"); and from the more general discussion of "People Without History" (McIntosh, McIntosh, and Togola). Archaeologists and art historians of all periods and places would do well to read carefully and consider the many issues raised by Brent in "The Rape of Mali"; to think about

---

[2]The Society for Amercian Archaeology's recent Special Report, *Ethics in Amercian Archaeology: Challenges for the 1990s*, edited by Mark J. Lynott and Alison Wylie, makes several papers on the subject readily available to land-based professionals.

the unfortunately timely problems of cultural property in times of war and social unrest (all of Part III); of the impression archaeologists make on the local people when and where they do fieldwork (Scott, "St. Lawrence: Archaeology of a Bering Sea Island"; McGuire, "The Gringo Stigma"); and of our responsibilities to make public the results of that fieldwork (Chase, Chase, and Topsey, "Archaeology and the Ethics of Collecting"; Fagan, "Archaeology's Dirty Secret"). None of the issues raised in this collection is unique to a particular geographical area or specialty within the field. These are worldwide issues.

About half the students in my class this year chose to end their papers with the same quote. It seems an appropriate choice with which to end this preface, as well.

"Ethical responsibility is not beside the point of archaeology; it is the only thing that will keep our discipline alive."[3]

ACKNOWLEDGMENTS

The editor and publisher would like to acknowledge the following for rights to reprint articles in this volume.

Chapter 1: Archaeology and the Ethics of Collecting, originally published in *Archaeology* 41:1, 56–60, 87 (Jan/Feb 1988). Reprinted with the permission of *Archaeology* magazine, copyright Archaeological Institute of America.

Chapter 2: Black Day at Slack Farm, originally published in *Archaeology* 41:4, 15–16, 73 (Jul/Aug 1988). Reprinted with the permission of the author.

Chapter 3: Daring to Deal with Huaqueros, originally published in *Archaeology* 45:3, 15–16, 73 (Jul/Aug 1993). Reprinted with the permission of *Archaeology* magazine, copyright Archaeological Institute of America.

Chapter 4: A Seductive and Troubling Work, originally published in Archaeology 46:1, 64–69 (Jan/Feb 1993). Reprinted with the permission of *Archaeology* magazine, copyright Archaeological Institute of America.

Chapter 5: Project Sting, originally published in *Archaeology* 46:5, 52–56 (Sep/Oct 1993). Reprinted with the permission of *Archaeology* magazine, copyright Archaeological Institute of America.

Chapter 6: Turkey's War on the Illicit Antiquities Trade, Turkey's Claims Abroad, and Flattery Will Get You Everywhere originally published in *Archaeology*

---

[3]K. Anne Pyburn and Richard R. Wilk, "Responsible Archaeology is Applied Anthropology," in *Ethics in American Archaeology: Challenges for the 1990s*, eds. Mark Lynott and Alison Wylie, page 76.

48:2, 45–50 (Mar/Apr 1995). Reprinted with the permission of *Archaeology* magazine, copyright Archaeological Institute of America.

Chapter 7: The Looting of Arkansas and Buying and Selling the Past, originally published in *Archaeology* 44:3, 22–30 (May/Jun 1991). Reprinted with the permission of *Archaeology* magazine, copyright Archaeological Institute of America.

Chapter 8: Enlightened Stewardship, originally published in *Archaeology* 48:3, 12–16, 77 (May/Jun 1995). Reprinted with the permission of the author.

Chapter 9: The Looting of Bulgaria, originally published in *Archaeology* 46:2, 26–27 (Mar/Apr 1993). Reprinted with the permission of *Archaeology* magazine, copyright Archaeological Institute of America.

Chapter 10: The Glory that was Angkor, originally published in *Archaeology* 47:2, 39–49 (Mar/Apr 1994). Reprinted with the permission of *Archaeology* magazine, copyright Archaeological Institute of America.

Chapter 11: Securing Sites in Time of War, originally published in *Archaeology* 44:3, 43 (May/Jun 1991). Reprinted with the permission of *Archaeology* magazine, copyright Archaeological Institute of America.

Chapter 12: Operation Scroll, originally published in *Archaeology* 47:2, 27–28 (Mar/Apr 1994). Reprinted with the permission of *Archaeology* magazine, copyright Archaeological Institute of America.

Chapter 13: Who Owns the Spoils of War? and the Limits of World Law originally published in *Archaeology* 48:4, 46–52 (Jul/Aug 1995). Reprinted with the permission of *Archaeology* magazine, copyright Archaeological Institute of America.

Chapter 14: St. Lawrence: Archaeology of a Bering Sea Island, originally published in *Archaeology* 37:1, 46–52 (Jan/Feb 1984). Reprinted with the permission of *Archaeology* magazine, copyright Archaeological Institute of America.

Chapter 15: The Rape of Mali and The Plight of Ancient Jenne, originally published in *Archaeology* 47:3, 26–35 (May/Jun 1994). Reprinted with the permission of *Archaeology* magazine, copyright Archaeological Institute of America.

Chapter 16: Champion of Aboriginal Art, originally published in *Archaeology* 46:4, 44–47 (Jul/Aug 1993). Reprinted with the permission of *Archaeology* magazine, copyright Archaeological Institute of America.

Chapter 17: People Without History, originally published in *Archaeology* 42:1, 74–81 (Jan/Feb 1989). Reprinted with the permission of *Archaeology* magazine, copyright Archaeological Institute of America.

Chapter 18: Reburial: Is It Reasonable?, originally published in *Archaeology* 38:5, 48–51 (Sep/Oct 1985). Reprinted with the permission of *Archaeology* magazine, copyright Archaeological Institute of America.

Chapter 19: Burying American Archaeology and Sharing Control of the Past, originally published in *Archaeology* 47:6, 64–68 (Nov/Dec 1994). Reprinted with the permission of *Archaeology* magazine, copyright Archaeological Institute of America.

Chapter 20: Bones and Bureaucrats and Stories the Bones Will Tell, originally published in *Archaeology* 47:6, 28–38 (Nov/Dec 1994). Reprinted with the permission of *Archaeology* magazine, copyright Archaeological Institute of America.

Chapter 21: The Arrogant Archaeologist, originally published in *Archaeology* 46:6, 14–16 (Nov/Dec 1993) Reprinted with the permission of the author.

Chapter 22: The Gringo Stigma, originally published in *Archaeology* 47:4, 72 (Jul/Aug 1994). Reprinted with the permission of *Archaeology* magazine, copyright Archaeological Institute of America.

Chapter 23: Archaeology's Dirty Secret, originally published in *Archaeology* 48:4, 14–17 (Jul/Aug 1995). Reprinted with the permission of the author.

Appendix A: Codes of Ethics of Society of Professional Archeologists, Archaeological Institute of America, and Society for American Archaeology reprinted with permission of those organizations.

INTRODUCTION

I stumbled into the complicated and fascinating subject of archae-ological ethics in the early 1970s. Late in the term, a student who had never spoken in class before, raised his hand. The class had just read Plato's *Symposium* and then gone to the local art museum to find objects and representations of everything they would have needed to host a similar event. The young man, to my surprise, began by reminding me of my lecture early in the term about the permitting procedures that archaeologists must go through in Greece before conducting any kind of archaeological fieldwork and the fact that we were forbidden by law to take any of our finds out of the country—indeed, needed additional permits to get into the storerooms to study the material we had excavated or recovered in surveys. If that was the case, he said, how did the museum get all its neat stuff out of Greece?

After a stuttering initial response, I remember coming back to the class with a gallery sales catalogue (could I have written to one of the galleries that used to advertise in *Archaeology*?), absolutely stunned when it sank in that anyone with enough money could buy ancient Greek objects. And those objects were better preserved, more nearly intact examples of some things than I had ever seen before. Since they were intact pieces, I suspected they came from looted tombs, which was bad enough; but I also wondered how the looters could find better examples than people conducting careful, systematic archaeological excavations.

Yes, I, too, was naive about such things, but in the early 1970s most archaeologists were. We'd never seriously thought about why Greece, and other countries, had such tough permitting and export laws. They were simply an annoying fact of doing archaeology abroad. We were busy discovering environmental and ethnoarchaeology, designing water sieves and theoretical models. But at least for those of us working outside of North America, it was precisely those new methodological concerns, which focused our attention very clearly on precise excavation techniques, records, and context, that eventually made us see that the "said to be from" pieces in museum galleries are not the "best examples of," but represent the incredible and permanent loss of information from looted sites.

Pursuing a response to my student's question led me to the UNESCO Convention on Cultural Property, which the U.S. Senate had ratified in 1972. I became involved, with a number of colleagues, in working on and for the U.S. implementing legislation. In doing this, many of us received our first direct experience in the fascinating and frustrating process of lawmaking in the U.S. Congress. We learned about the needs for compromise, the many interested parties, the pressures of lobbies and election politics, the power of numbers, and the lack of a broad public understanding of just what archaeology is and does. As most Americans did, and probably still do, I had assumed that if it was illegal to export artifacts from Greece or any other country, it was illegal to import them into the United States. Stolen goods are stolen goods. In fact, it isn't so simple—at least, not for antiquities. That point remains one of the stickiest in all cultural property law. My layperson's explanation will probably not satisfy any legal scholar, but here it is.

Most countries, including Greece, have antiquities laws in which the government claims ownership of all archaeological materials, whether in state or private museums and collections, or as yet undiscovered in buried archaeological sites. Sometimes the laws allow private individuals to buy and sell such materials within the country.[1] That is, individuals may legally *possess* the objects, but the state *owns* them and controls where they may go.[2] Exporting any archaeological material without a government permit, therefore, constitutes theft *in*

---

[1]Hence the ancient objects for sale in tourist shops in Greece and elsewhere.

[2]The tourist shops may or may not tell you that if you buy an ancient object, you still need to get a government export license to export it legally, and you probably won't be granted one.

that country, under that country's antiquities laws. But no nation automatically agrees to enforce all the laws of any other country. Think about it, and you'll come up with lots of examples: the first ones that enter my mind are the manuscripts that were smuggled out of the former Soviet Union and legally published in the free world. In many cases of antiquities removed illegally from a foreign country, nothing more than an honest declaration of age and value to U.S. Customs is required for legal import into the United States.

The legal issues revolve around questions of ownership. If the imported antiquities can be verifiably documented as having been stolen from a previous owner, then U.S. courts will consider the case, subject to all the complexities of stolen property law. Thus, if an object was inventoried and photographed in a way that it could be uniquely identified as having recently been in the collection of the National Museum in Athens or the excavation storerooms for Mycenae, there would be little question in a U.S. courtroom that the object now in the United States was stolen from Greece. In this way, the Cypriot Orthodox Church, able to document with earlier publications the presence of the Kanakaria mosaics in a church in Kanakaria, Cyprus, prior to their being offered for sale in Indianapolis, Indiana, made their case compelling.[3] Similar concerns no doubt prompted the Ward Gallery lawyers to inquire of the Greek Ministry of Culture whether they recognized the pieces in Ward's collection as having come from Greece.[4] When the answer was negative, the lawyers felt justified in claiming the objects were not stolen (Rose 1993, 28).

That brings us to the more common and difficult situation regarding ownership and theft of antiquities: how does one prove that objects never even seen in modern times (i.e., looted objects) came from a specific country, much less a specific site? How could the Greek, or

---

[3]On the Kanakaria mosaics case, see Dan Hofstadter, "Annals of the Antiquities Trade: The Angel on her Shoulder (Part 1)." *The New Yorker*, 13 July, 1992:36–65. (Part 2) *The New Yorker*, 20 July, 1992:38–65.

[4]Mark Rose, "Greece Sues for Mycenaean Gold." *Archaeology*, (Sept/Oct 1993): 26–30, and Mark Rose, "Mycenaean Gold Returned," *Archaeology*, (March/April 1994): 19.

any other authorities, recognize or document as stolen the objects in the Ward collection if they had been looted and smuggled out of the country, since only the looters could have known that the pieces existed? The same issue determined the outcome of the Sevso case, in which neither Croatia nor Hungary could prove that the Roman treasure had been excavated within its borders.[5] It is this inability to prove the specific origin of previously undocumented—indeed, unknown—material that ultimately allows museums and others to claim legitimately that their acquisition of looted antiquities is legal under U.S. law. It is the problem that allows the illicit antiquities market to flourish, that opens doors for forgeries to circulate unde-tected, and that, to date, has stumped all legal efforts to stop the trade in looted archaeological materials at the point of sale.

Of course, once materials have reached the point of sale, their archaeological value has already been compromised, and the site of origin (assuming the pieces are genuine) destroyed. Much as we may applaud efforts such as Turkey's (see the article by Rose and Acar, "Turkey's War on the Illicit Antiquities Trade") to recover materials from abroad, restoring objects to their country of origin does not undo the damage done by the original undocumented excavation. Turkey's strategy, ultimately, is to make the acquisition of illegally exported Turkish antiquities potentially so expensive because of the likelihood of protracted lawsuits, that museums and individuals will cease acquir-ing illicit Turkish artifacts, the market will dry up, and thus, the looting in Turkey will come to a stop.

The antiquities laws of all nations are important and should be studied, adhered to, and used by archaeologists to bring public atten-tion to the many layers of issues they encompass (see the articles by Neary, "Project Sting," and Bailey, "The Looting of Bulgaria"). The laws may even get through to individuals who are unimpressed with ethical and moral arguments, but persuaded by the threat of an arrest

---

[5]Barbara Hoffman, "The Sevso Follies of 1994." *Archaeology*, (May/June 1994): 42–43. On this case, see also David D'Arcy. "Shadow of the Sevso Treasure," *Vanity Fair*, (October 1993): 151–52, 154–68 (even pages only).

and fine or jail sentence. Archaeologists might also want to work for laws that would reward the conservation of sites, rather than penalize offenders after the damage is done. But laws and their enforcement alone are not going to preserve archaeological information and sites. As archaeologists, we need not worry over much about our legal expertise and understanding of the intricacies of the laws regarding archaeological materials. Rather, we should be finding ways to put our own special archaeological expertise to work on the problems. We might begin by looking at ourselves and our profession. Are we doing things that could be contributing to and encouraging the destruction of what we are pledged to preserve? (See the articles by Elia, "A Seductive and Troubling Work," Harrington, "The Looting of Arkansas," and Fagan's and McGuire's papers in Part VI.) Exploring that question is what takes us into the much broader field of archaeological ethics, which encompasses not only our professional responsibilities to materials, sites, and colleagues, but also to the many people who are affected by archaeological work.

One need not be trained in philosophy, an expert in cultural property law, or even have followed closely the fast-growing body of literature on the subject, to be qualified to teach a course on archaeological ethics. Any serious and conscientious archaeologist will discover that she or he harbors a wealth of relevant experience as soon as the readings and discussions begin. We've all been guided by and are practicing some level of professional ethics all along, whether or not we've examined them explicitly and critically.

Considering how we have contributed to current problems means looking at everything we do as professionals, from developing peoples' interest in antiquity, to how we treat our students and peers, to the impact of our work on descendant people and the local communities in which we work (see Parts IV and V). Once we start talking and thinking seriously about the implications of all that we do, the subjects not tackled directly in this collection will come up. I am convinced that the result will be a stronger and more effective discipline that will contribute in even more significant ways to the changing world in which we live and practice.

21

We should remember, too, that ethics are culturally based and vary from place to place, profession to profession, and over time. Professional archaeologists and colleagues in related disciplines have developed, or are developing, codes of professional standards and practice for today (see Appendix A). You might find it interesting to look at other codes—earlier statements and those from other societies, professions, and countries. These, too will change, as the issues facing us change and as new ideas and approaches emerge. Context is as meaningful to our ethical discussions as it is to our archaeological research. We may soon look back on reburial and the stringent export laws of the 1990s with the same sense of disbelief we now feel looking at the dealers' ads of the 1960s in *Archaeology*. But if we are to find better solutions and maintain and develop archaeology as a proud, contributing discipline, we must make responsible, thoughtful, aware behavior an essential part of our training and experience.

Today almost everyone, archaeologist and nonarchaeologist alike, is "against" looting, but on close examination it turns out that we have many different ideas about what exactly constitutes looting and what precisely is wrong with it. Nonarchaeologists often say that looters break things, steal, miss important material, don't always know what is important, or don't keep records. Archaeologists, on the other hand, generally decry the loss of "contextual information." That phrase conjures up a wealth of meaning for fellow archaeologists, but few nonarchaeologists fully comprehend what we mean and understand by "contextual information" and, thus, the extent of the loss when a site is looted. Just such a misunderstanding underlies a legal scholar's recent suggestion for a way to legalize the market in antiquities.[6] I think that this failure of communication is also responsible for much of the antagonism among interested groups in this country, and is largely the fault of professional archaeologists. We have a large, interested audience who are fascinated by the adventure of archaeology, by the thrill of digging buried treasure, by the beautiful and

---

[6]See Lisa J. Borodkin, "The Economics of Antiquities Looting and a Proposed Legal Alternative," *Columbia Law Review*, (March 1995): 1–36, especially page 17.

strange objects that we find and they see in museums and the media (and sometimes in our offices or homes), by the high-tech tools that magically reveal unexpected turns, and by the stories we weave about ancient peoples. "Context," to them, means finding deer bones inside a big pot sitting on a pile of charcoal—a rare, if spine-tingling event.

Ultimately, archaeologists are responsible for the public's image of archaeology. If we don't convey in our writings and public talks (and too often still don't even use fully in our own research) the many ways in which carefully documented, stratigraphic excavation and analyses contribute fundamentally to our work and results, then how can we expect nonspecialists to understand and respect our laments about loss of context? The modern discipline of archaeology is a dramatically different animal than the one I studied as a graduate student 25 years ago. We've made tremendous leaps in sophistication and sensitivity, but we have, by and large, failed to bring the public with us, to find vivid ways of conveying the complexity of the work, and to make very clear the roles that context plays in all of it.

I certainly don't claim to have all the answers, or even good ones. But I do try, in classes, in my research and writing, and in public talks about my research, to illustrate the role of contextual information, and to demonstrate *how* we arrive at our conclusions, not just what those conclusions are. I try to show that it is not the individual object that produces the story, but the whole process of how it came to be where it was buried. An example that makes an impact on students comes from the site I have worked on most extensively—Franchthi Cave in southern Greece. I tell it here (see the case study following the introduction) to encourage readers to discuss the role of context in archaeological work *before* you go on to digest and discuss the many other issues that are covered in this collection. Every archaeologist will have other, probably better, examples from his or her own experience, or will have ideas about how to get the message across in a vivid, compelling way. It is my hope, in presenting this collection, that readers will be inspired to share those examples widely; indeed, that you will come up with constructive responses to the many questions raised in the pages that follow.

PALAEOLITHIC OBSIDIAN
FROM FRANCHTHI CAVE: A CASE
STUDY IN ARCHAEOLOGICAL CONTEXT

Franchthi is a large prehistoric cave on the southern tip of the Argolid on mainland Greece, with occupation extending from the Upper Paleolithic through the Neolithic. It was excavated in the late 1960s and early 1970s, using many techniques that were quite innovative at the time. All the excavated soil was passed through a sieve, much of it through a water sieve, the first in Greece. The 5mm mesh sieve produced small mountains of what looked like pea gravel, all carefully labeled as to stratigraphic origin, and in need of laborious sorting into its components. Everyone on the project took a turn, sitting with a pile of "residue" and a paintbrush, moving the pile, piece by piece, into smaller piles of marine or land shell, carbon, flaked stone, ceramics, bone, etc. Some years we hired local teenagers to work steadily on the sorting. We devised elaborate systems of sampling, so that we might have useful information available before we all reached retirement. Meanwhile, we went ahead with our analyses of the larger materials recovered from the trenches.

In 1978, years after we had stopped excavating, we had the first of several symposia in Bloomington, Indiana, for all members of the publication staff to get together, exchange, and compare information from our analyses to date. Fifteen or twenty of us sat around the large seminar table, already exhausted from the intensity of several days of discussion (and as a local, I didn't suffer the additional jet lag of my European and West Coast colleagues). We were considering the sequence of excavated units that removed the Upper Palaeolithic and earliest Mesolithic deposits in the cave. We had heard Bill Farrand, our geoarchaeologist, present his analysis of the rate of sedimentation for the deposits. Nancy Whitney had reviewed their land snail content. Judith Shackleton had graphed the changing patterns of marine shell remains. Bas Payne had told us of the variety of mammalian fauna and the changes that appeared to be taking place as he moved up the sequence. As each of the specialists made his or her report of preliminary observations, unit by unit in the sequence, a pattern began to emerge, a convergence of the various kinds of data that was extremely exciting.

Then it was Catherine Perlès' turn to report on her work with the lithics. Working, at the time, without access to field excavator's notebooks, or even final stratigraphic sections that showed superimposed units of excavation, she had noted flakes of obsidian in units that should have come from Mesolithic and Palaeolithic deposits. Since some of those units also had very un-Palaeolithic ceramic sherds, she had assumed, initially, that the obsidian chips, like the ceramics, were drop-ins, accidentally knocked from higher up on the 30- to 40-foot, loose, friable scarps. As we went around the table, hearing about each other's work, she had noted which units had anomalous materials for other specialists, and what the superimposed sequence in the deepest Palaeolithic trench was.

Obsidian is black volcanic glass and was used extensively in the Greek Neolithic, as elsewhere, for the finest chipped stone tools. The natural sources of obsidian in the Aegean area are in the Cycladic Islands, especially on the island of Melos. Tjeerd van Andel's work on prehistoric sea-level changes in the Mediterranean had shown that, among other things, Melos had been an island, separated by some distance from the mainland, even in Palaeolithic times. Thus, if obsidian flakes were found *securely stratified* in Palaeolithic deposits on the mainland, they would have far-reaching ramifications. Their presence in the Palaeolithic deposits at Franchthi would imply that people had been making sea voyages on the Aegean millennia earlier than we had ever imagined they had the technology and skills to do so.

As that realization sank in, I think the initial response of everyone around the table was skepticism. How could we claim the beginnings of seafaring based on a couple of chips of stone that were less than 5mm in maximum dimension, too small and simple even to have distinguishing typological characteristics? Something that small could so easily have fallen unnoticed from a scarp, or accidentally been left on a table after sorting one batch of residue and then picked up with a later batch sorted on the same table. How could we settle this—because the implications, if valid, were very far-reaching? What followed was certainly one of my most exciting experiences as an archaeologist. Everyone around the table pitched in with ideas and ways to test the hypothesis that the obsidian chips had been recovered *in situ,* that is, in a context that had not been disturbed since its original deposition. We looked at the pattern of occurrence of the obsidian chips: one flake in the lowest excavated unit in the series; one in the unit above that; none in the next unit up; then a few more units with, some without; and finally, a pattern of increasing frequency throughout the remaining deposits in the cave.[7] We looked at every other category of material from the same excavated units, on the assumption that it was highly unlikely that an obsidian chip, which was rare enough in superimposed deposits, would be the only thing to be knocked from a scarp, repeatedly. If the obsidian in the various Palaeolithic and Mesolithic units had been knocked from the scarps, there should be some other materials that were knocked with it, which would show up as equally out of place.

We looked carefully and critically at the stratigraphic sections, to see if there was any sign, any indication at all, of an intrusive pit, a rodent hole, or other disturbance. We reviewed the process of sorting residue, the sequence in which bags of residue from different contexts had been sorted, and by whom. Steve Diamant, who had excavated the deposits, thought he remembered finding a piece as he excavated, and confirmed that memory through reviewing the trench notebooks. And so we went on, checking every possible alternative explanation for the presence of the tiny bits of obsidian in apparently Palaeolithic and Mesolithic contexts.

In the end, we compiled sufficient, independent lines of evidence and reasoning to convince us all that the obsidian was indeed *in situ* and did, indeed, constitute evidence for Palaeolithic seafaring. Today, we take that conclusion as a given, although we and many other scholars are still working on the implications: the kinds of seagoing craft, the technology of their construction, the development of navigational skills, the impact of waterborne transport on the movements

---

[7]For full details see Catherine Perlès, *Les industries lithiques taillées de Franchthi (Argolide, Grèce).* Tome I. *Présentation générale et industries paléolithiques.* (Bloomington, Indiana University Press)1987: 143 and Document XIII.3.

of people, goods, and ideas in the early prehistoric Mediterranean and elsewhere. We can't even keep track of all the studies and information, the excitement and interest, that have followed on that discovery from the symposium. And it was a discovery made, not in the field, not at the side of the trench when an amazing, beautiful object was uncovered, but years after the excavation, from a series of unremarkable tiny chips of stone whose significance came entirely from their context. It was the result of carefully excavated and recorded, undisturbed deposits whose total environmental and cultural context is being thoroughly explored by rigorous, demanding, and patient scientists and humanists.

Similar painstaking analyses of the upper, Neolithic, deposits in the cave showed signs of considerable disturbance in recent times, possibly by looters looking for the showy, decorative pieces of pottery and other items that characterize the Greek Neolithic.[8] Or perhaps, ignorant of its absence in early Neolithic sites, they sought the gold that is often assumed to be what archaeologists seek (see the article by McGuire, "The Gringo Stigma"). These pits stop right at the boundary between Neolithic and Mesolithic, the point at which major items of potential interest to the antiquities market cease to occur. Had the diggers gone a few feet farther into the Meso- and Palaeolithic deposits, even if they had removed nothing, they would have destroyed the evidence of all the environmental materials, the bones, seeds, shells, pollens, and soils that gain their explanatory power entirely from their stratigraphic context. We might still be convinced that Palaeolithic people were ignorant of the sea. Who knows, however, what equally significant information about the Neolithic has been lost to those pits? At least careful stratigraphic excavation, detailed record keeping, and subsequent analyses allowed us to separate the disturbed from the undisturbed and avoid misinterpreting the entire deposit as intact.

---

[8]Karen D. Vitelli. *Franchthi Neolithic Pottery*. Volume 1, (Bloomington, Indiana University Press 1993): 33, 34 note 13.

Stratigraphic excavation, detailed record keeping, rigorous questioning, painstaking analyses: these are what trained archaeologists bring to their endeavors and what makes archaeology work. These elements are lacking in the hasty digging of looters. Looters sometimes find beautiful and curious objects. They always destroy much more. Their efforts deprive us all of the chance to learn the meaning of and the story behind the beautiful objects and the small simple chips of stone.

K.D.V.

PART ONE
LOOTING
AND COLLECTING

For most of the early history of archaeology, archaeologists, museums, and collectors worked closely together, seeing themselves as partners in preserving the past. In recent decades, however, as collecting has become increasingly commercial and archaeology increasingly scientific, the partnership has, in many cases, been replaced by antagonisms and direct conflicts. The articles in this section introduce the rationales for the recasting of the relationship and some of the problems that follow from it.

CHAPTER ONE
ARCHAEOLOGY
AND THE
ETHICS OF COLLECTING

by Arlen F. Chase
Diane Z. Chase
and Harriot W. Topsey

The article reviews various aspects of collecting antiquities and the related responsibilities of archaeologists and museums. It includes a brief history of the discipline of archaeology and how past actions and standards have contributed to present problems, the many responsibilities that follow from a commitment to a particular field project, and problems that stem from using unprovenienced objects in scholarly studies.

A major magazine recently ran on its cover a photo of a handsome Maya jadeite mask, suggesting that the piece had originally been dug up by looters. The magazine also reported that the piece was for sale at an exorbitant price. The cover depicting this object and an article within the issue in defense of private collecting rocked the archaeological community, and underscored the growing rift between scientific archaeologists and art historians and epigraphers, who often use looted material in their research. The controversy also raised some ugly questions about the discipline of archaeology, the majority of them revolving around the deprivations caused by the intertwined evils of collecting and looting. It is important to ask, for instance, if the portrayal of a looted artifact on the cover of a national magazine raises its value on the illicit art market. Or is its appearance offset by educating the public about the serious problem of a burgeoning black market in looted antiquities? Even more controversial, however, is any stance sanctioning the collecting of illicitly recovered objects.

Some archaeologists feel strongly that every artifact shown publicly or used as a kingpin in arguments about ancient societies must have an archaeological pedigree—it must have been properly excavated. They must know precisely where it comes from to tell its story. Without any indication of its origins and context, it is deemed worthless by some, or at best unreliable. Many institutions, the Archaeological Institute of America among them, have taken strong stands against illegal traffic in antiquities and will not knowingly publicize looted objects for fear of increasing their market value.

The controversy concerns not only intent, but results. How can one defend, either directly or indirectly, the rape of the past? Doesn't buying the fruits of such an enterprise only make the collector an accomplice in the crime? Today's private collectors, however, usually point to the beginnings of archaeology to justify their attitudes.

In its infancy, the discipline was primarily concerned with collecting artifacts. A number of prominent individuals of the 1800s were indeed antiquarians or collectors. In that era, collecting was believed to be both a mode of science and a way to increase knowledge. But while the destructive excavation methods of the antiquarians may have been similar to those in use by looters today, even then antiquarians usually recorded at least some details about the context of their finds—something looters don't do.

By World War I, archaeology had grown out of this stage. Today, an archaeologist "collects data" and, more important, "collects" context. Collecting objects is not, in and of itself, scholarship. It is the collecting of information in a scientific way that characterizes archaeology. To liken the archaeologist and the looter to one another—as some have done—is to project a false and simplified version of what archaeology is all about. The ethical and moral responsibilities involved in carrying out archaeology are found in neither the world of the looter nor that of the collector. In fact, the looter and collector are so intertwined that neither could exist without the other. The case of the robbery of Mexico's National Museum of Anthropology on Christmas Eve 1985 serves as a grave warning. Here, the looters stole certain objects "on order", much as big-city car thieves steal a given make and model of auto. When people will rob an institution to satisfy the collector's greed, no cultural resource in the world is safe.

But where do these heated differences of opinion come from and who are the various parties that are concerned with ancient artifacts? Archaeologists, art historians, epigraphers, museums, government officials, collectors, looters and dealers each have their own concerns. But who are the rightful guardians of the past and what are the responsibilities that go hand-in-hand with such guardianship? Professional obligations cannot be ignored. Looted or fraudulent pieces have sometimes been made respectable by noted scholars, either through publications or exhibits. The authentication and valuation of non-pedigree pieces constitutes irresponsible behavior.

The archaeologists of today have inherited the consequences of the methods and attitudes of the researchers that went before them. The first big archaeological and anthropological museums developed out of the antiquarian attitudes of the 1800s. For them, amassing artifacts was one way to increase their prestige and reputation. They therefore sent out expeditions to collect large numbers of pieces. With the advent of foreign nationalism in the 1950s and with the beginning of scientific archaeology in the 1960s the traditional collection-related roles were re-defined. Most archaeological and anthropological museums broke away from their previously mandated role. Now expeditions were sent out less to collect pieces than to make spectacular finds and collect data. By the early 1970s many museums openly discouraged looting and actively hindered unfettered collecting: they did this by refusing to purchase or acquire by donation collections devoid of archaeological context or pedigree. Yet even then these same institutions had not yet fully broken away from the collecting mentality. Once they had gained prestige by mounting a large long-term archaeological expedition that continually "collected" significant discoveries, many sponsoring institutions did not then go on to provide sufficient post-field support: they failed to process the mountains of collected data, or even to fully publish their findings in a timely manner. Archaeology may be defined as "controlled destruction": whatever is excavated must be fully recorded because it can never be precisely restored to its exact context. Full publication of archaeological investigations allows a recreation of this context. To put it simply, archaeologists do not and should not dig unless they can expect to fully record and then publish their findings. These go far beyond the pretty pots and objects that form the sole interests of the collector.

Not writing up and not publishing findings is irresponsible. However, nonarchaeologists need to understand that for every day spent in the field, *at minimum* seven days are required for processing, analyzing and writing. Projecting these post-field rates, it is not surprising that it takes years for final reports to appear. If one's emphasis is solely on collecting, the rest of the data are expendable. Today's archaeologist and, indeed, today's responsible institution, does not take such a narrow view. Rather, whatever is collected needs to be placed into its context to be understood; this takes time and forms the basis of the scientific enterprise. The end result of this long-term procedure is a final report that not only deals with past ways of life and cultural processes, but also permits the reader to recreate the excavated archaeological record and cross-check archaeological interpretations.

Modern archaeologists have a series of commitments, contracts and responsibilities that they did not have in the past. Most often these ethics or rules of conduct are understood by working archaeologists, but the general public is largely unaware of them.

While the primary task of archaeology is to answer scientifically questions about ancient societies, through their research archaeologists become enmeshed in a wide network of relationships that involves not only their work but the plans and goals of their colleagues, the local public and the government. Once an archaeologist begins to work at a site, he or she has usually made a commitment not only to the collection of data from that locale, but also to the physical preservation of the site once excavation ceases. Preservation of a site is accomplished either through backfilling of all excavations, or consolidating the site for viewing by tourists, in conjunction with

33

government offices in charge. Such a stabilization and reconstruction program is part of the ethical responsibility of modern archaeology.

Apart from responsibilities to the site being worked on, the archaeologists also submits published reports on his or her research to the government offices in charge of archaeology and to colleagues within the overall discipline. In a wider sense, this responsibility also extends to guardianship of data. Archaeologists recognize that they do not physically own any of the items they are digging up. Rather, these items generally form part of the patrimony of the country in which the excavation is taking place and they rightly belong to the people of that country. Likewise, the data collected through archaeology ultimately should be used by the wider profession and the public. These data, however, must remain fully in the hands of the archaeologist until full publication. Only then can such material be placed in a permanent archive, preserved for use by other scholars.

Perhaps the most obvious responsibility of modern archaeologists centers on the published articles, public lectures and museum exhibits that should result from their activities. For these are the only ways that archaeologists can fulfill their primary obligation to the public—in return for public funds. Still, major questions are currently being raised by archaeologists about just how to do this and how much to tell. Should all data be made openly available to everyone or should some finds be hidden? Does the open display of national treasures encourage looting and collecting? The archaeologist must attempt to educate the public concerning its collective responsibility to the past patrimony. This responsibility should involve the open sharing of data with nonarchaeologists through lectures, exhibits and newspapers. Nothing found in or by archaeology should be intentionally hidden.

In certain countries there has been a recent trend in the opposite direction. Rather than fully educating the people as to their past, news of important finds made by archaeologists is sometimes suppressed from public dissemination. Pictures of rare finds are not shown in public forums and archaeologists make no mention of them.

Suppression of data can create a dangerous situation by making archaeologists and government officials untrustworthy in the eyes of the public. If the data are not made available, some might unknowingly ask how the archaeologist is different from a looter. And who is to know where these unpublicized finds might end up? A lack of openness or honesty is not in keeping with ethics of scientific archaeology. But still there is sometimes fear that increased knowledge will lead to even more looting and destruction.

In Belize, there is a concerted effort to educate all Belizeans as to the necessity for preserving the past. This effort is being carried forward by the Department of Archaeology, archaeologists working there and the Association for Belize Archaeology, a local group interested in prehistory. Major new finds are presented in public archaeological displays throughout the country's districts and archaeology is being taught in elementary school. This enlightened approach is raising the consciousness of the nation about the importance of preserving the past. As a result, the public is increasingly helpful in preserving both sites and artifacts.

Beyond the problems involved in excavation, analysis preservation and dissemination of information, the archaeologist is faced with another dilemma. Should looted pieces and collections be used side by side with carefully excavated material? Archaeologists who do not include unidentified objects in their interpretations share an outlook that embodies three major points: First, these looted or collected items do not provide the full story; they are not associated with other artifacts or a particular location that can provide a context.

Second, non-provenanced material originally derives from illegal excavation and using these objects indirectly legitimizes the artifacts and the looting from which they are derived. Professionals are concerned that the use of such objects may also drive up market value and increase looting.

Third, because of the high demand for archaeological objects in the public sector, many of the looted pieces on the art market today are either fakes or repainted vessels that bear little resemblance to the originals. There is no assurance that the interpretations made from them are valid. It is in fact often difficult to distinguish a fraud from the real thing.

Some collectors and art historians feel that a rich world of iconography and glyphs has been opened up by the collection of looted pots of unknown provenance. Any responsible archaeologist would question this assertion, for it is not known whether such materials are real or repainted. The use of iconography founded on non-provenanced vessels is likely to introduce false interpretations, for the modern forger is just as skillful and inventive as the ancient artist. Even if some of these vessels should prove genuine, a much richer world of iconography and associations has been destroyed by removing the vessels from their contexts. Archaeologists do not ignore or discard data that can be utilized by epigraphers and art historians, even though their goals are different. This collection of all data by the archaeologist leads, in fact, to the problem of lag time between data collection and full publication.

Epigraphers, by definition, are predominantly interested in hieroglyphic texts while art historians are primarily interested in single vessels and their iconography. Such information can be rapidly disseminated because it comprises such a small amount of the data recovered through archaeology. Yet hieroglyphics and single objects form only a part of the repertoire that the archaeologist seeks to publish.

Collecting is big business. Archaeology is not. Business ethics, in which the dollar is supreme, is not compatible with archaeological ethics, where contextual data are worth more because they provide a fuller picture of ancient peoples not discoverable solely from the iconography of decorated artifacts. These interpretations of prehistoric life are the goals of archaeological science. The collector of artifacts needs to be made more aware of the invaluable nature of archaeologically collected pieces—and of the fact that information gathered about the relationships and meaning of such items may be worth far more than the object itself. It would be far better if collectors could be persuaded to spend their time and money in support of legitimate archaeological research. Such work would not only produce beautiful objects, but would also result in the contextual data needed to make archaeological interpretations of the past. And more important, collectors could experience the thrill of discovery, and the multitudes of meaning, that can be derived from the accurate placement of objects in their context. This experience might prove far more satisfying than mere ownership of a looted plot.

Today, collecting and profit go hand-in-hand. The unfortunate truth is that if collectors were not willing to pay exorbitant amounts for artifacts, destructive looting would not be so rampant. Nor would fraudulent archaeological materials so often be introduced into the marketplace. The argument that collecting "saves the past" only clouds the issue. A looter is not salvaging materials. He is only helping to destroy the past—for a profit. Most sites are not in danger from any other source but the looter's pick. And untouched archaeological sites are rapidly becoming an endangered species. Private collecting simply encourages further looting and from an archaeologist's viewpoint it is wrong.

Some would argue that the responsibility for curtailing looting lies not with the collectors but with government officials. But many countries are only now realizing the invaluable nature of their past. Most countries have solid laws against such activity, but not the manpower to enforce them. The responsibilities to curb looting, however, go beyond enforcement and educating the nation's people. They also rest with the country to which the looted items ultimately go. The simple fact that customs checks are made when one is entering but not when leaving a country means that the country entered has more of a chance of detecting a looted piece than the country of departure. Beyond this, curbing of looting requires an educated public unwilling to purchase items not rightfully for sale.

The dispersal of looted artworks into the world is a direct result of the existence of an art market to support such activity. Responsible museums and individuals have recognized that their obligation to the public precludes the ownership, authentication and valuation of such objects. It is now time for collectors, also, to realize their responsibility to the cultural patrimony of the world.

Arlen F. and Diane Z. Chase teach anthropology at the University of Central Florida and do field work in Belize.

Harriot W. Topsey was the Archaeological Commissioner for Belize until his recent death in an automobile accident.

DISCUSSION QUESTIONS

1. Is an artifact without a pedigree (i.e., archaeological provenience) worthless?
2. Why is the idea of stealing artifacts "to order" so offensive?
3. Does publicizing looted artifacts increase their market value?
4. Do archaeologists have a legitimate claim to being the primary guardians of the past? What other groups might contest the claim?
5. Does authentication and valuation of nonpedigreed pieces always constitute irresponsible archaeological behavior?
6. What should be done (and by whom) if an archaeological team cannot fully record and publish its finds with reasonable speed? What is "reasonable speed"?
7. Why don't archaeologists publish more quickly?
8. What should/can be done about slow publication by archaeologists?
9. What are the complex obligations (and to whom) of an archaeologist engaged in fieldwork?
10. Should all archaeological data be made available to anyone who wants it?
11. What are the archaeologist's obligations to public education in the locales of fieldwork?
12. Should looted objects be studied alongside excavated objects? (See "Publication Policies of Professional Journals" Appendix B.)
13. What are the differences between archaeological and business ethics? Between archaeological ethics and cultural property law?
14. Can any kind of collecting of antiquities be legitimately justified as "saving the past"?
15. Who is responsible for curtailing looting?
16. What are the responsibilities of collectors, including museums, to the archaeological record?

FURTHER RESEARCH

See also: "Is There a Legitimate Role for an International Market in Antiquities?" *The Art Newspaper*, 53 (November 1995): 22–23.

CHAPTER TWO

BLACK DAY
AT SLACK FARM

by Brian Fagan

After the death of Mrs. Slack, whose family had long protected the important contact period site on their Kentucky property, new owners leased the land to pot-hunters, who bulldozed graves and habitation deposits for fun and profit. The discussion in this article of what we might have learned about Mississippian culture and early European contact if looters hadn't destroyed the Slack Farm site provides one vivid example of the destruction of information caused by looting everywhere.

Like most archaeologists, I have, over the years, developed a numbness to the orgy of site destruction that surrounds us on every side. But a recent story about Slack Farm on the front page of *The Los Angeles Times* has opened old wounds afresh.

"Plunder for Profit," "Looters Rob Old Graves and History"—the headlines leaped out at me with sickening familiarity. But it was only when I read on that I began to realize the full horror of the events at Slack Farm.

The Slack Farm site lies near Uniontown, Kentucky, on land just opposite the confluence of the Ohio and Wabash rivers. The Slack family, which had for many years owned a house and farm at the site, had allowed no digging for artifacts, although on occasion people stole into the corn fields at night to dig illicitly.

Archaeologists had known about the site for years, knew that it was a large, relatively undisturbed Late Mississippian settlement. Judging from surface artifacts, the site dated to sometime between A.D. 1450 and 1650. The farm was of special importance, for it straddled the vital centuries of first European contact with the New World. Cheryl Ann Munson of Indiana University stresses the significance of the farm: she has studied every other large site of this period both up- and downstream. All the other sites have, Munson reports, long since been ravaged by pot-hunters. Yet through last fall, Slack Farm had, remarkably, remained nearly intact, a unique archive of information about Late Mississippian lifeways.

But no more. With the death of Mrs. Slack the property changed hands. The tenant farmers on the site did make some attempt to keep people from looting the place. In 1987, however, ten pot-hunters from Kentucky, Indiana, and Illinois paid the new owner of the land $10,000 for the right to "excavate" the site. They rented a tractor and began bulldozing their way through the village midden to reach graves. They pushed heaps of bones aside, and dug through dwellings and the potsherds, hearths, and stone tools associated with them. Along the way, they left detritus of their own—empty pop-top beer and soda cans—scattered on the ground alongside Late Mississippian pottery fragments. Today, Slack Farm looks like a battlefield—a morass of crude shovel holes and gaping trenches. Broken human bones litter the ground, and fractured artifacts crunch under foot.

Two months passed before local residents complained about the digging. Eventually the Kentucky State Police stepped in and arrested the diggers under a state law that prohibits desecrating a venerated object, such as a human grave. The looters pleaded not guilty to the charge—a misdemeanor—and now await trial. But whatever the court decides, the archaeological damage is done—and it is staggering.

No one knows how many graves were ravaged, what artifacts were removed, what fine pots or funerary ornaments vanished onto the greedy antiquities market. No signs of the dwellings, hearths, and other structures they disturbed remain. A team of archaeologists from the Kentucky Heritage Council, Indiana University, and the University of Kentucky, aided by many volunteers, is now trying to assess the damage and record what is left of the site. They are cleaning up the pothunters' holes, recording what intact features remain, and collecting artifact samples to document and date the settlement more precisely.

The ravagers of Slack Farm had no interest in science or prehistory. They were hunting for artifacts for their personal collections and for money. There is a flourishing market in pipes, pendants, whole pots, and other Mississippian grave furnishings. Under these circumstances, pot-hunting can be addictive.

Prehistoric artifact prices are staggering, and rising steeply as the illegal supply—especially from overseas—becomes scarcer. A stone ax can fetch as much as $1,000, a pipe up to $5,000. A looter who finds a rare type of Mississippian pottery bottle or an embossed copper plate can name his price, and expect to get it. The marketplace is so hungry for antiquities of every kind that a lively underground market in very high quality forgeries grows daily.

In some ways, one can hardly blame landowners for cashing in on the potential of such hidden treasures. They lease rights to companies to mine their land for coal. Why not lease rights to pot-hunters to dig for artifacts? Both coal and artifacts can be regarded as wealth underfoot. But in the case of the prehistoric past the issues are much more complex.

This point was underlined for me when I showed the newspaper account of the Slack Farm tragedy to some friends at a coffee break. I was horrified by some of the reactions. "So what?" shrugged one coffee shop acquaintance. "It's a free country." He expressed what turned out to be a widely held view: it's up to landowners what they do with their property. In my numbness, I had forgotten that many people see nothing wrong with private landowners ravaging the past for profit—as long as laws are not broken.

We have a strange relationship with the prehistoric past in this country. Most Americans, like my friends, have no direct cultural identification or emotional tie with North American prehistory, with Mesa Verde, Cahokia, or the many other brilliant achievements of the American Indian. As far as most people are concerned, history (and North American archaeology, for that matter) began with Leif Erikson, Christopher Columbus, and the Pilgrim Fathers. Anything that predates European contact is considered somewhat irrelevant, and often ignored in school.

So most Americans of non-Indian descent tend to think of prehistoric Indian sites in impersonal, remote ways. Most would protest vigorously at the destruction of an important, privately owned, historic site from pioneer days, or shudder at the very thought of someone looting their neighbor's great-grandmother's grave. But a long-abandoned prehistoric Indian village and the graves of the people who once lived there are a different matter.

It would be naive to think that Slack Farm is an isolated incident. Looting and pothunting have been endemic in the Southeast since the Depression days of the 1930s, and were rife in the Southwest in the early years of this century. Reports from elsewhere in Kentucky, and from Illinois, Indiana, and Ohio, testify to widespread vandalism directed against archaeological sites of every time period over the entire length of the Ohio Valley.

But there is far more to the Slack Farm tragedy than the material destruction of hundreds of prehistoric graves—or of an entire archaeological site. For days after reading the news stories, I was haunted by the staggering scientific loss at Slack Farm.

To understand the dimensions of that loss one must realize that the Mississippian culture was a brilliant efflorescence of late prehistoric life in the Midwest and the South. Cahokia, Moundville, and other great centers testify to that culture's extraordinary elaboration of public constructions and brilliant art traditions in ceramics, copper, and shell. The first Mississippian communities appeared after A.D. 750, at just about the time when maize farming took hold in eastern North America. Mississippian culture was past its apogee in many regions when Europeans first penetrated the Midwest in the seventeenth century.

Many questions about this ancient society remain unanswered. Most excavations have focused, fairly naturally, on a few town sites and their mounds and spectacular monuments. Very few villages or cemeteries have been investigated—especially with the full apparatus of modern, hi-tech archaeology. The well-preserved deposits at Slack Farm offered one of the few chances for such a painstaking investigation.

As in other Mississippian communities, the people who lived at Slack Farm probably enjoyed close and constant economic, political, and social relationships with other villages and hamlets up and down the Ohio. But most of these sites also have been destroyed by looters. Until this tragedy, Slack Farm had been our best chance to study the dynamics of this Mississippian society.

Some of the fine Mississippian pots from Slack Farm so coveted by collectors are identical to vessels made in Arkansas, far from the Ohio Valley. Some of the copper and marine shell ornaments prized by looters attest to even more distant trade—for copper either with the Great Lakes area or the Appalachians, for marine shells with the Atlantic or Gulf coasts.

It may be news to looters, but the fragmentary bones they cast aside are a treasure trove of potential information on Mississippian diet and disease, of vital genetic data about the biological relationships between prehistoric Americans, of evidence on ancient warfare. We now have the scientific techniques to probe such questions. Unfortunately, most of the vital clues for doing so vanished when the site was destroyed.

Slack Farm straddles the vital centuries of European contact with American Indians. We know this because glass beads, brass tinklers, and other European artifacts have come from the surface of the ravaged settlement. These finds testify to some form of indirect, or perhaps even direct, contact between the Slack Farm people and early European traders and explorers. Studying such imports requires a detailed knowledge of their precise archaeological context. The looted holes at Slack Farm remind us that we may never understand the true nature of these early contacts.

Christopher Columbus's quincentennial has passed, yet we still know little about the complex relationships between Europeans and Native Americans five centuries ago. What changes in culture resulted from European contact? Did exotic diseases decimate midwestern populations? Were the Late Mississippians in the Ohio Valley the ancestors of one of the historic tribes of the Midwest and Southeast? What goods were traded between whites and Indians, and how did this new trade affect relationships between indigenous societies? The looted burials and village deposits at Slack Farm might have helped find some of the answers to these questions. They cannot help us now.

When historians look back at the history of archaeology in the late twentieth century, they will be struck by a tragic irony. The seventies and eighties were the decades when archaeologists finally developed the scientific technology to attack fundamental questions about the past. Yet the same scientists were powerless to stem the tidal wave of destruction that swept away the very data they could now study to its full potential.

The only bright side of the Slack Farm affair is the public outcry aroused locally by the looting. This protest led to new state legislation in Kentucky, which now makes it a felony to desecrate a human grave, regardless of the race or antiquity of the person buried. Yet, in Indiana similar legislative efforts failed. In surrounding states, no one is tackling the legal, ethical, and archaeological problem of site vandalism.

It's not making front page headlines, but looting on the scale of Slack Farm is commonplace in nearly every state—from the Bering Strait to the U.S. Virgin Islands, especially on private lands. The fact is that we and our friends are not making enough noise about this insidious scandal society tolerates in its midst. No one else is going to do it for us, so we had better raise our voices very loudly before it is too late.

In a way I feel like Nero, blithely fiddling while Rome burns. Only this time it is not Rome that is at stake, but the priceless and finite past. The Slack Farm affair has made me wonder for the first time if, perhaps, it is already too late.

AN UPDATE ON THE SLACK FARM SITE
by David Pollack and Cheryl Ann Munson

Archaeological investigation of the damaged areas of the village and its cemeteries followed the arrest of the looters and demonstrated that they disturbed more than 700 burials. Despite the extensive damage to the site, the archaeological work showed that the looters were stopped before much of the residential areas and the smaller cemeteries were destroyed. Additionally, archaeologists recovered new information concerning the lifestyles of the late Mississippian people who occupied this site and neighboring settlements along the Ohio River. Analysis of the materials and records from the site is ongoing, and there is a great deal of local interest in preserving the Slack Farm site as a unique protohistoric Mississippian village.

Though initial legislative efforts to prevent looting were met in the Indiana legislature by successful protests from artifact collectors, continued looting changed the laws there too. Less than a year after the Slack Farm depredations, illicit diggers struck again nearby. This time their target was a Hopewell Mound (the GE Mound) on the Indiana side of the Ohio River. Once newspapers picked up the story, the public outcry that followed the Slack Farm looting was renewed. As a consequence, Indiana's governor signed a law in the spring of 1989 that was designed to help land managers and landowners protect burial sites and other types of archaeological sites on public or private lands from illicit excavation and from accidental damage. Changes in laws have not brought an end to looting in Indiana and Kentucky, of course, but we believe the incidence of destruction has begun to decline thanks to continued public concern.

Brian Fagan teaches archaeology at the University of California, Santa Barbara. He is a well-known author of archaeology textbooks and a contributing editor for Archaeology.

DISCUSSION QUESTIONS

1. What is the relationship between the availability of antiquities from overseas and the market for U.S. antiquities?
2. How could we find out whether the market for high-quality forgeries is increasing?
3. Do landowners have rights to exploit subsurface resources, whether coal or antiquities? Should they have such rights?*

---

*See also: Cheryl Ann Munson, Marjorie Melvin Jones, and Robert Fry, "The GE Mound: An ARPA Case Study," *American Antiquity* 60 (1995): 131–59.

4. Is the lack of direct cultural identification with the buried past for most (i.e., non-Indian) Americans a primary reason for the looting of prehistoric sites in the United States? (Compare the situation in the United States with that in other countries.)
5. What is the market overseas for American antiquities?
6. Are archaeologists powerless to "stem the tidal wave of destruction"?
7. What are the laws in your state regarding desecration of graves?**

**The federal government's NAGPRA regulations on treatment of burials may be found at http://www.cast.uark.edu/products/NADB/.

CHAPTER THREE

DARING TO DEAL WITH HUAQUEROS

by Carol L. Howell

Olaf Holm, director of the government-owned Anthropology Museum of the Banco Central of Ecuador, believes that working with huaqueros, or looters, is better than ignoring them. He argues that even unprovenienced artifacts contribute to the variety of the collections; that buying from looters keeps antiquities in their country of origin, providing access to their own history for locals and attracting foreign archaeologists to the museum; and the collections in Ecuador provide opportunities for employment and research for native archaeologists. An innovative program has been successful in transforming some of the huaqueros into archaeologists.

"Want to buy some old things?" the young woman asked. I was visiting a Guayaquil museum, and this brazen offer was made as I waited for an appointment with the director, Olaf Holm, with whom I wanted to discuss a research project. I refused her offer and watched as she disappeared down a flight of stairs. It occurred to me that the woman might be a disgruntled employee who had decided to sell some of the museum's inventory.

"No, she's just another *huaquero,*" Holm explained as he asked me into his office. "They still come in, even though I buy nothing anymore. It is nice of them to let me see these things before they go to Bogotá, don't you think?"

Did he say *anymore?* This was the Anthropology Museum of the Banco Central del Ecuador, a government-owned institution, not a private museum built to house collections of dubious provenience. Given the archaeologist's mantra of "context and provenience," how could he justify dealing with looters?

A Danish expatriate, Holm has devoted the better part of his past 50 years to the archaeology of his adopted land. During that time he developed an unusual relationship with huaqueros, those who dig into ancient mounds (*huacas*) hunting for decorated vessels (*huacos*). In doing so he was able to acquire many unique pieces for the museum before they were lost to the international market.

"I have done my share of the fieldwork," he says. "I appreciate the differences between a purchased collection and one that has been scientifically excavated." But Holm believes that, even without the benefits of provenience, artifacts still lend breadth and subtle variation to a collection. And researchers, it appears, are eager to study this material, which leaves Holm impatient with what he terms "the hypocrisy of the scientific community."

Since 1965, the Banco Central has financed eight anthropology museums throughout Ecuador. Before they were built, scholars interested in Ecuadorian archaeology had to travel to the United States or Europe to study collections there. "Foreign scientists now visit our museum collections," Holm says with pride.

"In the late 60s," the director recalls, "a particular huaquero would come by routinely. He took pride in his knowledge of the artifacts and on one occasion allowed me to visit 'his site' and make excavations under his guidance. Those collections are now in the possession of the bank."

With amused exasperation, he concedes that not all huaquero acquisitions have been completed so successfully. In one instance, he was contacted by a huaquero whose "brother" had found a skull with gold-studded teeth. The Jama-Coaque people of the northern coast of Ecuador were masters of metal-working. They would drill their teeth to adorn them with gold studs, a practice that still continues in some isolated communities. From the time that the Spanish discovered the riches of the Jama-Coaque, this region of mangrove swamps, estuaries, malaria, and dengue fever has been continuously "mined" for such treasures. As a result, few artifacts from the area now exist.

Holm says he expressed an interest in seeing the skull and advanced the huaquero bus fare to have it brought to his office in Guayaquil. Within a week the huaquero returned with a handful of gold studs. No effort had been spared to extract and crush the teeth in the misguided belief that Holm, like the Spanish conquistadors, was only interested in gold.

Several years later another such skull surfaced. This time Holm asked to be shown the whole skull. He was glad to meet the huaquero's steep price. Holm paid for the acquisition with his own money, only to find that Banco Central administrators would not reimburse him. Austerity measures were in force, and no money was to be spent on acquisitions. Because of limited government resources, the museum has acquired little in the past ten years, but contact with the huaquero community continues. By keeping abreast of their activities, Holm feels he can at least maintain some record of Ecuador's heritage as it undergoes the metamorphosis from artifact to exportable art. Disheartened, he speaks of a postcard he has just received from the Netherlands showing an intricate golden figurine studded with emeralds. "We have nothing like it in Ecuador . . . it came from the Río Jama area on the Ecuadorian coast. I hope it is well cared for by the curators at Rotterdam's Museum voor Volkenkunde."

Holm has seen to it that at least some archaeological projects continued to be financed by the state's meager budget. The Banco Central is virtually the only place where Ecuadorian archaeologists can find employment within their country. Many are hired to curate or study collections, while others receive bank support for fieldwork.

The Guayaquil collection that has been assembled under Holm's guidance is as extensive as it is diverse. It addresses many different facets of the country's past cultures: its unique costumes, musical instruments, tattoo-like body adornment, weaving technology, and metallurgy. Regrettably, scarcity of state funds has limited the dissemination of this work—the publication of archaeological research is now about three years behind schedule. Although the profession will benefit as this material becomes available, the publishing may paradoxically stimulate the antiquities market as collectors become better informed.

In the early 1960s the Banco Central diverted a percentage of its profits to support Ecuadorian anthropology. The destructive consequences of buying looted artifacts, were poorly understood, and the bank's director was given a blank check to acquire as much as he could for the country's first anthropology museum in Quito. Acquisition of artifacts by lot spawned a looting industry. While the Banco Central openly dealt with looters to build collections, the relationship between them was never a pleasant one. Sellers had to wait for hours for an appointment, then were reprimanded for being looters. Some had to wait weeks for their money. Angry huaqueros repaid the government with misinformation about the provenience of artifacts.

Fellow archaeologists are quick to attest the discretion of Holm's acquisitions for the Guayaquil museum, comparing his efforts favorably to those of the Banco Central administrators who bought for the museum in Quito. He is credited with being more intelligent in his dealings; he treated the huaqueros well and purchased far more selectively.

Meanwhile, the recent installation of an oil pipeline along the forested coast required the bulldozing of a swath of land 15 feet wide and 100 miles long. Previously unknown archaeological sites were quickly discovered, leveled and looted. Holm's reliable informants alerted him to the destruction, which has kept him busy marking sites for future salvage and maintaining a record of new artifacts flooding the market.

Holm has also put the support of the Banco Central behind an imaginative effort to stem the practice of looting. Agua Blanca, a small village located in the foothills of Ecuador's central coast, was the center of a sophisticated prehistoric maritime trade network. In modern times, its economic base has consisted of mining the extensive ruins for marketable artifacts. The situation changed with the arrival of Colin McEwan, a graduate student from the University of Illinois in 1984. With financial backing from the Banco Central and field support from the Programa de Anthropología para el Ecuador, a private research foundation, McEwan was successful in turning huaqueros into archaeologists.

The residents of Agua Blanca became enthusiastic students. As they learned about their cultural heritage, they willingly undertook a program of rigorous training in archaeological techniques. The residents drew an initial map detailing prehistoric Agua Blanca as it stretched across more than a square mile of overgrown and rugged terrain. These reformed huaqueros now carefully excavate test pits to understand the lives of their ancestors; how scarce resources were used; and the relationships among merchants, divers, shellworkers, fishermen, agriculturists, and priests. Holm has brought together resources from the Banco Central, the British Council, and the Ecuadorian State Enterprise of Petroleum to finance the construction of a museum in Agua Blanca.

During a stay in Salango, a five-hour ride northwest of Guayaquil, I learned of an important stela that had just found its way onto the antiquities market in Quito. I was told that only two or three stelas had appeared since boatloads were crated off to the Museum of the American Indian (Heye Foundation) in New York earlier in the century. I questioned several Ecuadorian archaeologists about their attitude toward such a valuable piece: "If Olaf's budget for acquisitions was somehow magically funded, should the museum make an effort to acquire the stela?" At first their responses were little more than textbook clichés about "perpetuating the destruction of sites."

"Suppose it were headed out of the country," I asked, "destined to become an exotic lamp base for a prince?" One archaeologist responded to this worst-case scenario by conceding that "this is where the argument [to deal with huaqueros] starts working," and the Banco Central should at that point pay the $8,000 that the dealer was asking. Another maintained that, because the piece lacked provenience, most of its value to anthropology was lost.

"Look at it this way," one argued. "Suppose that $8,000 was put toward looking for things in context." In this economy, the thought of what could be accomplished with these funds is breathtaking. From surveys to excavations, research to publication, each could rapidly formulate a wish list. One archaeologist concluded: "The stela is an art object. As soon as you label something a 'museum piece' the implication seems to be that it's worth obtaining. I would maintain that it's not worth obtaining. What should be in the museums are not pieces or things but information about the culture, using objects of the culture to interpret that information."

Curators of antiquities the world over face an ethical dilemma in acquiring objects that may have been looted. Men and women of sound integrity have been humbled by choices that eventually compromised the reputation of some of the United States' best-known museums. The problem is even more acute in art-rich developing countries, where local museum curators must purchase illegally excavated artifacts or watch as they vanish onto the international antiquities market. I applaud the career of Olaf Holm and concur with those who feel he has established an invaluable archaeological resource for Ecuador. I also share in his outrage at having to clip auction catalogs in order to record Ecuador's disappearing heritage. Risking professional reproach, Holm chose to accept artifacts for preservation, many devoid of context. His only alternative was to preserve a fraction of the archaeological record.

Carol L. Howell is a free-lance writer and photographer with archaeological interests.

DISCUSSION QUESTIONS

1. Is the scientific community hypocritical (and/or self-defeating) in its stand against working with looters and treasure salvors?
2. What are the pros and cons of dealing with huaqueros?
3. Is there an important difference between dealing with looters directly, in the country of origin, and with their middlemen, after the materials have left their country of origin?
4. What is the difference between the huaqueros described here and treasure salvors licensed to work on underwater shipwrecks?*
5. Is it possible to turn looters into archaeologists?
6. How might archaeologists unintentionally be encouraging looters?

---

*See: Ricardo J. Elia, "The Ethics of Collaboration: Archaeologists and the Whydah Project," *Historical Archaeology* 26 (1992): 105–17.

7. How would you answer the question of whether Holm's museum should buy the stela?

8. Should museums collect objects or information, and which do they, in fact, collect? Are there different considerations for different types of museums, for example, art museums and anthropology museums?

9. What is your local museum's policy on the acquisition of antiquities by purchase? By gift? By loan?

FURTHER RESEARCH

See also the article by Bailey in Part III, "The Looting of Bulgaria."

CHAPTER FOUR
A SEDUCTIVE AND TROUBLING WORK
by Ricardo J. Elia

Reviewing Colin Renfrew's, The Cycladic Spirit: Masterpieces from the Nicholas P. Goulandris Collection,* *Elia calls the distinguished archaeologist to task for publishing this unprovenienced collection of artifacts from a private collection (now a private museum). Elia points out the (partially documented) destruction caused by the demands of the art market for Cycladic marble figurines, the likelihood of fakes in the corpus, the damage to scholarship on the Early Bronze Age and to the scholar himself, and the scholarly biases introduced when a scholar (client) publishes materials in a private collector's (patron's) possession.*

During the Third Millennium B.C. , small communities of Early Bronze Age agriculturalists developed a distinctive culture in the group of rugged Aegean islands known as the Cyclades. Like their contemporaries in mainland Greece, Crete and Anatolia, Cycladic craftsmen fashioned implements of obsidian, copper, and bronze and made vessels of fired clay. But these islanders also created remarkable objects out of local marble: bowls, cylindrical containers, and especially human figurines.

In the nineteenth century, when European travelers and antiquarians first encountered these strangely shaped Cycladic "idols," they regarded them as primitive, rude, and even ugly. Their abstract forms and the absence of naturalistic features offended the aesthetic

---

*New York: Harry N. Abrams, in association with the N.P. Goulandris Foundation, 1991.

sensibilities of art historians weaned on the Classical ideal of Greek sculpture. As recently as 1925, Gustave Glotz, in his account of Aegean civilization, referred to rare Cycladic figures such as the flautist and the harpist as "monstrosities."

But fashions in art change, and during the 1950s and 1960s the art world acquired an appetite for Cycladic sculptures. In response, looters in the islands, eager to satisfy the greed of collectors and museums, undertook one of the most systematic episodes of archaeological pillaging ever as thousands of Cycladic graves were vandalized in the search for figurines. Predictably, the lust for Cycladic marbles, coupled with a dwindling supply of unplundered graves, spawned a major industry in counterfeit sculptures. Workshops in places like Paris, Athens, and Naxos (where sources of actual Cycladic marble were at hand) profitably flooded the market with fakes. This frenzy of looting, faking and unprincipled purchase has placed approximately 1600 objects identified as Cycladic figurines into private collections and museums throughout the world. For the vast majority we know nothing about where they came from, what they mean, and even if they are authentic.

One of the largest and most prominent private collections of Cycladic material was assembled during the 1960s by Dolly and Nicholas Goulandris and now constitutes the Nicholas P. Goulandris Foundation-Museum of Cycladic Art in Athens. All of the objects in the Goulandris Collection were purchased either in Greece or on the international art market; not a single specimen has an archaeological provenience. *The Cycladic Spirit*, written by the prominent British archaeologist Colin Renfrew, showcases this collection in a lavishly illustrated publication that will surely be welcomed by art historians, collectors, and traffickers in antiquities.

Renfrew has written many important studies on various topics in European prehistory. He has published extensively on Cycladic archaeology and sculpture, including, in 1969, what has become the standard stylistic typology of Cycladic figures. His association with the Goulandris Collection dates back to the 1960s, when, as he tells us, he was given free access to the "wonderful collection" in the Athens apartment of Dolly Goulandris. Renfrew's relationship to this collection was personal and intimate: he recalls "creeping out from the adjoining bedroom" during the night with a flashlight for a private viewing of the collection, which was on display in the drawing room.

In *The Cycladic Spirit*, Renfrew dons the cap of the art historian and offers a personal and aesthetic appraisal of Cycladic figures. As the subtitle of the book indicates, these are treated not as artifacts, but as masterpieces of art. To be sure, part of the book describes what is known about Cycladic society and material culture, a topic that derives from archaeological research, much of it desperate salvage carried out at newly plundered sites. But *The Cycladic Spirit* is essentially Renfrew's personal appreciation of Cycladic sculpture ("there is, after all, no other way," he says).

In typically eloquent fashion Renfrew sets the stage by summarizing our understanding of Cycladic culture. He describes the "canonical" form of Cycladic figurine: usually a standing nude female, arms folded across the stomach, the depiction executed in a simplified, abstract manner. Several stylistic varieties or types of figures are illustrated. More difficult is trying to understand what the figures meant in Cycladic society: Renfrew speculates that the monumental figures represented deities, while the smaller ones might have served as votive offerings in public or private cults.

Renfrew next discusses several aspects of Cycladic art, including who made the figures and whether individual sculptors can be identified; to what degree they were originally painted; how the sculptors seem to have followed certain rules on proportions in carving the human form; variations in the treatment of anatomy; and the monumental figures. Renfrew's final essays offer his appreciation of Cycladic sculpture in the context of modern aesthetics and artistic taste: here Renfrew is at ease in a wide-ranging discussion that includes Classical, Byzantine, and Renaissance art, African tribal figures, and the artistic expressions of Picasso, Modigliani, and Brancusi.

There are, however, several pitfalls facing the scholar who chooses to study looted artifacts. The basic problem can be briefly summarized. Collectors cause looting by creating a market demand for antiquities. Looting, in turn, causes forgeries, since forgeries can only remain undetected where there is a substantial corpus of antiquities without proper archaeological provenience. These two problems—looting and forgery—fundamentally corrupt the integrity of the field of ancient art history.

One might expect that these problems would merit the special attention of scholars working with collections. Unfortunately, many art historians choose to ignore the corruptive effects of the illegal art market on their study. Their basic assumption seems to be that looters are bad but collectors are good. Scholars who work with looted material regularly condemn looting, while in the same breath they laud the enthusiasm of the collector who, directly or indirectly, financed the looting.

Another assumption made by those who study private collections is that forgeries are only purchased by *other* collectors. Each collector, of course, is unwilling to believe that he or she has been duped by a forger, and few scholars have the courage to suggest that the collection they are studying contains forgeries. This attitude produces an absurd and impossible situation, nowhere more keenly illustrated than by Cycladic sculpture. Everyone admits that forgeries are rampant but few have been so identified. One Greek archaeologists told me he believed that as much as 30 to 40 percent of all known Cycladic figurines are forgeries; the most disturbing thing about this statement is not that it cannot be proved, but that it cannot be disproved.

The reluctance of scholars to deal with the problems that are inherent in the study of private collections springs from the fact that the relationship of scholar to collector is essentially that of client to patron or guest to host. The obligation owed to the collector—for hospitality, access, and sometimes financial support—tends to compromise the researcher's objectivity and corrupt his or her intellectual honesty. An added complication is the fact that the scholar's publication of a collection inevitably serves to authenticate the collection and increase its market value.

How then, does a serious scholar like Colin Renfrew deal with these problems in *The Cycladic Spirit*? He clearly does not sidestep the problem of looting and its effects. In his introductory chapter, Renfrew describes the unparalleled looting of Cycladic cemeteries and asserts: "The damage is irreparable, the loss incalculable." He also addresses the question of whether archaeologists should avoid dealing with artifacts that lack provenience, but he rejects such a solution as "inappropriate," and states that we cannot afford to ignore the Cycladic sculptures because they "represent one of the great moments of human achievement."

Renfrew is careful to avoid offending his hosts: although he repeatedly points out how little is known because of the lack of archaeological evidence, he never suggests that the act of collecting might be directly responsible for the looting. Instead, he praises the "energy," "enthusiasm," and "initiative" of Dolly Goulandris in assembling the collection. He also praises the Goulandris Foundation for keeping many Cycladic objects in Greece and for making them available to scholars and the public. "They have," he says, "escaped the international art market."

To be sure, the foundation has established a museum and has supported Cycladic research. But Renfrew's defense rings hollow: the Goulandrises made their purchases from the international art market, both in and outside Greece. Renfrew never acknowledges the likelihood that the Goulandrises' collecting actually promoted the looting of Cycladic sites. During the 1960s the couple must have been well-known in the islands as major buyers of Cycladic sculptures. Dolly Goulandris herself says, in the foreword of the first publication of the collection in 1968, "I found my own fascination in asking the villagers on the islands to show me antiquities and ruins . . .," and she states how she and her husband "concentrated our efforts in collecting" Cycladic figurines. Renfrew asks the reader to think of the Goulandris Collection as "rescuing Cycladic figurines from the international art market: more likely, looters plundered Cycladic graves with the specific intention of selling their booty to the Goulandrises.

One can only guess at the cost of forming the Goulandris collection in terms of archaeological sites destroyed and information lost. Renfrew notes that less than one tenth of all excavated Cycladic burials contained marble figures: if we assume, hypothetically, that a grave will contain no more than one figurine, then the 46 Cycladic figurines from the Goulandris Collection illustrated in *The Cycladic Spirit* represent about 460 destroyed graves.

The issue of forgeries remains unaddressed by Renfrew. Forgeries are mentioned by Christos Doumas—the Greek archaeologist who first published the Goulandris Collection—in a chapter contributed to the present work on the history of archaeological investigations of Cycladic culture. Doumas explains how "a veritable industry producing fakes" developed when the voracious demand of museums and collectors outstripped the supply of available Cycladic figures. Entire collections were built up almost entirely of fakes, leading Doumas to wonder if the forgeries were not some sort of "divine retribution."

But Doumas, who, like Renfrew, owes a debt of gratitude to the Goulandrises for being allowed to publish their collection, never mentions what troubles this reader: Since a flood of fakes was infiltrating the art market when the Goulandris Collection was being formed, is it not possible, even likely, that some of the Goulandris marbles are fakes? Unfortunately, Renfrew, who elsewhere shows a keen awareness that in archaeology all assumptions must be made explicit and all evidence carefully evaluated, here simply ignores the question and presumes that all the objects in the Goulandris Collection are authentic. In fact, Renfrew touches upon the issue just once in the book, when he suggests that a particular sculpture in a Berlin museum is a fake; there he mentions the "widespread existence of modern fakes" of Cycladic figures.

One of the most troubling aspects of the study of Cycladic sculpture is that, because the figurines appeal so much to modern aesthetic sensibilities, their ancient context hardly seems to matter. In fact, many art historians and collectors seem to prefer to contemplate the abstract Cycladic figures unencumbered by any concern for their original function, as they might a work by Modigliani or Brancusi. The figurines seem, after all, so very modern. Indeed, many are.

For Dolly Goulandris, the appeal of the figurines lay in "their timeless forms and mysterious origins." The mystery, of course, is largely a consequence of the clandestine and illegal way the objects were obtained. This viewpoint is rather typical; for example, a curator at the Museum of Fine Arts in Houston, where the Goulandris

Collection was exhibited in 1981–1982, praised the "beauty of their timeless forms," which makes them "prized today for aesthetic qualities that speak to us across the ages." Their original functions, and the ancient culture that produced them, have become irrelevant, or worse, "mysterious," a tag that enhances their marketability.

Even Renfrew eventually succumbs to this modernist perspective. Renfrew the archaeologist struggles to understand what place these figurines might have had in Cycladic society. In the final analysis, however, it is Renfrew the art critic who describes the collection in the effusive terms of the connoisseur, for whom the context does not matter: marble vessels are "elegant," "exquisite," and "splendid," marble figurines are "masterpieces," "beautiful," "delightful," "vivacious," a "tour de force." One can only wonder how they might have seemed to a Cycladic farmer: Magical? Frightful? Awesome? Holy?

The Cycladic Spirit is more than art criticism by Colin Renfrew; it is also a coffee-table book beautifully illustrated with John Bigelow Taylor's photographs of artifacts and figurines. There is something both seductive and troubling in this format. The Cycladic figurines are photographed against a black background: one might be looking at a display case in a Madison Avenue art gallery, so completely are these objects divorced form their context. And throughout the book are uncaptioned and tiny color scenes of the Cycladic land- and seascapes; these evoke not so much a real sense of place but a mood. The overall impression of the illustrations is of "timeless" museum pieces with only the most distant connection to the land from which they were untimely ripped.

Colin Renfrew has missed an excellent opportunity to educate collectors and art historians about the barbarity of collecting. How effective it would have been to include in the book photographs of plundered sites and despoiled graves.

The Cycladic Spirit is a disturbing book because the author, a prominent archaeologist, perpetuates an attitude that is all too typical of the way art historians treat collections of looted material. Those who have personal and professional ties to the art market tend to lose a fundamental and priceless element of their objectivity and, in certain areas of inquiry, their critical acumen as scholars is diminished. This book, written for a non-specialist audience, can only reinforce the notion that looting is something that just happens, while collecting is a noble and worthwhile pursuit. The truth is that collectors are the real looters.

Ricardo J. Elia teaches archaeology at Boston University. He is the editor of the Journal of Field Archaeology.

DISCUSSION QUESTIONS

1. What are the pitfalls for scholars who publish unprovenienced materials? The rewards?
2. What do we lose if we ignore unprovenienced materials?
3. Can one prove an object is a forgery?
4. How is authenticity determined?
5. What, and of what value, is a "certificate of authenticity"?
6. How common are forgeries? How could we determine this?
7. How do forgeries affect the marketplace? How do they affect scholarship?
8. What message is conveyed by the choice of illustrations in an archaeological publication? (Examine some publications intended for a non-specialist audience with this question in mind.)
9. Is it fair to say that collectors are the real looters?
10. What are the consequences for the discipline of damning collectors as looters? (Consider extant sources of funding for individual archaeologists, students, museums, professional organizations; jobs outside of academe; new responsibilities that follow from these consequences; etc.)
11. Do textual and epigraphical antiquities require a different ethic? The Dead Sea Scrolls are perhaps the most well publicized and studied of recent textual materials that have come from undocumented archaeological contexts. Should scholars have refused to study and publish them?*

---

*See: Peter S. Allen's review of *Secrets of the Dead Sea Scrolls* in "Films," *Archaeology*, (Jan/Feb 1992): 70–72. For a New World example, see Angel M. H. Schuster, "Case of the Suspect Stela: Scholars Debate the Authenticity of a Post-Olmec Commemorative Stone," *Archaeology* (Sept/Oct 1994): 51–53.

FURTHER RESEARCH

See also: Colin Renfrew, "Collectors are the Real Looters" and "Ricardo Elia Responds," *Archaeology* (May/June 1993): 16–17; and, for a rare example of an attempt to document the effects of the art market on archaeological scholarship, David W. J. Gill and Christopher Chippindale, "Material and Intellectual Consequences of Esteem for Cycladic Figures," *American Journal of Archaeology* 97 (1993): 601–59.

PART TWO
RESPONSES
TO LOOTING

L ooting, along with economic development and modern farming practices, is destroying the nonrenewable archaeological
record of the past far more rapidly than archaeologists can study
that record. To slow the destruction, modern nations have turned,
first, to legal remedies. Some of these are discussed in the first two
articles in this section. But while laws may be helping, they are clearly
insufficient protection. The third and fourth articles present other
creative approaches. Still others are needed.

CHAPTER FIVE
PROJECT STING
by John Neary

Neary describes a day in the life of a National Park Service undercover agent, executing a sting operation to catch traffickers in stolen antiquities. U.S. Park Service and Bureau of Land Management agents pose as dealers and, in one case, the spoiled mistress of a collector, to catch people dealing in illegally acquired artifacts. They hope their undercover work will not only bring some major offenders to trial, but also make everyone dealing in these materials wary of everyone else, thus making the practice less attractive.

It's Wednesday morning, and Judy Reed looks ahead to a busy few days of oddly melodramatic work for an archaeologist. A National Park Service undercover agent and the 41-year-old mother of two daughters, she frequently goes into the field with other agents to set up and execute sting operations intended to catch traffickers in stolen artifacts. On this day, with Park Service undercover specialist Phil Young, Reed flies from her home base in Sante Fe, New Mexico, to Austin, Texas, where she picks up from a federal museum a small satchel containing artifacts from Mexico and the southwestern United States, bait for a sting planned for that evening.

She and Young then drive to a motel in northern San Antonio, where they rendezvous with Park Service agent Al DeLaCruz and their boss Bill Tanner. Young, Tanner and DeLaCruz next drive to a motel on San Antonio's south side, leaving Reed to put identifying code numbers on the artifacts. DeLaCruz checks in, taking two rooms, one for the sting, the other for surveillance. They quickly set up a radio receiver and tape recorder and begin testing them to make sure they pick up conversations through the microphone that Young has planted—along with his .357 magnum pistol—under the bed pillows in the room two doors away. Meanwhile, because Young is not sure whether their target might bring some friends, if he shows up at all, two more Park Service agents, Don Philpot and Dan Steed, arrive to provide backup. Reed, en route with the artifacts, calls over her car phone to request help finding the motel. The powerfully built DeLaCruz, his faced scarred from years in the ring as an amateur prize-fighter, will lead the questioning of their target if the sting works. He straps on a shoulder holster, then changes from jeans into a business suit, the better to intimidate his quarry. Philpot hitches up his gun belt below his bulletproof vest and checks his handcuffs as Tanner readjusts the recorder. Young—slim, disarmingly youthful, and easy-going—slips into the room to give a last-minute briefing, explaining that the target is a "dealer in prehistoric antiquities," a middle-aged real estate entrepreneur who augments his income from negotiating oil leases by trading in artifacts. It was Tanner who had first spotted their target at an antiques show in Kentucky. "I go to all these shows," he says, "and look for people who buy and sell artifacts. If a person indicates any sort of willingness to do business illegally, we pursue it. Right now we probably have a hundred such cases we could pursue."

Young has no fixed appointment with the dealer, but had arranged days before to call him when he was in town. He had told the dealer he was selling artifacts, items taken from somewhere in the huge Amistad National Recreation area, a vast reservoir and forest on the Mexican border near Del Rio, Texas. The dealer had expressed an interest in seeing them.

Reed arrives with the artifacts, takes them to Young's room and spreads them out on the bed. They include three clay figurines from Jalisco, Mexico, and seven painted pebbles, three sandals made of woven yucca fiber, a piece of mat, a bit of wooden flute, a stone bead, a painted deer scapula, a tiny snare net, all from the Amistad. Reed leaves, and Young, now in his undercover role as convicted felon and trader "Shawn O'Hara," telephones the target and invites him to come over. At 8:02, hunched over their tape monitor, the agents hear a faint knocking. Shawn O'Hara's visitor has arrived. Showtime.

"Looks like a little net used to catch a mouse when it comes out of a hole," a strange voice drawls as Young's guest admires the artifacts on the bed. "Little bamboo flute. You got any papers on this?"

"No, but I can get 'em," Young replies, and the agents two doors away listen intently as the bargaining begins, O'Hara asking $1,500 for the whole batch, the trader laconically countering, "I don't think everything here is worth $250." The agents are waiting for the trader to make his buy and for Young to say, "Hope we can do business again," the code words that will signal the agents to rush down the hall and handcuff the trader—and cuff Shawn O'Hara too, to protect Young's undercover identity.

The bargaining goes on for more than an hour, interspersed with good ol' boy banter about bass fishing and the hard, long highway miles it takes to be a trader. At last a deal is struck. At 9:22, Young accepts $100 in cash and an I.O.U. for $300. He says he hopes they can do business again. DeLaCruz, Steed and Philpot speed down the corridor and grab the dealer as he is about to leave Young's room. "Federal officers!" DeLaCruz barks, "Back inside!"

But the evening is far from over. Questioning of the dealer goes on for about two hours. He is released, pending further interrogation, and warned that he faces a possible federal indictment. The agents hope he will choose to cooperate with the government and name others involved in the artifacts trade. Around midnight the agents return to their motel to review the day's work. "Good job," Young tells them. "I'm really pleased, because the ultimate goal is to get this guy to lead us to other people—and it looks like he will. Texas has a lot of collectors. He's been a collector and a minor dealer for a number of years. We want him to identify his business friends." Tanner tells the agents the next morning at breakfast, "When we get back to Sante Fe, we'll sit down and figure how to milk this guy."

But before that happens, Judy Reed has another job back in Sante Fe preparing diagrams that will enable a federal court jury in Albuquerque to understand the damage another trafficker in artifacts has done by looting a rock-shelter in the Gila National Forest. She will explain to the jury how digging inside the shelter has diminished its archaeological integrity and the value to scholars of the artifacts taken from it. Confronted by her testimony and the rest of the evidence against him, the accused, a building supplies dealer from Milan, New Mexico, will abandon his efforts at a defense and plead guilty. He will be fined $5000, given three years probation, and ordered to perform 300 hours of community service. Reed's role in this case began more than a year before when she posed as the mistress of a wealthy collector, a ruse invented to explain where the money was coming from to buy the stolen artifacts—more than $10,000 worth before the sting was over—and to pay for a helicopter to take the agents to the rock-shelter in question.

Reed began working on such cases two years ago, after the body of a 35-year-old Sante Fe artifacts trader was found on secluded land near the village of Tesuque outside Sante Fe. The trader had shot himself in the chest with a .22 caliber rifle. Hearing that the dead man kept a stash of antiquities in a rented storage unit, Park Service agents checked out the lead and discovered a bonanza of looted artifacts along with journals and maps indicating where they had come form and to whom some had gone. It was a virtual client list of collectors and dealers.

A Park Service field director busy at the time with an exhaustive survey of the Native American ruins that dot Bandelier National Monument, Reed was asked to drop that assignment and undertake an inventory of the dead trader's collection. It was a tough job, made even more difficult by the fact that she had known the trader and his family for years. In time, she catalogued 2,952 artifacts worth $178,550, and traced each one to the site from which it had been taken. From the trader's files and journals, she and her fellow agents, working as a Park Service/Bureau of Land Management task force, created a wall map showing the whereabouts of more than 200 of the trader's clients throughout the country—and began investigating them.

Only once did Reed feel herself to be in danger in the field. A team member working undercover on a tip from an informant had visited a remote ruin southwest of Socorro, New Mexico. He had watched looters dig, but an assessment of the damage by an expert was needed to buttress the case. On a trip to the site, Reed was naturally apprehensive that the culprits might turn up at any moment, spoiling for a fight. "We drove from Sante Fe," she recalls, "taking the back roads and avoiding the small towns. These Broncos we use have antennas all over them, blacked-out windows, you can spot 'em a mile away. We parked at the drop-off the looters used, in the open. The five of us walked up through the trees to the ruin, up on a ridge 20 to 40 feet above the surrounding flatlands. Everybody else had a bullet-proof vest. I didn't! I was thinking, if there's trouble, where should I be—under a tree? I'd never been in a position where my life might be in danger." The assignment required two visits and eight hours of study, and helped obtain the convictions of a rural store owner and his son who pleaded guilty to federal charges of artifact theft. They were sentenced to probation of two years and one year, respectively.

In the rock-shelter case, Reed had to gain the confidence of the looter so she could go along on the helicopter ride. She felt the risk was worth it to get to the remote site and assess the damage. "I was supposed to be the spoiled mistress of a collector," she recalls. Her undercover teammate, BLM agent Mike Moomey posing as a scout for a wealthy export company owner, told the target, "Don't talk to her. She's a real bitch!" To live up to her advance billing, the slender five-foot six-inch Reed dolled herself up in hiking boots, a tank top and Lycra tights under a long sweater that concealed a wire—"I wore a harness with two mikes and a recorder in back, so he wouldn't detect it if he touched me on the shoulders. I frowned a lot."

Reed recalls with undiminished astonishment the time she drove to the home of a California looter who told her and another under-cover agent, "I've got skeletons in my closet." She laughs. "He really did!" The man had been excavating Chumash burials around Santa Barbara, and there in his utility room were two human skulls. The skeletons were in the basement. "I just can't believe that people can live with skeletons in their house!" she marvels. The looter was fined $2,500, given a five-year suspended jail term and 18 months of probation and ordered to perform 300 hours of community service with the Santa Barbara Trust for Historic Preservation. The skeletons were sent to the anthropology department of the University of California at Santa Barbara, pending their return to the Chumash.

A specialist in Pueblo ceramics, Reed signs a log every time she opens and closes the locked room that serves as the evidence vault in the suite of Sante Fe offices her team occupies but will soon vacate. The task force, having blown its cover over the course of two dozen criminal investigations, is being disbanded. Park Service and BLM agents, between whom there had been considerable friction, will pursue their undercover work separately. Inside the vault, carefully swathed in blisterpak and plastic zip-loc bags, nestled in acid-free paper and cardboard boxes, are more than 4,000 artifacts, a miniature museum of the cultures of North, Central and South America. Some of them get the special treatment that their status as cultural totems requires. Reed once invited a Navajo medicine man to inspect a ceremonial mask and to advise her on proper storage procedures. He told her the mask should be stored alone in a box, not rolled in paper, and kept face up—and that nothing should obstruct its vision. Mylar was okay. A plastic lid was eventually chosen.

Reed wears white cotton gloves so the oil of her skin won't contaminate these relics, which include a prehistoric ivory pin from Alaska; textiles, a comb still bearing the reddish hairs of its long-dead owner, copper money, a ceramic whistle in the shape of a bird effigy, a duck-shaped pot, a tripod-shaped stone metate and an intricate stirrup-shaped mano, and spindles from Peru; charred tubes of wood once smoked as cigarettes by the Hohokam; tiny purses made from the bodies of rodents; a magnificent 2,000-year-old turkey feather robe from a cave in Utah; a hunter-warrior's oak bow; and a delicate wooden circlet enclosing a web of yucca fibers used by its Apache owner to snare bad dreams.

"I've seen more beautiful things than I probably would have otherwise," says Reed, "even in a museum." Her work imposes an emotional toll, the price she pays in the anger she feels. "Some people wouldn't want to do this at all, it irritates them so much, seeing all this contraband. They can't hold their temper." Packing a tiny woven cotton sandal from southeastern Utah, she murmurs, "Archaeologists *never* find these. *We* find little bits of cloth. Now I know why.

Somebody's already been there!" She resents the targets she and her teammates pursue, especially the dealers. "They view these things as art rather than as things that lose their value when they lose their provenance."

Reed's boss, Phil Young, says stings like the San Antonio operation, in which artifacts Reed has authenticated as stolen are presented for sale—and identified as hot—are having a chilling effect on the trade. Says Young, "We don't want 'em even to trust the people they went to high school with!" But what is really needed, he adds, is a new law prohibiting the possession of stolen artifacts, period. "Until then," says Reed, as she prepares for her next court case, "We've got to concentrate on education, teaching people to respect things. It will take a long time. You won't see a return on it right away. It's like committing to research. There are all sorts of things people could do. But it means changing people's values."

Carefully, Reed packs up her cache of artifacts, some to be repatriated to their countries of origin, the rest destined for federal and tribal museums and storehouses. Meanwhile, Phil Young waits for a fresh supply to use in a new round of stings.

John Neary is a free-lance writer living in New Mexico.

DISCUSSION QUESTIONS

1. Who enforces U.S. antiquities laws? Who should enforce them?
2. What are the penalties for breaking those laws?
3. What happens to confiscated antiquities when the source cannot be determined?
4. What would a law that prohibits the possession of stolen artifacts accomplish?*
5. What are the problems in proving that an artifact is "stolen"?
6. What are the "papers" referred to here, and where do dealers get them?

---

*For a view on a recent Italian attempt to deal with this issue, see Umberto Allemandi, "Come Declare Your Antiquities and If We Fancy Them, We'll Hav'em," *The Art Newspaper*, 53 (November 1995): 23.

CHAPTER SIX

TURKEY'S WAR ON THE ILLICIT ANTIQUITIES TRADE

by Mark Rose and Özgen Acar

"America's museums have been the partners of thieves, smugglers, and unethical dealers and collectors in the looting of Turkey's cultural heritage." Turkey is one country that has committed substantial funds to fighting back. The article discusses the Lydian Hoard (with additional references), the Boston Museum of Fine Arts' Herakles, the San Antonio Art Museum's Domitia, Dumbarton Oaks' Byzantine church treasure, the Elmali Hoard, the Garland sarcophagus, and other "gifts" to the American-Turkish Society. The supplements mention similar cases in European countries, including the Altar of Zeus from Pergamon, currently in Berlin, and Priam's Treasure; and the competition for, and courtship of, collectors by museum curators.

America's museums have been the partners of thieves, smugglers and unethical dealers and collectors in the looting of Turkey's cultural heritage. Anyone who doubts this need only walk through the archaeological museum in Antalya on Turkey's southern coast. Here one finds the lower half of a statue of Herakles; the upper half is in the Museum of Fine Arts, Boston. In one gallery are some of the silver pieces belonging to a Byzantine church treasure; the rest are at Harvard University's Dumbarton Oaks Research Library in Washington D.C. Displayed in yet another gallery is a reassembled sarcophagus that looters had broken up so they could sell its individual carvings for greater profit. a placard below one carving notes that it had been acquired by the J. Paul Getty Museum in

Malibu, but was returned when Turkish archaeologists identified it as stolen. Elsewhere in the museum is another sarcophagus, with rich carvings of cupids holding up heavy garlands. Stolen from Turkey, it was displayed at the Brooklyn Museum, but was returned last year. No one knows precisely the value of antiquities stolen from Turkey each year; it may be as high as $100 million. To get an idea of the immense profits that can be made, consider a single piece, a stolen Hellenistic statue returned to Turkey last fall. Smugglers paid the farmer who found it the equivalent of $7,400. In New York it went for sale for $540,000. A list of stolen antiquities seized by authorities in Turkey between February and September 1991, published in the Instanbul newspaper *Cumhuriyet*, illustrates the scale of the looting: 3,489 Roman and later coins; 390 Hellenistic bronze coins and several Roman glass bottles; 421 ancient silver coins; a Roman sculptural frieze; five Roman grave reliefs; 14 classical marble sculptures and heads; and a cache including more than 1,260 coins, bronze arrowheads, and small terra-cotta statues.

The high prices commanded by such plunder are hardly surprising. What is news is that Turkey is doing something about it: In a series of high-profile cases it has served notice to the players in the illicit antiquities game that it means business. No other country had pursued its plundered heritage as aggressively or as tenaciously. "There is a willingness on the part of Turkey to commit substantial resources in the fight to recover stolen antiquities," says Lawrence Kaye, head of the Art Law and International Law Practice Groups at the law firm Herrick, Feinstein, which represents Turkey. Some cases may be settled amicably, others will certainly end in protracted legal struggles.

Turkey has used fundamental principles of Anglo-American common law as the basis for its cases in the United States, claiming that the antiquities involved are stolen property and that a thief cannot convey title. It bases its ownerships of these antiquities on Turkish laws that, since 1906, have established its proprietary interest in all antiquities found on or in its territory.

Of Turkey's victories so far, the most impressive has been the repatriation of the Lydian Hoard, also known as the Croseus, Lydian, or East Greek treasure, in October of 1993. The return ended a

25-year effort to recover the material and a six-year legal struggle with New York's Metropolitan Museum of Art. Consisting of 363 artifacts—gold and silver vessels and jewelry, a pair of marble sphinxes, and wall paintings—the "hoard" came from several sixth-century B.C. burial mounds in the Manisa and Usak regions of Turkey that were plundered in early 1966. (Authorities later recovered about 100 objects that were left behind.) The looters were arrested and prosecuted. Some confessed and later assisted in attempts to trace the hoard, which had been smuggled out of Turkey and sold to dealers George Zacos of Switzerland and John Klejman of New York. The Metropolitan purchased the antiquities between 1966 and 1970 for $1.5 million. It made no formal announcement of the purchase, and, as late as 1986, provided no information about the hoard in its central catalogue, a public inventory of its holdings.

According to Karl E. Meyer's investigative study of the illicit antiquities market, *The Plundered Past* (1973), the Metropolitan had plans to unveil the treasure in its 1970 centennial year. An article in the Boston *Globe*, however, hinted that the museum had acquired a Lydian treasure. This prompted a request for information from a Turkish official, which the museum apparently ignored. Plans to exhibit the entire hoard were dropped, but the museum did display a silver wine pitcher and four other pieces in the show "Masterpieces of Fifty Centuries." The five objects were omitted from the exhibition catalogue, and were returned to the museum's vault after the show closed. A second inquiry by Turkey followed a 1973 article in the *New York Post* that again brought up rumors of a Lydian treasure at the Metropolitan, but it, too, received no response.

Former Metropolitan director Thomas Hoving, in his 1993 memoir, *Making the Mummies Dance*, gives an account of an acquisitions committee meeting dealing with the Lydian hoard, indicating that the museum knew where the treasure came from:

> Houghton [trustee Arthur Houghton, Sr.] swiftly cut in to move ratification of two appropriations for Greek and Roman purchases made before my arrival, the last remaining objects in a hoard of Greek sixth century B.C. silver found in Turkey—$14,500 for a gold ring, a silver alabastron, and a silver beaker, and $25,000 for two

marble sphinxes that had come from the tomb in Anatolia where the treasure had been unearthed. Curator Dietrich von Bothmer explained that the works constituted the final pieces of what he described as the "Lydian hoard."

Hoving describes a subsequent meeting with vice-director Theodore Rousseau, John Buchanan (his assistant), von Bothmer, and Ashton Hawkins (the Metropolitan's legal counsel) to plan their response to Turkish inquiries:

> Dietrich von Bothmer asked what we should do if any damaging evidence were found that our East Greek treasure had been excavated illegally and smuggled out of Turkey . . . . I was exasperated. "We all believe that the stuff was illegally dug up," I told him. "Drew Oliver [curator Andrew Oliver] has strong evidence. He went to the tomb and says he identified the lower parts of the pair of sphinxes which are now hidden in your storeroom. For Christ's sake, if the Turks come up with the proof from their side, we'll give the East Greek treasure back. And that's policy. We took our chances when we bought the material.

The museum's policy was, simply, not to help the Turkish investigation, but to return the hoard if the Turks could prove it had come from the tombs in Usak. After the retirement of Metropolitan president C. Douglas Dillon in 1983, Hoving claims, "the museum bent and ultimately broke that policy and when the proof was forthcoming, the Met persistently refused even to discuss the return or sharing of the treasure . . . ."

In June 1984 the Metropolitan finally displayed more than 40 of the objects as a group, labeling them the East Greek Treasure, and described them in a catalogue titled *A Greek and Roman Treasury*. With the catalogue's photographs, the Turkish authorities were able to establish, for the first time, that the museums pieces were Lydian and were similar to the objects they had recovered from the thieves. Turkey began building its case, rechecking the tumuli, re-interviewing the looters, and obtaining customs documents.

In 1985, and again in 1986, the Metropolitan attempted a legal "end run" by sponsoring a bill in the New York state legislature that would have changed the time at which the clock began running on the state's three-year statute of limitations regarding stolen antiquities:

from three years after the first demand for the return of an object by its owner and a refusal of that demand by the possessor to three years after the first public notification of the acquisition of the object. The museum apparently hoped that such legislation would block any claim Turkey made to the hoard. The bill was vetoed both years by Governor Mario Cuomo, who argued that its "provisions do not provide a reasonable opportunity for individuals or foreign governments to receive notice . . . before their rights are extinguished."

In July 1986 Turkey's Director General of Antiquities and Monuments, in a letter to the Metropolitan, formally demanded the return of the Lydian Hoard. A later meeting between museum officials and Turkish Consul General Murat Sungar and lawyers Harry Rand and Lawrence Kaye proved fruitless, and on May 29, 1987, the Republic of Turkey filed its lawsuit against the Metropolitan. The following years were occupied with hearings and other legal proceedings. The museum moved for dismissal of the suit, claiming that it had purchased the items in good faith and that the statute of limitations had expired. Turkey countered, arguing that it had been unable to determine that the objects in the museum were from the looted tombs until after the Metropolitan published its 1984 catalogue. In 1990 U.S. District Judge Vincent L. Broderick accepted the Turkish position and refused to dismiss the suit. With this decision, the case entered the pretrial discovery stage. A team of scholars selected by Turkey's Ministry of Culture was allowed to study the objects. Included were the Turkish archaeologists Ekrem Akurgal, Kazim Akbiyikoglu, Güven Bakir, and Burhan Tezcan; Crawford Greenewalt, director of excavations at Sardis which is near the tumuli; and Machteld Mellink, a Bryn Mawr College professor and an authority on Anatolian archaeology. Given access to the material, Turkey soon amassed considerable evidence indicating that the Metropolitan's treasure had been taken from the tomb. Wall paintings were measured and shown to match gaps in the walls of one tomb. Looters cooperating with the investigation described particular pieces at the Metropolitan that they had stolen. Minutes of acquisition committee meetings made it clear that the museum had known the material was illegally excavated and smuggled out of Turkey. Had the case come to trial, there would likely

75

have been testimony from former Metropolitan officials, including Hoving and von Bothmer.

Faced with the possibility of losing the case should it come to trial, the Metropolitan tried to negotiate a settlement. Hoving's account was published in *Art & Auction* magazine:

> . . . a delegation of Met officials led by President William Luers and including Director Philippe de Montebello and Lawyer Hawkins traveled to Turkey around Christmas 1992 to talk to Minister of Culture Fikri Saglar and surrender. The plan was to admit—for the first time since 1974—that the treasure was Turkish and did belong with the pieces left behind and to make a deal to share the objects, say five years in New York and five years in Turkey. Angered, the minister refused to talk to the men from the Met, who returned home saying only that inadequate hotel accommodations had forced them to cut short their trip before a meeting could be arranged.

In fact, the Turks felt it was inappropriate for the minister to meet with the Metropolitan's delegation, which did speak with Engin Özgen, Turkey's Director General of Monuments, and attorney Kaye. Finally, in September 1993 the Metropolitan relented and agreed to return the Lydian Hoard to Turkey. The lawsuit was dropped and the artifacts were sent to Ankara, where they were put on display that November in the Museum of Anatolian Civilizations. Philippe de Montebello, director of the Metropolitan, explained in a press release that the museum's decision to return the objects was prompted by the fact that:

> Turkish authorities did provide evidence that most of the material in question may indeed have been removed clandestinely from tombs in the Usak region, much of it only months before the museum acquired it. And second, we learned through the legal process of discovery that our own records suggested that some museum staff during the 1960s were likely aware, even as they acquired these objects, that their provenance was controversial. Under this unique set of circumstances, the Metropolitan has chosen to follow the only course that it feels fitting and proper.

There are, however, unresolved questions. If the Metropolitan's own documents showed that the hoard was taken from Turkey, why did it engage in a six-year legal battle to retain it? Why did the museum

hide in its basement for 25 years one of the most important archaeological finds of the century, preventing anyone from studying the
material and preventing the public from seeing it and appreciating it?
Some of the objects, the wall paintings for example, remained
unrestored until they were returned to Ankara and prepared for
exhibition there.

Turkey had sufficient evidence to prove that the Lydian Hoard
was removed from its territory in violation of its patrimony laws. The
Museum of Fine Arts in Boston seems to be hoping that Turkey
doesn't have such evidence in the case of a Herakles statue in its
collection. The object in dispute is a Late Antonine (A.D. 170–172)
sculpture of the type known as the Weary Herakles, which shows the
tired hero leaning on his club. The upper half of the statue is jointly
held by Leon Levy and Shelby White, New York collectors and
husband and wife, and the Museum of Fine Arts. The lower half is in
the main lobby of the Antalya Museum, along with photographs of
the statue fragment in Boston and copies of articles about it from
Turkish and American newspapers.

In 1980 Jale Inan, director of excavations at the ancient city of
Perge, northeast of Antalya, heard rumors that something important
had been stolen from the site. Later that summer, while excavating a
Roman villa, Inan discovered the bottom half of the Herakles statue,
as well as several other statues that were complete. By 1981 the top
half of the statue had been acquired by Levy, who gave a half-interest
in the sculpture to the Boston museum. The statue was displayed at
the Metropolitan from late 1990 through early 1991 in an exhibition
of White and Levy's collection titled *Glories of the Past*. Turkey learned
of the Levy-White Herakles from the exhibition catalogue (for which
Boston's curator Cornelius Vermeule had written an entry on the
statue) and from a photograph that was faxed to the Antalya Museum.
Articles in *Connoisseur* magazine and *The New York Times* showed the
upper and lower halves of the statue photographically rejoined.

Following this publicity, three attempts were made to prove that
the two halves of the statue matched. First, a thin plaster cast of the
top surface of the lower half of Herakles was made in Antalya and
shipped to New York. Because the top half of the sculpture was still

mounted on its pedestal, it was impossible to do more than compare the sizes of the cast and the statue top. A second and more substantial cast was then produced and taken to Levy and White's apartment, to which the upper half of the sculpture had been moved. The piece had been taken off its pedestal, but the metal post by which it was fixed to the stand had been left in place, preventing an attempt at fitting cast and statue together. Finally, in 1992, complete casts of both top and bottom were brought together at the Museum of Fine Arts. Representatives of Turkey and the museum watched anxiously as the cast of the upper half was lowered onto that of the lower half. They fit perfectly. Vermeule is quoted by Thomas Hoving, in *Art & Auction* magazine as saying: "I'm shocked. I'm so surprised! Well, I never . . . ." He then, according to Hoving, asked the Turks, "Say, would you be willing to discuss a shared loan?"

Despite the fact that the two halves match, the Museum of Fine Arts has nonetheless kept the upper part. In a 1994 *Los Angeles Times* article, Robert P. Mitchell, the museum's director of public relations argued that:

> The museum does not acknowledge Turkey's claim to ownership. There has never been any evidence that the statue was stolen, and allegations to that effect were entirely unsupported . . . Indeed, the break between the top and the bottom halves of the statue appears to be an ancient one, such that the top half could have been removed long ago from the territory that is now Turkey. In the unfortunate event that the current settlement discussions are not successful, a lawsuit would be necessary. Such a case would raise significant questions.

One question would be whether or not Turkey could prove that the upper half was still in its territory after its patrimony laws were enacted.

Turkey has been less successful pursuing a marble statue in the San Antonio Art Museum that possibly represents the empress Domitia. Carved ca. A.D. 90, the statue has been loaned to the museum by dealers Fuat Üzülmez of Munich and Fritz Burki of Zurich. The two are reportedly trying to sell it for $1.8 million. The statue's recent past is difficult to reconstruct, but according to articles in *Connoisseur* it was smuggled out of Instanbul in either September 1987 or April 1988. Its trail was picked up in June 1988 when a KLM cargo official in Istanbul opened a crate that seemed too heavy for its listed contents, plaster models for dolls. Inside the crate was a marble statue of the goddess Demeter. Authorities traced the sculpture to Fuat Aydiner, who, wanted for questioning by Turkish police and Interpol concerning the smuggling of a coin hoard, had fled Turkey. Aydiner's nephew, Sait, who had arranged fraudulent shipping papers for the sculpture, escaped to Canada, but was convicted in absentia. Evidence produced during his trial showed that a second crate had been sent from Instanbul to Fuat Üzülmez's Munich gallery, Artemis. In that crate, suggested *Connoisseur*, was the Domitia statue. American expatriate dealer Robert Hecht, Jr., in a February 1991 interview in the British newspaper *The Independent*, claimed that the statue came to America in early 1988, before April, and was shipped to the Getty Museum, which declined to purchase it. According to Hecht, the statue was then sent to the Acanthus Gallery in New York before being shipped to San Antonio. After publication of an October 1990 *Connoisseur* article that suggested the statue was looted, Hecht, acting for Burki, notified the San Antonio museum that he intended to remove it. The museum requested a delay and he gave them until the end of December. In January 1991 a U.S. Customs agent found Hecht at the Union Club in New York. The agent had documents authorizing the seizure of the statue, which was taken off exhibition and stored pending determination of ownership. Turkey is reported to have withdrawn its claim to the statue, which the museum has again put on display. One problem with Turkey's case was an affidavit, alluded to by Hecht in *The Independent*, that a Munich museum director saw the statue at the Artemis Gallery in 1986, two years before it was supposedly smuggled out of Istanbul. Apparently Turkey felt it was more worthwhile to focus its efforts elsewhere than to pursue the matter. Meanwhile, the statue is still on loan to the San Antonio Art Museum.

One case that may be settled amicably concerns a church treasure, part of which is at Harvard University's Dumbarton Oaks Research Library in Washington, D.C., the other is at the Antalya Museum.

In 1963 looters at Kumluca, the ancient city of Corydalla west of Antalya near Turkey's Mediterranean coast, stole silver and bronze vessels, candlesticks, and other liturgical objects from the ruins of a sixth-century church. Subsequent excavations by Turkish archaeologists yielded more treasure. Inscriptions and stamps on the objects indicate that they had belonged to a monastery named Holy Sion and that they dated to between 565 and 575. Karl E. Meyer, in *The Plundered Past*, traced the stolen treasure to Istanbul antiquities dealer George Zacos, who had purchased it and then contacted John Seymour Thacher, director of Dumbarton Oaks, home of one of the finest collections of Byzantine art in the United States. Thacher reportedly met Zacos in Switzerland and bought the treasure for $1 million. In 1964 Nezih Firatii, an Istanbul Archaeological Museum curator studying the legally excavated part of the treasure, made inquiries at an international meeting of Byzantine scholars in Greece, but learned nothing. In the fall of 1964 Dumbarton Oaks put the treasure on display. In 1967 it published a catalogue of its Byzantine collection that identified the objects as part of a church treasure from a site near Antalya. According to Meyer, Turkey applied diplomatic pressure and denied research permits to Dumbarton Oaks scholars. Eventually negotiations were opened and seemed to be heading toward a settlement in the 1980s, only to be broken off over technicalities. In the wake of the publicity surrounding the Metropolitan's return of the Lydian treasure, talks between Dumbarton Oaks and Turkey have resumed.

At issue in the Decadrachm or Elmali Hoard case are nearly 2,000 Greek and Lycian silver coins, among them 14 Athenian decadrachms, possibly a commemorative coin struck after an Athenian victory over the Persians. Before the hoard was found, only 13 decadrachms were known to exist, and the last one to be sold had been auctioned in 1974 for $270,000. The value of the entire hoard is estimated at more than $10 million. Turkey's case, filed in 1989, has been fought aggressively by the defendants, including multimillionaire William Koch, Johnathan Kagan, and Jeffrey Spier, and their consortium known as OKS Partners. The name OKS derives from Oxbow, a Dedham, Massachusetts corporation owned by Koch, a former board member of the Museum of Fine Arts, Boston; Johnathan Kagan, a Harvard graduate interested in numismatics who received an M.A. at Oxford and then joined an investment banking firm in New York; and Jeffrey Spier, a Harvard classmate and fellow numismatist who received a Ph.D. from Oxford in 1988. Repeated motions for dismissal have been decided in Turkey's favor, and the case may go to trial next year.

According to a 1988 article in *Connoisseur*, the hoard was found April 18, 1984, by Bayram Sungur, Ibrahim Basbug, and Ahmet Ali Sentürk. The three were treasure hunting at Bayindir near Elmai, north of Antalya, when Basbug, using a metal detector, discovered coins in an ancient jar near the surface. How the hoard came to be buried there is unknown. It may be associated with the presence of Athenian forces in the area after the defeat of the Persians at the Eurymedon River near Elmali in ca. 468/467 B.C. The looters were arrested and later revealed much about the subsequent history of the hoard. Sungur and Basburg flew to Istanbul and met with Fuat Aydiner, who purchased 1,889 coins from them for $692,000. How the hoard was carried out of Turkey is unknown. Documents from the looters' trial name Edip Telli, a Munich based Turkish dealer, as a conspirator. Ayinder is said to have sold the hoard to Telli for $1.325 million. Turkey issued an arrest warrant for Telli through Interpol in early 1985. He apparently escaped custody in Italy and returned to Munich, where he was left undisturbed by German authorities, notwithstanding Turkish efforts to extradite him.

OKS partners bought 1,746 coins for $2.7 million in 1984. It began selling them in 1987. According to *Connoisseur*, Anton Tkalec, a dealer in Switzerland, purchased 60, including three decadrachms, for more than $1 million. He reportedly resold most of these to the Numismatic Fine Arts (NFA) gallery, owned by Bruce McNall. NFA was to auction ten of the coins in early March 1988, and described them in its sale catalogue as "South Anatolia (Decadrachm) Hoard, 1984." That NFA labeled the coins so openly is puzzling. Lawyers for Turkey stopped the sale of the coins, and McNall turned over to them the ten coins. In a 1994 interview with *Vanity Fair* magazine McNall explained: "For me to be sued by the government of Turkey, can you imagine the problems, the press?. . . I can't handle the publicity or the litigation. I tell all my people, 'If there's a whisper [from Turkey], give it back.'" Why, given this cautious policy, would McNall advertise the source of the coins so openly?

If anyone was hurt by the raided auction it was OKS. By surrendering the coins immediately, McNall established a precedent that would make any sale of the coins difficult. Why would McNall attack OKS? Perhaps he resented their acquisition of the hoard. After all, McNall was the man who bought the last Athenian drachma before the hoard was discovered. He described in *Vanity Fair* the effect that the purchase had had on his career as a dealer: "That took me into a different league. All of a sudden I became the biggest buyer in the world. All of the dealers in Turkey and Greece, and all of their middlemen, started giving me first glances at the new hoards." Had McNall been waiting for the asking price of the Decadrachm Hoard to come down when OKS snapped it up?

So far, Turkey has recovered 19 coins from the hoard, including the ten McNall handed over. For the rest, either OKS will return them voluntarily, or the court will decide who gets them.

There are avenues other than legal action for the repatriation of cultural property. On April 24, 1994, a Roman-era sarcophagus smuggled out in 1986-87 was returned to Turkey, first being displayed in the archaeological museum in Istanbul and now in Antalya. The piece had been donated to The American-Turkish Society, a nonprofit tax-exempt organization that subsequently loaned it indefinitely to Turkey.

Dated to ca. A.D. 150, the intact marble coffin is known as the Garland Sarcophagus from the sculptured decoration on its sides and ends: small cupid figures holding up a heavy garland above theatrical masks. Damon Mezzacappa, a New York collector and investment banker who worked with Johnathan Kagan, had loaned the Garland Sarcophagus to the Brooklyn Museum, which placed it on display in 1987, labeled "anonymous loan." According to the Istanbul newspaper *Cumhuriyet*, Mezzacappa bought it for $1 million from Nevzat Telli, brother of the Munich-based dealer Edip Telli. *Connoisseur* identified Johnathan Kagan and Jeffrey Spier as middlemen in the deal. As

Turkey was considering going to court to recover the sarcophagus, Mezzacappa offered to give it to the Brooklyn Museum. A donation to a tax-exempt nonprofit foundation would have allowed Mezzacappa to deduct the full market value of the sarcophagus, which he placed at $11 million. Concerned that the sarcophagus might have been illicitly excavated, the Brooklyn Museum turned down the offer. A factor in its decision was the reported discovery of modern Turkish newspapers stuffed up under the lid of the sarcophagus, an indication that it was taken out of the country recently. In December 1991 Mezzacappa donated the sarcophagus to the American-Turkish Society, which promotes commercial and cultural relations between the Republic of Turkey and the United States. The amount Mezzacappa was able to write off as a tax deduction is unknown.

Hoving, in his *Art & Auction* article, saw the tax write-off as an opening many would take advantage of: "When this hitherto-unknown news leaks out, can one expect a rush of goodies to the [American-Turkish] society? . . . And will we soon see catalogue entries noting, say, the American-Peruvian Society or the American-Mexican society or the American-Whatever-Aggrieved-Country Society? One can fairly bet on it." While the flood of donations predicted by Hoving has not materialized, the American-Turkish Society has received at least one other statue, a second-century B.C. marble sculpture of Marsyas, who, as punishment for challenging Apollo in a music contest, is about to be flayed. The sculpture was found in May 1988 by a farmer, Abdurrahim Çetin, while plowing a field near the village of Baglica (the site of ancient Philadelphia) in western Turkey. Çetin's tractor broke the statue, originally the leg of an ornate Hellenistic table, into three pieces, but the farmer mended it. Çetin sold the sculpture to dealer Ali Kolasin for $7,400. The statue was smuggled out of Turkey and next appeared at Atlantis Antiques Gallery in New York with a price tag of $540,000. Johnathan Rosen, who ran Atlantis, was presented with evidence that the statue was stolen from Turkey (the farmer had photographed the statue in his living room). Rosen forestalled litigation by donating the statue to the American-Turkish Society, which, after displaying it in the Princeton University Art Museum, sent the statue to Turkey in August 1994 in the care of Engin Özgen, Director General of Monuments and Museums. Kolasin and three others were prosecuted in Turkey for their roles in smuggling the statue. Similarly, The Society for the Preservation of Greek Heritage was presented a collection of Mycenaean jewelry by New York's Michael Ward Gallery. The jewelry was probably looted from Aidonia in southern Greece.

Turkey's aggressive pursuit of stolen artifacts has been highly effective. In December 1993 Sotheby's in New York withdrew a torso of a kouros dated to ca. 500 B.C., from sale after Turkey claimed it was stolen. A second-century A.D. Roman frieze block depicting a mask of a youth, stolen from Aphrodisias, was identified by an archaeologist who saw it at Fortuna Fine Arts, a New York gallery. Seized by the FBI, it was returned to Turkey in August 1994. In January 1995 another sculpture stolen from Aphrodisias was returned to Turkey: a first-century A.D. marble head of a young man with curly locks, it had been cut from a block of the monument known as the Sebasteion sometime in early 1993. Discovered at Fortuna Fine Arts, it was on consignment for a Munich dealer.

The pillaging, however, continues. Interpol reports that from December 1993 to December 1994 seven classical marble statues and heads, four Roman marble frieze blocks, three Roman marble grave stelai, several carved column capitals and bases, one Hellenistic marble relief of a woman, and one Byzantine fresco were stolen from Turkish archaeological sites and museums. Nonetheless, Lawrence Kaye detects a "chill in the illicit marketplace," and notes that museums and dealers are being more careful and more cooperative. "Turkey's vigilance had paid off," says Engin Özgen. "Many treasures have been brought home and are now in their rightful place—on display in Turkey's museums where they are carefully maintained and can be viewed in their proper context. But despite our successes, we cannot and will not rest until the illicit trade in Turkey's heritage is stopped once and for all. At the same time, we intend to continue our efforts to share Turkey's vast cultural heritage with the rest of the world through temporary exhibitions of our treasures in the United States and other nations."

TURKEY'S CLAIMS ABROAD

Turkey has not singled out the United States in its crusade to recover stolen antiquities. In September 1994 Minister of Culture Timurçin Savas met with the German ambassador, Jurgen Oesterheldt, to request help in the return of three artifacts in Berlin museums: a statue of a fisherman from Aphrodisias, a sphinx from the Hittite capital of Hattusas, and a thirteenth-century prayer niche taken from Beyhekim Mosque in central Turkey. Meanwhile, Great Britain and Germany remain home to some of the most impressive monuments of ancient Anatolia. The British Museum has sculptures from the Mausoleum of Halicarnassus and the Temple of Artemis at Ephesus. It also holds the Nereid Monument and reliefs of the Harpy Tomb from the Lycian city of Xanthos. Turkey has made no formal claim to these.

The Altar of Zeus from Pergamon, with its Hellenistic sculptures depicting a battle between gods and giants, is a different matter. Turkey claims that it was illegally excavated by German engineer Carl Humann and smuggled to Berlin between 1868 and 1878. Except for a period from 1945 (when it was taken to the Soviet Union) to 1956 (when Khrushchev ordered its return to East Germany), the altar has been in the Pergamon Museum in Berlin. In a show of popular support, the mayor of modern Pergamon (Bergama) has collected 15 million signatures asking for its return.

A similar case is brewing concerning Priam's Treasure, a collection of Early Bronze Age jewelry and other artifacts, found by Heinrich Schliemann at Troy in 1873. Priam's treasure and other artifacts were taken from Berlin by the Soviet Army. Their existence in the Pushkin and Hermitage museums was a closely guarded secret until 1991. Russian president Boris Yeltsin has promised publicly that the treasure will be exhibited in Greece in the future, but has made no official statement concerning either Turkey or Germany's claims to the material. Engin Özgen and other Turkish scholars were allowed to inspect the material in December 1994. Russia's plans for the treasure after its own exhibition in Moscow in early 1996 are unknown.

FLATTERY WILL GET YOU EVERYWHERE

Competition between museums for major acquisitions can be traced to institutional rivalries of the nineteenth century. Then, as now, galleries in major cities vied with one another, as well as with Europe's national museums, for prestigious collections. "Intermuseum as well as international contests have been pursued vigorously," wrote Karl E. Meyer in *The Plundered Past*, "so much that museums have acquired the outlook of indepenent principalities, each with the jealous sensitivity of a royal court." Meanwhile, affluent private collectors, a major source of funds and acquisitions, have been vigorously courted by competing museums. A 1994 report in *The Art Newspaper* explains why:

> U.S. tax law continues to favour gifts to charitable bodies by allowing deductions based on the full appreciated value of donated property. As a consequence, art museums and their publics have profited handsomely from gifts that account for not only the bulk, but the best, of the objects that entered American museums this year.

Among the law's beneficiaries in 1994 was New York's Metropolitan Museum of Art, which was bequeathed more than 800 Precolumbian objects from Peru and Mexico.

Museums have clear goals: establish close ties with wealthy collectors and encourage them to donate funds or antiquities. In *Making the Mummies Dance*, a memoir of his years as director of the Metropolitan, Thomas Hoving writes:

> Walter Baker, a New York banker married to a woman of great means and a sympathetic heart, Lois, had also developed a passion for Greek and Roman objects, and Dietrich [von Bothmer, a Metropolitan curator] had helped him assemble the tresures, gently, never acting pushy . . . . Baker was ill and Dietrich had begged me to join him at the banker's apartment to raise his spirits . . . . Walter Baker had, of course, long ago commited his fine things to the Met, but Dietrich wanted that final visit just to be sure. It is the mark of an excellent curator to keep nudging the donor.

Donations to museums are morally and legally acceptable, even praiseworthy, provided the objects donated were not stolen and were legally exported. For unscrupulous museum officials, however, donations may represent a way to circumvent official acquisition policies prohibiting the purchase of stolen artifacts and may provide a level of deniability should a donated object be claimed later by a foreign nation. In his book, Hoving also recalls that "aggressive collecting curators were more than a little larcenous. To land something great, they were perfectly willing to deal with shady characters."

Aside from the tax benefits, what do collectors gain from their relationship with museums? British scholar Sir John Boardman offered the following explanantion in a recently published catalogue:

> The motivation may be a matter of status or even investment, it may be a scholarly interest stimulated by a variety of causes, not themselves necessarily scholarly, but to a greater or lesser degree it usually entails that common propensity of man (and even some other members of the animal kingdom) to assemble objects that delight the eye and comfort the mind.

Introductions and acknowledgments in such catalogues suggest that collecting satisfies basic emotional needs; love, pleasure, ad excitement are words often used to describe collecting. ". . . we were as impressed by the collectors' love and warmth for all their pieces, from the tiny sealstones to the tall pithoi, as by the antiquities themselves," reads one introduction. "The excitement of collecting has been not only the joy of possessing a beautiful object but the fascination of discovering the links between that object and its place in history," reads another.

Meanwhile, museum directors heap lavish praise on collectors who, we are told, in catalogue after catalogue, express a unique personal vision in their collection of ancient objects. A selection of such flattery illustrates the point:

> . . . it almost stretches our credibility to acknowledge that these are not the holdings of a large museum but, in fact, a panoply of treasures assembled with relentless perserverence, according to a very personal vision.

or

> . . . in the assembly of private collections every whim can be exercised at will, and the preferences of the collectors tirelessly pursued and indulged: the result is fresh and often surprising because it reflects the collectors' personal taste and a sense of risk and adventure.

Even the collector's exhibition catalogue may be praised with fulsome hosannas:

> This spendid catalogue is a wonder for scholars, students, collectors, and lovers of the ancient world. Like a rainbow, the exhibition is a glorious but ephemeral moment. This book, on the other and, is a lasting moment.

It is praise to make the head spin and the purse strings open.

Mark Rose is an archaeologist and managing editor of Archaeology.

Özgen Acar is former editor of the Turkish national newspaper Cumhuriyet *and has been pursuing antiquities-related cases for several decades.*

DISCUSSION QUESTIONS

1. How can major U.S. museums get away with buying and exhibiting objects that have so clearly been looted?
2. Why do U.S. museums "take their chances" when they have good reason to believe they are acquiring looted materials?
3. What alternatives to major additions to their collections might museums consider that would attract public attention and support?
4. How common is the practice of denial of research permits to scholars associated with institutions that hold looted or stolen material?
5. Who pays (or absorbs the financial loss) when art objects are repatriated?
6. Given the intrigue and adventure of big-time international collecting, is there any way to control big egos at play?
7. What role does U.S. tax law play in museums and international repatriation cases? Could tax laws be used to improve conditions?
8. What is the effectiveness (and cost) of pursuing antiquities related cases in the courts?
9. What impact does repatriation have on actual looting?

10. How might the Garland sarcophagus case (or the Ward Gallery case*) have played out if the owner had not had the option of donating the sarcophagus to a nonprofit organization and taking a tax deduction? What is gained by such arrangements? What is lost?

11. Are the collectors described in "Flattery..." different in kind from those noted in Neary's "Project Sting" or Harrington's "The Looting of Arkansas"?

FURTHER RESEARCH

Note: The dealer Robert Hecht, Jr. is a recurring figure in the stories of looted antiquities. See, for example, Bryan Burrough, "Raider of the Lost Art," *Vanity Fair* (April 1994): 72,78, 80–90 (even pages only), 93–94, 96.(The article also discusses Bruce McNall's role in the Elmali Hoard case.)

For a mind-boggling account of acquisition practices at the New York Metropolitan Museum of Art, see Thomas Hoving, *Making the Mummies Dance: Inside the Metropolitan Museum of Art* (New York: Simon and Schuster, 1993).

---

*For a discussion of the Ward Gallery case, see Mark Rose, "Greece Sues for Mycenaean Gold," *Archaeology* (Sept/Oct 1993): 26–30; and Mark Rose, "Mycenaean Gold Returned," *Archaeology* (March/April 1994): 19.

CHAPTER SEVEN

THE LOOTING
OF ARKANSAS

by Spencer P.M. Harrington

Harrington explores Arkansas' problems with looting and responses to it through public outreach and visits to landowners who allow pot-hunting on their property. He summarizes the Arkansas Archaeological Survey's annual training program for avocational archaeologists and the tremendous amount of work the graduates contribute. To counter the destruction caused by farming techniques, the Soil Conservation Service has a training program that gives farmers sufficient knowledge to recognize and record cultural resources. Service benefits to farmers are contingent on adherence to the cultural resources policy.

I am standing with Charles Lowrance III in front of and old meat locker in the back of his real-estate office about a mile outside of Wilson, a small town in northeastern Arkansas. This part of the office is now a kitchen, but the meat locker, the high ceilings, the gray concrete floor, and the nearby farmland suggest that the building has some former agricultural use. The office has a sink, a refrigerator, a table, and some straight-backed chairs. Hanging on a wall are the heads of three bucks that Lowrance shot and mounted. It is a Saturday afternoon in mid-June and the office is empty.

Lowrance takes a key and unfastens the large padlock that secures the locker door. He pulls a chain, snapping on a bare light bulb overhead. What I see makes me gasp. Stacked side by side on pine shelves are more than 200 Native American artifacts: bowls with appliquéd moldings and rim ornaments in the shape of human and animal heads; frog, duck, and cat effigy pots; red-and-white polychrome pots; and a shattered dog effigy that was once shaped like a teapot. On the floor is a large metate, a stone used in grinding seeds or corn.

"This here stuff is not all that fancy," Lowrance says as I examine different pieces. He is a successful plantation owner, a tall, thin man in his mid-60s with a full head of gray hair. He started collecting when he learned of the value of some of the pots his farmhands were often plowing up. His most exotic pieces, he says, are at home, locked in an armoire.

Geographers divide Arkansas into three regions: the Ozark and Ouachita mountain areas in the north and west, the forests of the Gulf coastal plain to the southwest, and the Mississippi Valley, which forms the state's eastern border. The Mississippi River meanders north to south depositing silt along its banks. These deposits form ridges called levees. The levees provided fertile soil for the Native Americans whose culture, known as the Mississippian Tradition, flourished from A.D. 800 until contact with Europeans in the sixteenth and seventeenth centuries.

The Mississippian people were the first intensive growers of corn in the Southeast. Corn, along with beans, squash, sunflowers, and gourds, supplemented a protein-rich diet of fish and waterfowl. Their society evolved into chiefdoms led by elite families. There is evidence of elaborate burial ceremonies, and richly decorated pottery has been found in large townsites that prospered at the time of European contact. Certainly most, if not all, of Lowrance's artifacts, were associated with these Mississippian burials. The painted human-effigy head pot and dog-effigy "teapots" in his armoire are splendid examples of a sophisticated ceramic tradition.

Lowrance's home is only a half-mile from his real-estate office. There, sitting in a leather-bound easy chair, a rack of rifles on the wall behind him, he talks about "investing" in artifacts. "The objects in my armoire," he says, "will be worth $250,000 in ten years." He is proud of his artifacts, likes to show them to visitors, and tells me that he doesn't think Mississippian pottery is properly displayed in museums. He recalls visiting New York City. "I was staying at the Waldorf-Astoria, and I had a limousine take me to the Met to see how their collection compared to mine. But hell, they didn't have anything as far as pottery. I was so disappointed that I left."

Lowrance says that he has often bought his pieces from pot-hunters, who have appeared at his doorstep at all hours with pots still wet from the fields. He says that although it's cheapest to buy from diggers, he will not allow them to dig on his property. Part of his wariness may stem from an incident that occurred a few years ago when he hired some diggers to bulldoze an Indian mound on his land, the understanding being that they would split whatever was found. Within minutes there were 12 pot-hunters sinking probes into his mound. Lowrance subsequently papered his land with No Trespassing signs. He shuns prosecuting pot-hunters because "these people will burn your house down if you press charges."

The destruction of the mound prompted a letter of complaint from Dan Morse, a state archaeologist based at Arkansas State University in Jonesboro. Lowrance wrote back, informing Morse that the mound was on his property, that nobody could tell him how to use his land, and that "he [Morse] could consider it destroyed."

Archaeologists blame Lowrance and his fellow collectors for providing a market for diggers who eagerly plunder the state's archaeological resources. Collectors, on the other hand, feel unjustly vilified by archaeologists, and view the artifacts they collect as works of arts to be bought and sold. Joe Shurtleff, a digger and collector from Ashdown, a town in southwestern Arkansas, says he is bewildered by what he claims is a change in the attitude of state archaeologists. "They're almost totally against the amateur archaeologist," he complains. "These same people some years ago came to our homes, copied all our records, photographed all our artifacts and encouraged us to participate in publication. And those same people are now calling us looters and you name it. That kind of hurts a little bit."

The conflict between archaeologists and collectors is by no means exclusive to Arkansas. It is symptomatic of a country that by and large has failed to define its national heritage or how to preserve it, a situation that has led to a spectacular amount of site destruction, a vanishing data base for scientists, and acts of gross insensitivity toward Native Americans.

In most of the world, antiquities are nationalized—that is, once discovered, they become property of the government. In the United States, property owners have historically determined the fate of archaeological sites on their land. So even though looting is a world-wide problem, the sanctity of private property here gives the issue a uniquely American cast. Is it "looting" to dig up a grave on your own property (or, with permission, on someone else's) and keep or sell the burial artifacts? In about half the states in this country the answer is no.

Until 1991, there were no laws in Arkansas to protect artifacts in unmarked burial sites on private property, nor were there prohibitions against the sale and transport of these artifacts across state lines. The result has been open season on Mississippian burials, particularly in the valley region of northeast Arkansas. Parts of the valley have been so thoroughly mined that pot-hunters from Arkansas have had to cross over into Mississippi, where they risk arrest for grand larceny if they disturb such graves without a permit.

To combat the looting of their state, the Arkansas legislature appropriates $850,000 annually for the Arkansas Archaeological Survey (AAS), a watchdog group of 20 professional archaeologists posted at research stations across the state. Assigned to specific counties, they are empowered to conduct surveys and carry out excavations, to keep records of all reported sites, to provide counsel to local amateurs, and to lecture to public groups. In addition, AAS archaeologists staff the Survey's annual training program for avocational archaeologists. This program was initiated in 1964 in an effort to raise public awareness of the state's vanishing heritage. Amateurs attending the two-week summer program learn methods of fieldwork and laboratory study. The program attracts as many as 100 participants, some of then from out-of-state. According to Hester A. Davis, AAS co-administrator, the training program "provides interested citizens with the opportunity to gain information on how to do archaeology 'right,' and multiplies manifold the eyes and ears of the few professional archaeologists we have." Davis points out that since 20 archaeologists can't find, much less record or protect, all archaeological sites, the Survey's best hope is public involvement.

The 800-member Arkansas Archaeological Society, an amateur organization supervised by the AAS, has been critical to the success of the state's archaeology program. Davis estimates that Society members volunteer more than 5,000 hours annually and that they have reported about a quarter of the sites found in the state. They routinely alert AAS archaeologists about site destruction, serve as liaisons between landowners and the AAS, and volunteer at short notice to undertake emergency salvage projects. Many society members take part in the summer field school and some are working toward a certificate in field archaeology.

Yet despite the Society's volunteer efforts, Davis concedes that AAS archaeologists have often felt helpless when confronted with the enormity of the state's looting problem. "It's been an uphill battle up to this point," says Davis. The AAS's procedures for stopping site destruction—public outreach and visits to landowners who allow pot-hunting—do not always show immediate results. "Landowners still have control over their land," she says, "and there's no way that making a righteous plea about preserving the past is going to get through to everybody." In the meantime, the AAS has been encouraged by the recent passage of a bill that outlaws the unauthorized excavation of unmarked graves on private land and the commercial trade of antiquities.

Arkansas is flat, poor, and sparsely populated. It's 2,350,725 residents have the third lowest per-capita income in the country. Arkansas ranks, however, among the top 15 states in agricultural revenues, with more than six million acres of harvested land. Soybeans, broiler chickens, rice, and cotton are the main agricultural commodities. The agricultural wealth of the state, however, has never filtered down to most farmers, many of whom were sharecroppers up until World War II.

There is no doubt that rural poverty in eastern Arkansas has contributed to a looting problem that stretches back more than 100 years, embracing a time when non-mechanized farming allowed Arkansas's farmers a close look at the ground they were plowing. The state's rich alluvial soil contains few stones, so archaeological remains were, and still are, easily identifiable. Early in this century a number of dealers became rich by buying the pots plowed up by farmers and selling them to collectors across the country. At about the same time, archaeologists with the Bureau of American Ethnology, the Philadelphia Academy of Sciences, and Harvard's Peabody Museum began state-wide excavations, searching for pottery to add to their collections. They also bought artifacts from local sharecroppers.

It was the grandaddy of Arkansas relic dealers, G.E. Pilquist, who in 1924 tipped off the Museum of the American Indian in New York City about a prehistoric cemetery in Yell County in northcentral Arkansas that was yielding vast numbers of burial artifacts. Pilquist led Mark Harrington, an archaeologist from the museum, to an area known as Carden Bottoms, where tenant farmers hired by Pilquist were hard at work digging the site. Harrington described the scene: "It was sickening to an archaeologist to see the skeletons chopped to pieces with hoes and dragged ruthlessly forth to be crushed underfoot by the vandals—who were interested only in finding something to sell, caring nothing for the history of a vanished people . . . What could I do? There was no way of stopping the . . . destruction of so much that might have been of value to science—so I made the best of it and bought from the diggers, and from those [like Pilquist] who had financed them, such of the artifacts as I thought we needed."

Native American pottery provided a readily available source of income for indigent farmers throughout the Depression years. Relic dealerships prospered, and it was Pilquist and a few other dealers in central Arkansas who provided a market for the looters who from 1933 to 1935 plundered the famous Spiro site, a Mississippian village with a huge ceremonial mound in eastern Oklahoma. In more recent times, the mechanization of farming has reduced the number of people tilling the soil. But while there are fewer farmers picking up artifacts on cropland, some of the new farming techniques—land leveling and deep subsoil plowing—have proved especially destructive to surface-level sites.

Nowadays, a whole host of people are probing the levees in the valley region. David Dye, an archaeologist at Memphis State University, separates pot-hunters into three categories: night diggers, digger-collectors, and hobbyists. "Night diggers," he says, "are people who go out after dark, leave holes in the fields, and sell everything they find. They're in it strictly for the money. They're often working for a dealer who wants certain kinds of artifacts. The second group are digger-collectors, people who are making some money out of their digging . . . it's not simply a hobby or a sport. They probably have small private collections. The third group are hobbyists who are doing it for the fun of going out there and discovering something. These people look on it much as they would fishing or hunting. They think of themselves as amateur archaeologists."

Harry Elrod of Bassett, a small town in the eastern part of the state, is a night digger who was arrested for pot-hunting in Mississippi. Elrod has been digging pots for ten years and selling them out of the service station he owns in Bassett. He says that good pots are getting scarce in his area but that some of the finest polychrome pots are still available in Mississippi. "I saw a polychrome walking-dog double-spout teapot bring $12,000," he says. "Anything that's polychrome, whatever it is, most of it brings $3,000 or $4,000. I went to Mississippi to dig polychrome and they put my ass in jail."

Elrod was arrested January 4, 1989, in Coahoma County, Mississippi, after he and two other Arkansas men crossed over the state line to dig polychrome pots. He was charged with a misdemeanor, fined $1,100, and spent 30 days in jail. He says that he "just about quit digging" after the experience.

Elrod works in the winter, when the earth is soft and the temperature is cool. He says he doesn't use archaeological site reports to find pottery—he's familiar enough with the areas he digs. He probes the levees with an automobile antenna. "On the end of that probe there is a little old knob," he explains. "When you hit something you twist it and pull it up a little on the end and you can tell what it is . . . you can tell whether it's a bone or whether it's pottery or whether it's rock or hard sand." With his probe Elrod can distinguish human bones and pots at gravesites.

"Usually the pottery is around the head, the stomach, next to the legs, the arms, the hands," he says. "You've got to know what you're followin' . . . whether you're gettin' rib bones, leg bones, the skull . . . if you can trace the bone you can lay the grave out right out on top of the ground there and just probe around it and find what you're lookin' for."

Elrod describes business as brisk. "I've had people come from all over the United States for my pots . . . I know some boys that make $20,000 in the wintertime digging pots. Ain't but just a very few diggers . . . they're farmers . . . they drive tractors and anything else they can do. They make enough money in the wintertime so they don't do nothin' in the summertime. They sit on their ass until next winter."

Elrod says that he doesn't "usually hardly fool with the bones" and that he doesn't have any moral qualms about digging the graves. "Here's my point," he says. "Big mounds are out here in these cotton fields. They're runnin' these big tractors over 'em, they're runnin' these big plows over 'em, and they're cuttin' this stuff up every day. They're bustin' it up, cuttin' it up. Hell, I'd just as soon see someone go out there and dig it up and preserve it."

Destructive farming techniques, such as chiseled plowing and land leveling, have posed perhaps the gravest threat to the state's archaeological resources. Farmers use chisel plows to break up fragipans, clays that are common in the soil near the Mississippi and Arkansas rivers. The procedure aerates the soil, which increases its productivity, but some plows claw through the earth at a depth of 16 inches, destroying all surface-level sites. Land leveling, a technique that has destroyed countless platform mounds that once supported Indian temples, allows rain to saturate the soil easily and with little runoff. Land leveling was a common practice from the 1950s through the late 1970s, when federal agricultural policy encouraged farmers to plant as much as they could for sale on the world market.

"That policy didn't lend itself to environmental parameters," says Michael J. Kaczor, an archaeologist with the Soil Conversation Service (SCS), a federal agency that provides technical assistance to farmers. The SCS conducts environmental studies and draws up plans for cultivating the arable land that a majority of Arkansas farmers uses when planting. Until the early 1980s, the SCS had only general guidelines for the protection of cultural resources. In 1989, however, it implemented an agency-wide training program aimed at avoiding or mitigating damage to the archaeological record when planning the cultivation of farmland. According to Kaczor, the program "gives our people a working knowledge of what the cultural resources are, how to identify them, how to describe them, and how to record them so professionals can take a look and determine whether or not a site is significant."

Kaczor says that SCS benefits to Arkansas farmers are contingent upon adherence to the agency's new cultural-resources policy. "If we see that a farmer is actively and intentionally damaging something, and he's requesting our assistance, we can pull back."

Archaeologists working in the Mississippi Valley region have long had an uneasy relationship with local collectors and pot-hunters. Despite the exchange of letters following the bulldozing incident, Charles Lowrance says he is one of the few collectors who maintain a cordial relationship with Dan Morse, his county's AAS archaeologist. "Most collectors can't stand Dan," says Lowrance of the man who for 25 years has been monitoring the 17 northeastern counties that constitute some of the most archaeologically rich land in the nation. Morse, concedes that "I'm pretty outspoken when I see a pot-hunter out there. I don't play around with them . . . I tell them exactly what I think." Morse estimates that there are 60,000 sites in his jurisdiction, of which he has recorded 7,400. He claims that in his area well over half of the Mississippian graves within the reach of a probe or a plow have been destroyed, although estimates are difficult because his region is largely under cultivation.

"We go out to sites and see up to 50 to 100 holes made in a period of one to two weeks," he says. "Sites get recultivated and holes covered up. We really don't know how much [looting] is going on, and I think some of us are reluctant to find out . . . reluctant to confirm our own worst fears."

Pots are the relics of choice among collectors. "People want pots," Morse says. "They don't want hammer-stones. They want pots. And then fine lithics, particularly projectile points." As with the collecting of antiques, and fine art, prices fluctuate to accomodate what type of artifact or style is in vogue. "There's not a high correlation between the value of an object to its historic importance," says Morse. "It's what people collect, it's what your neighbor collects . . . it's what becomes collectible."

Ironically, scholarly research influences the market. Says Morse: "If an archaeologist publishes something about an important artifact—say, end scrapers [a stone implement that has a blunt end for scraping]—then all of a sudden end scrapers become items that are sold . . . and all of a sudden people want them in their collections and bang! End scrapers are selling for five bucks apiece. People couldn't give them away before, and all of a sudden they're five bucks apiece. And that makes archaeologists awfully nervous, because everytime we publish we aid and abet the market that's costing us our data base." Morse says he has not written about a few sites for fear that they might be vandalized.

This fear is shared by archaeologists who are conducting ongoing excavations. David Dye directs a summer field school on an old plantation in Crittenden County in eastern Arkansas. Natural levees on the property have yielded evidence of a Mississippian town-site that existed near a large lake. He is reluctant to give the name of the site since that area continues to be a target for pot-hunters. Standing on a levee in the middle of a cornfield, Dye directs my attention to the original configurations of the Mississippian site, now mostly under cultivation. Soon we are on our hands and knees, examining debris that has been churned up by the plows and scattered between the rows of corn. Almost everything is archaeologically significant. Here and there are potsherds, bone beads, small animal bones and the vertebrae of a gar, a river fish eaten by the Indians.

Dye says that the property owner had allowed a pot-hunter onto his land provided that the Memphis State research team be allowed to photograph and document all of the objects removed from the earth. "It was a situation we weren't happy with," says Dye, "but otherwise the site would have been destroyed. The arrangement was short-term, and in the end the landowner decided not to allow the pot-hunter to continue digging." But even such marginal cooperation has exposed Dye to charges that he is aiding the pot-hunters. "I think most archaeologists make good use of whatever data they have available," he says. "You're trained to do that—you're trained to make the most of the data that are there." A week after my visit, the site was looted again. Dye found six holes and human bone strewn around an area where looters had been digging at night without the landowner's permission.

The local archaeological community, Dye included, finds little research value in artifacts with no provenience, i.e. knowledge of where and in what context they were found. Ann M. Early, an AAS archaeologist posted in Arkadelphia, says, "The study of unprovenienced artifacts poses too many liabilities without enough benefits. It can be the rarest, most marvelous artifact, but if it doesn't have any provenience it's of very little scientific value."

Research goals, however, may dictate how much interest an archaeologist will have in looted artifacts for which site provenience is known. Archaeologists who study looted collections say that having access to them doesn't mean you're legitimizing collecting. "Some questions," says Dye, "may never be answered if we restrict ourselves to scientifically excavated collections because the data base is just not there—it's too small or nonexistent." Dye also notes that some areas of inquiry—particularly stylistic analysis—compel the study of looted artifacts in private collections and museums. "If you're studying a particular stylistic theme, such as frog or fish effigies, you may need to see 50 pots to recognize redundancy and patterning in a particular collection. In order to get 50 bullfrog effigies, you're going to have to look at 1,000 pots out there, and I don't think you could do a study like that if you were working with collections that hadn't been looted in the recent or remote past."

Those who object to laws that would protect unmarked graves on private land argue that one's property is sacrosanct. The Fifth and Fourteenth Amendments to the Constitution guarantee the inviolability of private property, and property law generally allows a landowner to possess anything found under his soil, including burial sites of prehistoric Native Americans. The result, says Hester Davis, has been that "property owners' rights have enslaved the dead."

Landowners such as Charles Lowrance consider buried artifacts a saleable natural resource, and any governmental intervention is not welcome. While most states have passed legislation to protect archaeological resources on state land, only 28 have specific legislation protecting unmarked graves on private property. And many of these laws are new and as yet untested in the courts; their passage does not guarantee adequate enforcement. Some states without these laws, such as Texas, Alabama, and Kentucky, have public health and sepulchral provisions that protect prehistoric Native American graves on private property.

An unsettling reason for the lack of legal protection may be that the majority of Americans do not view Native American remains as being representative of their cultural heritage. "I think there's a certain amount of racism involved," says Dye. "I think there's a feeling among some landowners that it's just Indian stuff, so what's the big deal about digging it up."

Nineteenth-century Manifest Destiny was grounded as much in a belief in the ennobling effect of American democracy as in a belief in the savagery of the American Indian. These ideas provided a rationale for the displacement of indigenous cultures. And while attitudes have changed, the refusal of some states to pass legislation protecting unmarked graves reinforces a feeling of cultural alienation among Native Americans. "When it comes to Indians," says Carrie Wilson-Woodley, a Quapaw tribal representative, "most people just want to see us on horses or in canoes. They don't think of us as being part of contemporary society."

Although the United States may be divided over laws protecting unmarked graves on private property, the rest of the world is not. As of 1984, 73 countries and provinces had outlawed clandestine excavations on private property for the purpose of discovering relics, while many others had more general rules requiring governmental authorization of excavation and the reporting of finds. Israel, the United Kingdom, France, Belgium, Luxembourg, and some Swiss cantons even restrict the use of metal detectors. It is interesting to note that in other countries where English-speaking people have displaced indigenous groups (Canada, Australia, and New Zealand) the laws protecting aboriginal remains are generally more stringent.

Here at home there are signs of change. The Native American Grave Protection and Repatriation Act, signed by President Bush on

November 16, 1990, now allows Native American groups to reclaim identifiable human remains and associated burial artifacts from museums that receive federal support. The law, which represents a compromise between Native American organizations, museum curators, and archaeologists, obliges these museums to take inventory of their Native American human remains and grave goods and notify the appropriate tribes of what they have. These tribes can then make claims on objects of ceremonial significance, but are limited as to what they can repossess, and have to prove ownership. The new law also grants ownership to Native Americans of all human remains and burial artifacts excavated on federal or tribal lands, but it does not apply to burial remains found on state or private property.

As long as this discrepancy persists, no one involved with Native American antiquities can rest easy. Native Americans will worry that their ancestry, however distant, is being sold off piecemeal; collectors will worry about losing their artifacts or about being subjected to an onerous registration process; relic dealers will worry about losing their business; and archaeologists will worry that by the middle of the next century 98 percent of all (not just currently known) archaeological deposits dating to before the year A.D. 2000 will have been destroyed. The fate of this country's cultural resources is ultimately not only an archaeological question or a question of property owners' rights, but also an issue of how we will choose to perceive ourselves and our past.

BUYING AND SELLING THE PAST

Most dealers in Native American antiquities, from international auction houses to local one-man operations, say they acquire their artifacts from collectors. They also insist they are not responsible for site destruction. Archaeologists, on the other hand, contend that dealing in high-priced artifacts stimulates pot-hunting, which in turn does lead to the destruction of sites.

Bill Swan III operates The Relic Cache, a mail-order dealership in Signal Mountain, Tennessee, and edits a magazine for collectors called *The Artifacts News*. He guarantees his relics are authentic and insists on the same guarantee from those who advertise in his magazine. He says he pays taxes on all his transactions and claims that the media "have distorted the business 100 percent by describing it as a black-market, underground ring."

"Black market? There's no such thing," says Swan. "My job is not promoting looting and robbing . . . it's just legitimate trading between people."

The May/June 1990 issue of *The Artifacts News* featured six artifacts on its cover, five of which were found in Arkansas and are now in private collections. The most expensive item, a Mississippian red-on-buff head pot, sells for $25,000. The two walking-dog "teapots" on the cover go for $15,000 each. Swan attributes the high prices to "the fact that [the pots are] intact, the fact that there are so few of them, and the fact that there are so few with such a good history."

Swan says that he makes frequent trips to Arkansas, acquiring his artifacts from collectors or from the families of deceased collectors. "If a dealer sells a relic," he says, "that doesn't mean he has to hire somebody to go out and dig up a new relic to replace it. What happens is that the relics just keep changing hands. There are no more being added to the pile unless somebody gets lucky and stumbles across one."

Swan warns the potential consumer that "there are more fake relics than there are good relics" on the market. As a result, adequate site provenience increases the value of an object. He says that if a buyer isn't careful about provenience, "it's nobody's fault but your own . . . you could be buying a fraud. You can't sell artifacts without provenience . . . If a piece pops up and nobody knows where it comes from, you better watch out. It might be a fake."

Bernard de Grunne, director of Tribal and American Indian art at Sotheby's in New York City, estimates that 90 percent of the Mississippian artifacts he sees are fake. And, while most archaeologists and collectors in Arkansas believe there is a national, even worldwide, market for artifacts from the Mississippi Valley region, de Grunne claims that few Mississippian objects are being bought and sold in New York. "Most Native Amercian antiquities collecting is regional," he says. "People will try to collect objects from the area where they live . . . they will pay more for it there than anybody in New York." Mimbres pots from New Mexico, which have sold at Sotheby's for as high as $88,000, seem to be the only North American ceramics to have acquired national attention, says de Grunne, who adds that there is no significant foreign market for American Indian antiquities from any region.

Sotheby's conducts two auctions of Native American antiquities annually, and the two to four million dollars in receipts from those auctions constitute a "very small" share of the company's $3 billion business, according to de Grunne.

An art historian, de Grunne recognizes archaeologists' concerns about preserving artifacts in their context but he feels they can go too far: "With a lot of the pieces we find contexts are pretty meaningless—they were thrown away, they were destroyed, they were in garbage pits." He says that collecting indigenous art objects is "the easiest way for one culture to approach another" and maintains that it is a positive, harmless activity that reveals intellectual curiosity, interest, and respect. "We're a culture of the visual arts, visual things. You can defend both points of view, but I think that people who say that they [antiquities] can only be treated as cultural artifacts are stupid. Of course they weren't created for apartments on Fifth Avenue, but that doesn't mean we can't enjoy them on the mantelpiece."

Spencer P.M. Harrington is an associate editor of Archaeology *and has a degree in classics from Columbia University.*

DISCUSSION QUESTIONS

1. Consider the perspective of the collectors who used to work with archaeologists and now feel vilified by them. Are their complaints justified?
2. Are conflicts between archaeologists and collectors in the United States different from those in other countries?
3. How do U.S. laws and attitudes about private property give looting in the United States a special cast?
4. What archaeological programs does your state support?
5. To what extent does rural poverty, anywhere in the world, contribute to looting problems? Can archaeologists do anything about rural poverty?

6. What are the consequences of, and alternatives to, a "make the best of it and buy from the diggers" (or "if I don't buy it someone else will") approach?

7. Could archaeologists benefit from recognizing categories of diggers (or looters) and responding differently to different kinds, or is looting still looting, regardless of motivation?

8. What is the value of archaeological context for artifacts that were found in "garbage pits"?

9. How could we test the dealer's assertion that "relics just keep changing hands. There are no more being added to the pile unless somebody gets lucky and stumbles across one"?

10. If collecting antiquities, from any culture, contributes to greater appreciation of cultural diversity, is that worth the price of some lost scientific information?

11. Since tractors, bulldozers, and other farming and development equipment are digging through sites and destroying them anyway, why not extract the salable pieces?

12. If scholarly research influences the market, would it be better not to publish certain kinds of information and studies? What are some other countries' approaches to protecting burials, including those on private lands?

CHAPTER EIGHT
ENLIGHTENED STEWARDSHIP
by Brian Fagan

Sites on privately owned land in the United States survive largely at the whim of their owners (see the earlier article by Fagan, "Black Day at Slack Farm"). The Archaeological Conservancy, founded in 1980, purchases privately owned sites to maintain for the public on a permanent basis. The Conservancy also works closely with developers whose projects have the potential to affect prehistoric and historic sites, often managing to save sites and achieve positive benefits for the developer. Native Americans serve on the board and are consulted closely.

Federal and state laws give a measure of protection to archaeological and historic sites on public lands, and have resulted in the successful prosecution of several high-profile looting cases. But privately owned sites survive at the whim of their owners, with virtually no protection. The effect of tougher laws and more vigorous enforcement has been to divert looters and professional pot-hunters onto private lands. In many parts of the country archaeology is losing ground. Prices for fine Native American artifacts on the international antiquities market are rising. Inevitably, there are landowners only too eager to sell artifacts from their properties to the highest bidder with a backhoe.

"Saving the Past for the Future" has become a popular slogan in archaeological circles. But how does one do this on private lands? Fortunately, public awareness of the importance of archaeology is much improved over a generation ago. The Indiana Jones movies, more exposure in the media, and efforts at public education by the profession have all played their part. Big-budget movies such as *Black Robe* and *Dances with Wolves* have placed Native Americans at center stage. The 1990 Native American Graves Protection and Repatriation Act has also drawn attention to the complex relationship between archaeologists and Native Americans (see Chapter 18). We live in an era of rising respect for Native American culture, values, and achievements. Many property owners feel a deep respect and responsibility for archaeological sites on their land. Some states, notably Kentucky, have developed successful pledge schemes in which landowners promise to protect sites on their property. But such promises only last the lifetime of the owner—there are no long-term guarantees. Only one strategy is effective: continuous ownership and stewardship. This is the mandate of a remarkable organization, the Archaeological Conservancy.

Founded in 1980 by a group of private citizens and archaeologists dedicated to protecting the future of the past, the Archaeological Conservancy's mission resembles that of the much higher profile Nature Conservancy, but with a fraction of its resources. In purchasing privately owned sites, the Conservancy agrees to maintain them for the public on a permanent basis. President Mark Michel and his small staff operate out of a headquarters in Albuquerque and regional offices in Duluth, Georgia; Groveport, Ohio; and Sacramento, California, with a minuscule budget of $850,000 a year. In 14 years they have acquired 100 sites in 22 states. Their acquisitions range from Paleo-Indian sites to an early nineteenth-century Hudson's Bay Company trading fort.

The Conservancy's first purchase was Powers Fort, Missouri, a Mississippian cultural-civic-ceremonial center consisting of a small village and four mounds surrounded by an earthen embankment, dating to ca. A.D. 1350. Soon afterward, it acquired Savage Cave, Kentucky, where 18 feet of deposits extend into Paleo-Indian times. The Conservancy owns, or has owned, sites at Borax Lake, California; the Hopewell Mounds Group and Stackhouse Mound—a large, nearly pristine Adena mound complex—in Ohio; and Pueblo San Marcos, New Mexico, whose inhabitants once controlled the nearby Cerrillos turquoise mines. It is also responsible for five preserves in heavily looted areas of Texas and Oklahoma, where the mound-building Caddo culture flourished between ca. A.D. 700 and the mid-eighteenth century. Each spans a different Caddo period, allowing a continued research on this most important of early American chiefdoms. The 100th property, obtained in late 1994, is the three-acre Lamb Spring site near Littleton, Colorado, a Paleo-Indian hunting and game-processing area that may be one of the earliest of its kind in the United States.

The Conservancy accepts sites as gifts, and works closely with land developers whose projects impinge on prehistoric and historic sites. They have achieved some remarkable successes. In 1993 the Weyerhauser Real Estate Company was developing a planned community on the site of Fort Nisqually, a Hudson's Bay Company trading post founded in 1832. The Conservancy persuaded Weyerhauser to set aside the open space in the heart of its new community. E. I. duPont de Nemours Company donated an archaeological easement on the site of Old Mobile, Alabama, the first French settlement at Mobile (1702–1711). Such transactions benefit not only archaeology, but the developer, who receives a tax break and, more important, a positive public image. In other cases, the Conservancy purchases sites outright for the appraised value of the land. The funds come from its 13,000 members, corporate sponsors, and private foundations. In purchasing the Lamb Spring site, the Conservancy collaborated with the Denver Museum of Natural History. The two organizations raised matching funds against a grant of $100,000 from the Colorado State Historical Fund.

The Conservancy staff works closely with a national board of archaeologists, with interested lay people, and with local committees that recommend sites for acquisition. Native Americans serve on both the national and regional advisory boards, and the Conservancy consults closely with tribes before acquiring any site. Mark Michel spends much of his time traveling around the country, looking at prospective acquisitions and working with property owners, sometimes over several years, before purchasing a site. With 100 acquisitions to its credit, the Conservancy is a viable option for preservation-minded landowners who wish to sell their land. The Conservancy assumes it will own sites in perpetuity, but sometimes transfers them to a national or state agency to be developed into protected public parks. Such was the case with the Hopewell Mounds Group in Ohio, now part of the Hopewell Culture National Historical Park. The Conservancy approves research projects that have specific goals and are compatible with conservation of the site. For example, study of animal bone fractures at the Lamb Spring site may yield evidence of very early human occupation, perhaps before 9500 B.C.

The Archaeological Conservancy strategy *works*, and in the final analysis it is the best option archaeologists have in this country to insure permanent protection of sites on private land. The Conservancy is at a point of critical mass, where future growth and public support are likely to be exponential. Mark Michel hopes that large bequests will put the Conservancy's endowment and activities on a new footing. What better investment in the future of the United States than to help save its past. I urge everyone, archaeologist and nonarchaeologist, to join and support the Conservancy in its unique and highly success-ful work.

Brian Fagan teaches archaeology at the University of California, Santa Barbara. He is a well-known author of archaeology textbooks and a contributing editor for Archaeology.

DISCUSSION QUESTIONS

1. What other lessons might those interested in the preservation and management of cultural heritage learn from the environmental movement?
2. How might cultural and environmental heritage groups collabo-rate to their mutual benefit?
3. With what other groups would those concerned about cultural heritage have a natural affinity, and how might this be developed to mutual advantage?

4. How do the U.S. tax laws affect the protection of cultural property within the United States? Could these laws be used more widely and effectively to protect Americans' archaeological heritage? Do environmental groups currently have policies regarding the cultural heritage? Do archaeological organizations have policies regarding the environmental heritage?

PART THREE
CULTURAL HERITAGE IN TIME OF WAR AND POLITICAL UNREST

C urrent events provide an unfortunate and vivid reminder of the vulnerability of the world's cultural heritage during times of political unrest. We are horrified by TV images of bombed-out churches and mosques, ancient bridges and palaces. Some of us are sickened by an art market that exploits these situations, profiting from artifacts newly looted from an already suffering Bosnia or Cambodia. The papers in this section document such problems and their long history. They also help us understand that the record of the past is incorporated into the soul of a people; that it forms an essential part of their social identity. The articles, thus, underscore the significance and reach of archaeology, and goad us to respond.

CHAPTER NINE
THE LOOTING
OF BULGARIA
by Douglass W. Bailey

The plundering of the rich Bulgarian heritage has, ironically, speeded up under the new democracy. Money that museums once had to buy chance finds now goes to pay for guards and burglar alarms, so looters sell their wares abroad. Public education efforts include documentaries for the single TV channel, and changes in the laws, but the problem cannot be resolved entirely from within Bulgaria.

It is five minutes past midnight, and the townspeople of Vidin in northwestern Bulgaria are celebrating the New Year with toasts and liberal shots of *rachiya*, a clear plum brandy. Meanwhile, thieves take advantage of the moment and force their way into the local museum. Fifteen minutes later, in answer to the museum's alarm, police arrive to find a half dozen life-size Roman marble statues stolen. This museum break-in differs from those that make newspaper headlines in most European cities because in Bulgaria the looting of museums has reached epidemic proportions. In the three years since Bulgaria became a democracy, burglars have struck seven museums. Museums, however, are not the only targets of this new breed of criminal. Five thousand icons have disappeared from Bulgaria's churches during 1992.

Bulgaria has a rich cultural heritage. From the anthropomorphic figurines of the first agriculturists and the magnificent gold and copper ornaments of the first metal-users to the intricate craftsmanship of Thracian silversmiths, its peoples have left a superb artistic legacy. It is ironic that the plundering of this legacy should coincide with the onset of democratic government. In the wake of political upheaval few resources have been directed toward the protection of archaeological sites and museums. Before 1989, the antiquities business involved small groups of highly specialized looters servicing a limited foreign market. The subsequent relaxation of border controls and the consequent increase in opportunities for international travel and contact with Western countries have provided a context in which archaeological looting has flourished.

But the problems facing the museums and archaeologists of today's Bulgaria were developing long before Todor Zhivkov and his harsh communist regime were overthrown. Traveling exhibitions of gold from the Copper Age Varna necropolis on the Black Sea and Thracian gold and silver objects served as excellent, but unintentional, advertisements to Western antiquities collectors of Bulgaria's potential. Bulgarian archaeologists and local museums have added to the problem by openly dealing with looters and treasure hunters. Donors of finds are treated as cultural heroes, their photographs placed in local newspapers. By law, Bulgarian citizens are required to turn in any artifacts discovered while digging a garden or plowing a field. Provincial museums, however, encourage treasure hunters by buying antiquities. If not purchased, administrators fear that the artifacts will find homes in Western European collections. The negotiations accompanying such purchases seldom include rigorous investigations into an artifact's provenience. During the years of tight socialist price-and-wage controls and heavy state investment in the preservation of the nation's past museums were able to buy almost everything that was brought to them. Now, with money tight, museums have had to spend their limited funds employing guards and installing electronic burglar alarms; little money is left to purchase antiquities. The result is that looters now sell their wares in the West, and there is little that Bulgaria's museums can do about it. Furthermore, the end of price controls and the introduction of competitive management have led to severe inflation and unemployment. Dire economic times provide a fertile climate for the looting and selling of artifacts.

Laws pertaining to antiquities theft, developed in 1962, have failed to keep pace with the rapidly changing social and economic situation. The fine for the looting of an archaeological site is the equivalent of about $12.00, but the return on a few Roman coins, an icon, or a silver Thracian bowl can be hundreds, thousands, or even tens of thousands of dollars. One night's work with a spade and flashlight can buy five years' worth of food and drink, and a Volkswagen to boot.

The most troublesome aspect of the existing antiquities laws is that the onus of proof is on the police. In theory they must prove that a suspect artifact or icon has been looted from a site or stolen from a church, and not accidentally found, handed down from parent to child, or plowed from a field. In practice the police must catch a looter in the act of robbing a site, which is difficult without an elaborate network of informants.

An attempt to address the problems of looting and cultural crime is being made by a group of concerned academics and lay people in Sofia. Virginia Kostadinova and her colleagues at the newly formed Social Council for the Preservation of Bulgarian Heritage have begun publicizing the problem and educating the public about the national importance of the country's artifacts and sites. Kostadinova has produced three films for Bulgarian television. The first two, *Indiana Jones is not in Your Imagination* and *Chronicle of an Actual Disappearance,* were funded by a Bulgarian national newspaper and private donors and are awaiting air time. Lack of funds has stalled production of the third. In a country with one television channel, intense coverage of national political debates, and a new hunger for previously unavailable Western films and soap operas, it is not easy to convince programmers to schedule documentaries of this sort.

In addition to the campaign to educate average Bulgarians about the value and importance of their cultural monuments, Kostadinova has also called for new laws that would raise the penalties for looting and shift the burden of proof that an artifact has or has not been looted from the police to the collector. Ivan Panajotov, a member of the Archaeological Institute of the Bulgarian Academy of Sciences and president of the Bulgarian Archaeological Society, would like to see a regional authority with a mandate to investigate suspected crimes against the cultural heritage, to monitor the preservation of sites, and to restore some respect for the country's archaeological heritage. Panajotov admits that established collectors will continue to buy and sell artifacts and that new laws may need to include plans to accommodate the legal acquisition of cultural artifacts by private individuals and organizations.

Bulgarian archaeological authorities, however, realize that attempts to control and eliminate the looting problem within Bulgaria will only succeed if they are matched by a coordinated effort between Bulgarian customs officials and Interpol agents working the European art and antiquities markets and auction houses. Until they are assured that the drain of antiquities to Western markets can be stopped, many Bulgarian museums will continue to try to staunch the flow by buying artifacts, which of course will only stimulate further looting. Those with the Social Council for the Preservation of Bulgarian Heritage can only hope that their effort to break this cycle will be aided by an economic recovery and government cooperation.

Douglass W. Bailey is a post-doctoral research fellow at the Center for Slavic and East European Studies, University of California at Berkeley.

DISCUSSION QUESTIONS

1. What are the costs and benefits of international traveling exhibits?
2. Dealers and collectors argue that the international trade in archaeological materials contributes to greater international understanding and appreciation of other cultures. It would be interesting, in that regard, to document the extent to which today's market is handling (and profiting from) art objects that have recently come from areas of current political turmoil.
3. As elsewhere, Bulgarian laws basically require that police catch a looter in the act to prove objects came from looting rather than a chance find or an old family collection. What other approaches might antiquities laws take that would be more likely to preserve sites and objects *in situ*?

FURTHER RESEARCH

Compare the analysis here of the effect of museums buying unprovenienced finds from locals with the situation as presented for Ecuador (see the earlier article by Howell, "Daring to Deal with Huaqueros").

CHAPTER TEN

THE GLORY
THAT WAS ANGKOR

by Russell Ciochon
and Jamie James

*Since the late nineteenth century, scholars have been trying to rescue
these spectacular ruins—extending over a 124-square mile area and,
in stone tonnage, dwarfing the pyramids of Egypt—from the encroach-
ments of the jungle. That work has kept scholars so busy that there has
been little time for archaeological excavation. Now, art thieves are
looting at such a relentless pace that soon there may be little left to
conserve. Nevertheless, and amidst much disagreement over appropriate methods and procedures, international teams of conservators
are trying to combat vegetation and thievery to preserve this world-
class site.*

Before him lay a chaos of fallen stones, some of them lying flat,
but most of them upended; it looked like a mason's yard invaded
by the jungle. Here were lengths of wall in slabs of purple sandstone, some carved and others plain, all plumed with pendent
ferns. Some bore a red patina, the aftermath of fire. Facing him
he saw some bas-reliefs of the best period, marked by Indian
influence—he was now close up to them—and very beautiful
work; they were grouped round an old shrine, half hidden now
behind a breastwork of fallen stones. It cost him an effort to take
his eyes off them.

—André Malraux, *The Royal Way.*

For sheer immensity, Angkor is unsurpassed among the archaeological wonders of the world. In stone tonnage, its massive temples dwarf the pyramids of Egypt and Mesoamerica, and its sculptures are the artistic equals of the best of Classical Greece or Renaissance Europe. For 500 years, from the ninth to thirteenth centuries A.D., successive dynasties built their capitals here. Feuding among ruling royal families was commonplace, and succession was rarely peaceful. After a new monarch took control of the empire, he would build a new capital enclave with a temple-mountain at its center, as an act of piety and a symbol of his authority. When French explorers came upon these temples in the mid-nineteenth century, they were stunned by their magnificence. Visiting the site for the first time in 1860, French zoologist Henri Mouhot remarked, "In the province still bearing the name of Ongcor, there are ... ruins of such grandeur, remains of structures which must have been raised at such an immense cost of labor, that at first view one is filled with profound admiration and cannot but ask what has become of this powerful race, so civilized, so enlightened, the authors of these gigantic works." A modern explorer landing at the Cambodian city of Siem Reap, a few miles from the ruins, is just as awestruck by the sculptured stone towers and massive temples that rise from the lush jungle foliage for as far as the eye can see.

It takes days to undertake even a cursory study of Angkor. Its many cities extend across the 124-square mile archaeological district of Angkor. Its ruins—several hundred monuments built of laterite, brick, and sandstone—range in size from tiny pavilions to vast temples, the largest being Angkor Wat. This famous shrine, occupying nearly one square mile of cleared jungle, has been variously described as the largest stone monument and the largest religious building in the world. A work of unparalleled magnificence, it took 37 years to build. Millions of tons of sandstone used in its construction were transported to the site by river raft from a quarry at Phnom Kulen, 25 miles to the northeast. Its gracefully curved central tower rises to a height of more than 200 feet. The subtlety of its bas-relief sculptures, depicting stories from the great Indian epic poems, the *Mahabharata* and the

Ramayana, exceeded anything that had been created before. A walk to the center of Angkor Wat was a metaphorical journey of the spirit to the center of the universe. There, housed in the temple's inner sanctum, a space no more than 19 feet square, was an image of Vishnu, the preserver god of Hindu mythology to whom Angkor Wat was consecrated.

The all-pervasive Indian influence at Angkor gives the monuments an underlying continuity, a distinguished tradition of stone carving executed by generations of Khmer sculptors. The buildings themselves reflect this continuity of style, created by priest-architects who had their own independent lineages and who served a succession of rulers.

At the center of the district stands the six-square-mile walled city of Angkor Thom, the capital of the Khmer empire at its apogee, from the late tenth through the early thirteenth centuries. To enter this moated city, one must cross one of five massive bridges guarded by rows of stone gods. At the heart of Angkor Thom is the Bayon, a labyrinthine temple of corridors and courtyards. Huge sculptured faces smile enigmatically from its stone towers. Its reliefs chronicle exploits of war and scenes from the everyday life of the people. French archaeologist Henri Marchal wrote of the Bayon in his *Archaeological Guide to the Temples of Angkor* (1928): "This is a confused and bizarre mass, seeming to be a mountain peak that has been shaped and carved by human hands. The impression is both powerful and disconcerting. The complication of the plan of the Bayon makes it all the stranger. It is so impressive that one forgets the faults of its construction, and is entirely preoccupied by its originality. At whatever hour one walks around it, and particularly by moonlight on a clear evening, one feels as if one were visiting a temple in another world, built by an alien people, whose conceptions are entirely unfamiliar."

We first visited Angkor in 1989. It was almost completely deserted, a casualty of foreign invasions and civil war. Since the Khmer Rouge was still a military threat in the area, we had to hire government soldiers armed with bazookas, rocket launchers, and machine guns to escort us. In 1993, we revisited Angkor. A measure of political stability had been restored, and scholars and tourists were returning in large numbers. Five years ago, the only significant work at Angkor was being done by conservators with the Archaeological Survey of India (ASI). Today, the ASI continues its work at Angkor Wat, while Japanese, French, and American teams labor elsewhere at the site. Meanwhile, art thieves are looting Angkor so relentlessly that in time there may be little left to conserve.

When the French arrived in the nineteenth century, Angkor's temples and monuments were overgrown by jungle. Romantic images of vine-covered ruins in the writings of Henri Mouhot, Louis Delaporte, and other French explorers were largely responsible for the burgeoning interest in the site, which led to the founding in 1898 of the École Française d'Extrême Orient (EFEO), a French government research institution specializing in Southeast Asia. Rescuing the monuments and temples from the encroachment of the jungle has kept scholars busy ever since, leaving little time for spade archaeology. The most spectacular exception occurred in 1936, when the French archaeologist Maurice Glaize dug up the bronze torso of a reclining Vishnu from an island temple in a great reservoir called the Western Baray. One of Glaize's Khmer workmen had told him that he had dreamed that the sculpture was there. The seven-foot-long fragment is now one of the principal treasures of the National Museum of Cambodia in Phnom Penh.

The thrust of the French effort was to conserve and interpret the visible remains. Fig and silk-cotton trees, rooted between the stones, had become inextricably bound up in the monuments; in some cases they actually held them together. One early visitor, French novelist and naval officer Pierre Loti (1850–1923), wrote, "The fig tree is the ruler of Angkor today. Over the palaces and over the temples which it has patiently pried apart, everywhere it unfolds its smooth pale branches, and its dome of foliage." In some instances, French conservators would take a monument apart, clear away the vegetation, then reassemble the stones. In other cases, the monuments were too thoroughly penetrated by the foliage to attempt such an approach. One site, a vast twelfth-century complex called Ta Prohm, was left just as it was found, to show the state of the monuments when they were discovered.

The EFEO also did a great deal of structural work, some of it irreversible and, by modern standards, regrettable. French engineers used concrete pillars and struts to support roofs that seemed to be on the verge of collapse. In the inner courtyard of Angkor Wat, they erected clumsy flying buttresses to support a wall, and they secured sandstone pillars with iron bands that have since rusted. The best that can be said of these efforts is that they probably kept further deterioration in check.

In 1970 General Lon Nol seized control of the government, and the ensuing civil war put a stop to restoration. The subsequent takeover by the Khmer Rouge resulted in a four-year reign of terror during which more than a million Cambodians, including virtually all the nation's scientists, historians, and educators, were killed. Like the Fascists in Italy who venerated Roman civilization, the Khmer Rouge saw themselves as the inheritors of Khmer civilization, so they did not destroy the monuments of Angkor. In 1979 the Vietnamese invaded and ousted the Khmer Rouge, and some degree of social order was restored. The first archaeologists to return were ASI restorers, who in 1986 began to work at Angkor Wat. India was the first non-Communist country to recognize the government installed by Vietnam, and the invitation to work there was politically motivated.

An ambitious effort, the ASI restoration set out to remove all intrusive vegetation and clean the sandstone surfaces. During our visit in 1989, we observed an Indian team disassembling pavilions to get at the vegetation that had taken root between the stones. Supervised by ASI engineers, Khmer workers told us they were using the same construction techniques to reassemble the masonry that their ancestors had used to build the pavilions more than 800 years before. Side-by-side with diesel-powered cranes, primitive battering rams were being used to reassemble masonry. Criticism of the Indian work was swift in coming, centering principally on the method of cleaning the stones. Restorers removed the pervasive fungus and lichens with chemical fungicides. They then cleaned the stones with a weak solution of ammonia, applied by workers using nylon and rattan brushes. Finally, according to team members we met in 1989, they coated the surface with polyvinyl acetate, an impermeable sealant that some conservators believe can cause severe damage by allowing water to build up beneath the surface. The ASI now denies ever having used such sealants. Critics also claim that surfaces of some of the reliefs have been scratched by overzealous scrubbing. Martin Lerner, the curator of Indian and Southeast Asian art at The Metropolitan Museum in New York, concluded after a visit to Angkor that the scrubbing "has done some damage," and that "most experienced conservators wouldn't dream of using such a technique."

Some of the criticism of the ASI's work has been irresponsible. A French agronomist in Phnom Penh warned in 1989 that the Indians "were scrubbing Angkor Wat with sulfuric acid"—a garbled reference to the conservators' use of acid to kill intrusive vegetation. Others have complained about the use of battering rams, arguing that it may damage the stone. We witnessed one of the rams in action and it seemed harmless enough.

ASI project director Barkur Narasimhaiah naturally defends the Survey's work. "Let them come and see for themselves what harm we are doing. Are they ready to say that moss and lichen are very good for the monuments? We are not experimenting here. We experimented in India and were successful. We have been using the same chemicals at Angkor Wat for six years, and no harm has been done. The chemicals are not at all strong. I don't think these criticisms have any weight."

French epigrapher Claude Jacques has been a persistent critic of the Indian work. "The Indians think I am their biggest enemy, but that is completely wrong," he told us. "I know that the Indians are capable of very good work; I've seen it in India. But it was impossibly stupid to wash Angkor Wat. It was a waste of money, and so much water. The parts they have washed two years ago are already black again." In fact, the galleries we saw being cleaned in 1989 are once again covered with fungus and lichen.

John Stubbs, program director of the World Monuments Fund (WMF), a New York-based conservation group, applauds the Indians for their effort. "It was an act of courage for them to go in there at that time and take on the enormous task of working on the world's largest religious building," he says. "Yet perhaps because it is so enormous, they may have lost control of the project. Consistency and vigilant control are the most important aspects of any project, anywhere in the world."

The challenge at Angkor, as always, is to rescue the monuments from the choking vegetation. Many of the sites are as covered over today as they were when the French arrived more than a century ago. Now that political stability has been restored, other professional conservators are arriving. The EFEO has reopened its office there, with two architects in residence, but it has not yet begun a major project. A team from Sophia University in Japan has begun a modest conservation of a twelfth-century temple called Banteay Kdei. Last October, representatives from 30 countries met in Tokyo to organize an international effort to save Angkor. France and Japan led the way, pledging $10 million each to the effort.

One important project is that of the WMF at Preah Khan, a temple built in the late twelfth century by King Jayavarman VII. Preah Khan occupies nearly a square mile of heavily wooded land just north of the walled city of Angkor Thom. According to a dedicatory stele dating to 1191, the site housed 515 religious images, which were adorned with vast quantities of silk veils and golden jewelry set with diamonds, emeralds, and pearls. "The conservation and stabilization of Preah Khan is actually quite secondary," says John Sanday, the WMF project supervisor at Preah Khan. "Unless you have a compe- tent group of craftsmen and administrators, all the money in the world will never save Angkor." Sanday, a British architect who lives in Kathmandu, Nepal, says the WMF's main objective is "to establish the principles and procedures of practical conservation. Preah Khan was a partial ruin when we found it, and I have set as our task to conserve it as a partial ruin. There are very few areas that we believe should be reconstructed." In one courtyard, however, the WMF team has reassembled sculptured pediments, or frontons. "When we arrived, there was a deep pile of earth and debris," Sanday recalls. "We decided to start sifting through it. Well, lo and behold, all of this stonework came out of the pile. We have gone through the stones and figured out where they should go. Slowly, we have been able to piece together the frontons."

In the course of clearing the site, the WMF team discovered a shallow depression, the remains of a small basin next to a freestanding pavilion. Stubbs believes the basin may have been a reflecting pool. "A lot of this architecture was meant to be seen reflected in water," he says. "Angkor is all about water, the whole place. The roofs of the buildings were designed to throw off water, which was collected in courtyards and then conveyed by sophisticated subterranean channels to the larger reservoirs. Sculptures of water gods called *nagas* are present at almost every site at Angkor." The basins and pools may also have been used by worshipers in purification rituals and by astronomers to calculate the angle of the stars, planets, and the moon above the horizon.

American archaeologist Richard Engelhardt is UNESCO's representative in Cambodia and, like Stubbs, he is deeply interested in the role of water at Angkor. Aerial infrared photography of the ancient city has revealed many large rectangular reservoirs, called barays, which were used to collect water during the rainy season for use in rice cultivation. The largest of these, the Western Baray, is nearly five miles long and one and one-half miles wide. Still water-filled, it is a favorite year-round recreation area for the residents of the nearby city of Siem Reap. Its counterpart, the Eastern Baray, is now only partially filled with water during the rainy season. Engelhardt suggests that the barays originally may have been quarries for the laterite that served as the foundation for the larger monuments at Angkor, as well as for the roadbeds throughout the Khmer empire. "It makes sense that they were quarries that were just left to fill up with water," he says.

Engelhardt is critical of the arbitrary way in which archaeologists and conservators from all over the world have gone about seeking permission to work on the sites. "What people have been doing up until now, basically, is shopping around to find someone who will say yes to requests to work on the monuments. They ask [Prime Minister] Hun Sen, and if he won't say yes, they ask the Ministry of Culture, and if the Ministry of Culture won't say yes, they ask the Ministry of Foreign Affairs, and if they won't say yes, then they go to the province level. Eventually, somebody will say yes." According to Engelhardt, there is no central control over conservation efforts and no one to hold conservators responsible for poor or ill-advised practices. He believes that "the important thing to be done at Angkor is not to clean stones or put them back together but rather to put in place a framework for preservation." For him, this means the establishment of an administrative structure that would support conservation. He envisions something along the lines of the National Trust in Great Britain, which combines landmark protection with the powers of a park service.

Jonathan Wager, an English environmental planning consultant with UNESCO, is now in the final stages of zoning a national park at Angkor. It is an ambitious program that will eventually provide a network of visitor-orientation kiosks, a research institute, and even a hydroelectric dam to provide power for the region. The park will also seek to preserve the original flora and fauna of Angkor, reintroducing species where necessary. Plans have been drawn up, but the principal, and perhaps most elusive, element lacking is a government in Phnom Penh powerful enough to implement the program. For the moment, the main objective is to provide rudimentary security for the monuments.

Meanwhile, in the past few years thieves working at Angkor have become bolder, stealing major works of sculpture not only from the field but from places of supposed safekeeping. Archaeologist Fred Aldsworth was at Angkor last year working on the WMF project at Preah Khan when thieves broke into the Conservation d'Angkor, the central storage place for stone inscriptions and artworks from Angkor and the surrounding areas. "They just blew away the wall with hand grenades and a rocket launcher, and came in and took what they wanted," says Aldsworth. The thieves made away with 22 objects, including some valuable stone sculptures.

Major depredations of the site began during the French colonial administration. Perhaps the most famous looter of all was André Malraux, the French writer and Minister of Cultural Affairs, who was arrested in Phnom Penh in 1923 for stealing a relief from the temple of Banteay Srei. Today the government is a fragile coalition with less central authority than the tyrannical Khmer Rouge. Lieutenant Ou Em, of the provincial police, complains, "Before, under the Khmer Rouge, those convicted of stealing cultural treasures received very harsh punishments. But now often they receive light punishments." Em and his men are further hampered by rules that allow them to arrest only those who transport stolen goods, not those who receive and sell them. Moreover, they are powerless to act against the Thai military, which plays an active role in the trafficking. "The art thieves who come to Angkor now take photographs to show their customers," says Engelhardt. "They return to Thailand, where their clients make selections. I've been at a temple site where I've overheard Thai dealers discussing which pieces they're supposed to get for clients."

When we returned to Angkor, the extent of the looting that had taken place since our previous visit was heartbreaking. Everywhere we found scores of headless statues. We were frequently assured that some of these heads had been removed for safekeeping, but after the raid on the Conservation d'Angkor, that was small comfort. On a visit to the outlying temple of Banteay Samre, a contemporary of Angkor Wat, we saw a large Sculptured stone lintel that had been chiseled out of place and then abandoned, apparently too heavy to be carried away.

UNESCO estimates that artworks are being stolen from Angkor at the rate of one per day. If the gargoyles and sacred images of the cathedrals of Europe were disappearing at the rate of one per day, it is safe to assume that a major international effort would be made, regardless of the cost, to save those great cultural treasures. Yet a loss of equal magnitude is taking place in Cambodia, and very few people outside the region are even aware that it is going on. Angkor has survived invasion, Civil war, and teams of well-meaning conservators; one hopes it will survive the depredations of the greedy. Unless strong measures are taken, the destruction of this priceless cultural heritage of Southeast Asia will soon be out of control.

Russell Ciochon, an associate professor of anthropology at the University of Iowa, is author/editor of The Human Evolution Source Book, *published by Prentice-Hall.*

Jamie James is the author of The Music of the Spheres, *published by Grove Press. They are presently collaborating on a book about the rise of civilization in Southeast Asia.*

DISCUSSION QUESTIONS

1. Does the responsibility for protecting Angkor rest primarily with the Cambodians? Should they be primarily responsible?
2. Does the United States have an interest in contributing to the protection and preservation of this site? An obligation? Who should pay the costs, and how?
3. Would theft and looting at a comparable level in European cathedrals be tolerated by the world community?
4. Are works of art from Angkor making their way into collections and museums in the United States? If so, does their presence contribute to the destruction, create interest in preserving the sites, or both?
5. Use your answer to the previous question to suggest new and additional strategies for preserving this and other sites affected by similar conditions.
6. Who are the ones selecting, from the photographs, the art-to-order pieces? For whom are they being ordered (i.e., where do the art works end up)?
7. Where else in the world are political and economic conditions such that archaeological materials might be seen as an essential and accessible source of local cash income? Are objects from those places available on the U.S. art market?
8. Is the instant access to news from all the world's troubled spots making it easier for the international art market to exploit situations in which it can be assumed that people will be paying little attention to cultural heritage protection?
9. Is the international art market actually preserving materials that would otherwise be destroyed by modern warfare, postwar development, neglect, and the like?

FURTHER RESEARCH

See also: *Looting in Angkor: One Hundred Missing Objects*, (Paris: International Council of Museums, 1993); and for a recent update on UNESCO's role in Angkor, Denise Haywood, "Standing Back to Help Better," *The Art Newspaper*, 54 (December 1995): 24.

CHAPTER ELEVEN
SECURING SITES
IN TIME OF WAR

by Arlene Krimgold Fleming

The 1991 Gulf War, with strategic targets located close to, or on, important archaeological sites, made many archaeologists and others wonder if cultural monuments were ever considered during the war's planning stages. Their concerns reawakened interest in The Hague Convention of 1954 and long-standing international efforts to protect cultural property in times of war. This brief paper summarizes the efforts and some recent applications in the Near East, Nigeria, Honduras and El Salvador, Cambodia, India and Pakistan, Cyprus and Turkey, Iran and Iraq, and Kuwait.

D uring the Gulf War Iraqi targets were "taken out" by precision bombing in the most technologically sophisticated air campaign ever waged. Archaeologists knew that many of the targets were perilously close to some of the world's most important sites, and they naturally wondered if, during the war's planning stages, the Department of Defense had consulted anyone who had excavated in Iraq. In addition to standing monuments, thousands of sites yet to be explored were vulnerable to heavy bombing raids over open countryside. The Defense Department reportedly never gave these matters much thought, which is surprising, considering the international attention in recent decades to protecting cultural property in time of war.

The most comprehensive agreement, a UNESCO *Convention for the Protection of Cultural Property in the Event of Armed Conflict,* was signed at The Hague in 1954. Several countries in the Gulf War

(Egypt, France, Iraq, Italy, Kuwait, Morocco, Saudi Arabia, Syria, and Turkey) were among the 77 nations to ratify the convention. Although the United States was a signatory and an active participant in negotiations, it has never ratified the agreement. During the 1950s, some Pentagon officials were convinced that nuclear war with the Soviet Union was inevitable, and they didn't want to be burdened by the terms of the convention. Nonetheless, the basic principles of the agreement were integrated into U.S. Army field manuals after 1957, and most observers feel there would be no objections to the convention among the military services now. Meanwhile, the United States remains bound by an earlier series of conventions on warfare drafted at The Hague in 1907. These documents call for protection of historical monuments and buildings devoted to religion, art, science, and charity, provided they are not used for military purposes.

The 1954 convention stipulates that artwork, monuments, sites, and objects of cultural value should be protected during wartime. With the destructive horror of World War II fresh in their memory, the Hague conferees stated in their preamble that "damage to cultural property belonging to any people whatsoever means damage to the cultural heritage of all mankind, since each people makes its contribution to the culture of the world."

The convention requires that combatants safeguard and respect cultural property, which is not to be used for military purposes. Monuments placed under special immunity from attack are to be listed in a register kept at UNESCO headquarters in Paris. At the insistence of the United States, a clause waiving protection in the event of "military necessity" was included, over the opposition of some nations that thought it weakened the agreement. Another point left open to interpretation was a requirement that protected cultural property be located an "adequate distance" from military installations.

The convention has a separate protocol dealing with arrangements for returning cultural property seized during a conflict. It also includes a nonbinding resolution suggesting that each country establish an advisory committee to provide military planners with information on the location of cultural property in countries where conflict is imminent or underway. To date the convention has had only limited effect. Of the 77 parties that ratified it, only four have entered property on the register for special protection: the Vatican, the Netherlands, Germany, and Austria.

During the past three decades, UNESCO itself has been in contact with governments involved in armed conflicts. Under the provisions of the convention, Commissioners General were appointed to advise the governments of Jordan, Lebanon, Egypt, and Syria at the time of the Six Day War of 1967. In 1968, UNESCO provided advice on the protection of cultural property to both sides in the Nigerian civil war as well as to combatants in Honduras and El Salvador in 1969, Cambodia in 1970, India and Pakistan in 1971, Cyprus and Turkey in 1974, and Iran and Iraq during the 1980s. For the past 19 years, UNESCO has monitored historic sites in Israeli-occupied East Jerusalem.

Shortly after Iraq invaded Kuwait on August 2, 1990, UNESCO sent letters to the governments of both countries reminding them of their responsibilities as parties to the convention. In October, Kuwait told UNESCO that occupying Iraqi forces had removed material from its national museum; the Iraqis responded that they had done so for "safekeeping." Iraq later claimed that U.S. bombing raids had damaged an ancient church in the Mosul area, the two historic Islamic towns of Najaf and Karbala, and the Iraq Museum in Baghdad.

UNESCO hopes to send a mission of experts to Iraq and Kuwait to assess war damage. "In the case of Iraq," says Lyndel Prott, chief of UNESCO's International Stands Section, "it may be necessary to address humanitarian concerns first. But eventually we will discover just what effect this latest war has had on the cultural property of the region."

Arlene Krimgold Fleming is a communications consultant for several United Nations agencies.

Note: The United States is not a party to the Hague Convention, reportedly because, during the Cold War, the government was unwilling to promise not to bomb the Kremlin, a listed cultural monument. In 1994, the State Department was said to be ready to ask the Senate, with President Clinton's blessing, to ratify the Convention on its 40th anniversary, but the issue seems to have been dropped with changes in the makeup of Congress.

DISCUSSION QUESTIONS

1. Defense departments need to know well before developing military strategies what cultural monuments and sites exist in an area and must be protected. How might archaeologists help in this process?
2. In today's wars of "ethnic cleansing" might a list of major cultural monuments end up as a list of prime targets rather than places to avoid?
3. Realistically, what can be done to protect cultural monuments and archaeological sites in times of war?
4. What can field archaeologists do to secure their sites, storerooms, and records against political turmoil?
5. Is, after all, a free and open market in cultural property the best hope for preserving the world's cultural heritage?

FURTHER RESEARCH

See also: The Hague Convention (notes in Appendix B); and the section on Protection of Cultural Property in Wartime in the *Proceedings of the Fifth Symposium on Legal Aspects of the International Art Trade: Licit Trade in Works of Art. Vienna, 28–30 September, 1994* [forthcoming] (International Chamber of Commerce Publication).

CHAPTER TWELVE
OPERATION SCROLL
by Neil Asher Silberman

One month before the scheduled staged withdrawal of Israeli forces from the Gaza Strip and the Jericho region, "the Israeli Antiquities Authority launched an ambitious survey and excavation project dubbed 'Operation Scroll'." The project, which produced a meager harvest of finds because the area had been thoroughly looted by the Bedouin 30 years earlier, nevertheless raises larger questions for the post-Cold War world on the treatment of cultural property in occupied areas at a time when the boundaries of modern nation states are changing.

In Fall 1993, as Israeli and Palestinian diplomats edged toward a delicate agreement on coexistence, the archaeological landscape of the Holy Land became a political battlefield. On November 14, a month before Israeli forces were to have begun a staged withdrawal from the Gaza Strip and the Jericho region, the Israel Antiquities Authority (IAA) launched an ambitious survey and excavation project dubbed "Operation Scroll." At the very moment when Israeli and Palestinian negotiators were working out the details of the Israel-Palestine Liberation Organization understanding signed in Washington in September, 20 teams of Israeli archaeologists assisted by some 200 hired workers began searching for, and removing, ancient coins, pottery, manuscript fragments, and other archaeological finds from the caves and ravines of a 60 mile stretch of the lower Jordan Valley and the western shore of the Dead Sea. Though the precise size of the proposed autonomous Palestinian enclave around Jericho had not yet been determined, the timing and scale of Operation Scroll, carried out in the same general area, led many Palestinians and outside observers to condemn the IAA for making a crude, eleventh-hour grab for what they thought were rightfully Palestinian antiquities.

The urgency of Operation Scroll was certainly hard to fathom: though this was the area where the Dead Sea Scrolls and other ancient documents had been discovered, the last major manuscript find in this region took place in the early 1960s (the result of illegal digging by local bedouin who thoroughly scoured the area for marketable antiquities). The IAA explained the operation as an attempt to prevent looting in the area. Yet in recent years, other areas on the West Bank and in Israel have been far more seriously ravaged by antiquities thieves. An intensive archaeological effort *there* might well have been more understandable. Though the IAA spokeswoman denied that Operation Scroll had any political implications, its timing, at least, was awkward. "The French did the same thing before they left Algeria," charged Nazmi Jubeh, a technical advisor to the Palestinian delegation to the Washington peace talks.

There were, of course, some significant differences. The most important artifacts in the Operation Scroll dispute were not artworks or treasure, but ancient Hebrew and Aramaic documents whose emotional importance to the Israeli people was considerably greater than any attachment felt by the Palestinian people to them. Expeditions to the caves of the Dead Sea region in the 1950s and 1960s had uncovered—in addition to the vast collection of ancient, Jewish religious writings known as the Dead Sea Scrolls—letters, deeds, and hastily gathered belongings of ancient Jewish rebels, religious visionaries, and frightened refugees, who sought asylum in this remote and desolate region during the two great Jewish revolts against Rome in the late first and early second century A.D. Since the 1950s these finds have captured the popular imagination of modern Israel. The reaction to the Dead Sea Scrolls and the so-called Bar-Kokhba letters on the Jordanian side of the border was never quite so enthusiastic. In fact, in 1957, the Jordanian director of antiquities, Abdul Karim Gharaybeh, ordered the removal of one of the newly found Bar Kokhba letters from display in the Palestine Archaeological Museum in Jerusalem because "it served as open propaganda for the Zionists."

Yet in late 1993, with the prospect of independence looming, many Palestinians saw a necessary link between archaeological finds and territorial sovereignty. The unilateral action of the IAA was seen as the illegal plunder of cultural resources from lands that Palestinians hoped would become the nucleus of a state. Even some prominent Israelis believed that there should have been consultation with Palestinian authorities before Operation Scroll was sent out into the field. Knesset member Anat Maor of the leftist Meretz party put it succinctly: "We have to find a balance between our deep feelings regarding our own history and respect for international law."

The international law referred to is contained in the ponderous 1954 Hague Convention, some of whose provisions deal with the proper treatment of cultural property in occupied territory. According to the Convention, an occupying power must preserve and protect all antiquities, sites, and cultural treasures for the benefit of the inhabitants, restrict excavation to necessary rescue digs or salvage work, and remove no cultural property from the occupied territory. These guidelines were established to prevent wholesale looting of art treasures such as had been carried out with ruthless efficiency by Nazi forces during World War II. Unfortunately, the situation envisioned by the authors of the Convention—hobnail-booted occupiers pulling down Old Masters from drawing room walls and pilfering statues from museum cases—bears little relation to the far more complex conflict between Israelis and Palestinians.

The territorial situation is legally tangled. Rightly or wrongly, the Israeli government has always bridled at the blanket description of the West Bank as "occupied territory" since it never legally recognized the area's annexation by the Hashemite Kingdom of Jordan in 1948. To make the situation even thornier, the areas of the West Bank to be evacuated by Israel would not be returned to Jordan, but would be handed over for administration to the PLO. The real issue—and the issue that the Hague Convention was utterly unequipped to deal with—was not the physical possession of relics but the equitable apportionment between two peoples laying claim to them.

Are the Israelis justified in mounting an effort to retrieve documents and artifacts of direct and demonstrable relevance to their culture and tradition—even if those artifacts lay in disputed territory? Do Palestinians, on the other hand, have a right to claim ownership of ancient Jewish artifacts in their part of the country, even if those artifacts are of relatively little significance to them? And if the antiquities of the country are to be partitioned by cultural association, do the Palestinians thereby have a right to custodianship of Muslim holy sites within Israel?

As things turned out, Operation Scroll reaped a meager harvest, proving how thoroughly the local bedouin had searched the area 30 years before. The most noteworthy discoveries were some fragments of Aramaic papyri (probably deeds or other legal documents, hidden by Jewish rebels at the time of the second-century A.D. Bar Kokhba Rebellion); a warrior's grave (first proudly attributed to the Maccabean period and then quietly redated to the Bronze Age); and various installations, coins, and ancient textiles. These finds hardly seemed worth the massive effort—or all the controversy and bad publicity they gained for the IAA.

As of this writing, the Israeli withdrawal from the area around Jericho, which was scheduled to begin on December 13, 1993, has not yet been implemented. The archaeological dispute over Operation Scroll was clearly just a minor skirmish in the larger Arab-Israeli conflict, yet it highlighted the need for international organizations to address the problems of disputed cultural heritage in the changing circumstances of a post-colonial, post-Cold War world. As new nation states spring up in the ruins of the Soviet Empire and across Africa and Asia, the disputes over archaeological resources are likely to become more frequent. Conflicting claims about cultural property may well arise in places like Bosnia, Armenia, Kurdistan, the Ukraine, and other locales of ethnic, cultural, and political strife. Unfortunately, there is no easy solution to the politicization of archaeology. As long as ethnic groups and nation-states continue to find prestige and modern validation in the past, archaeology will continue to be a dependable source of patriotic symbols. And, as in the case of Operation Scroll and the Palestinian protests against it, ancient pottery, stonework, metal, and manuscripts will continue to be the stage props of international politics.

Neil Silberman is a contributing editor for Archaeology, *with training and interests in the relations of modern politics and the past.*

DISCUSSION QUESTIONS

1. Are the Israelis (substitute Bosnians, Ukrainians, Somalis, Navahos, etc.) justified in trying "to retrieve documents and artifacts of direct and demonstrable relevance to their culture and tradition—even if those artifacts lie in disputed territory?"

2. Do the Palestinians (substitute other groups) have a right to claim ownership of ancient Jewish (or other) artifacts in their part of the country, even if those artifacts are of relatively little significance to them?

3. If the antiquities are "partitioned by cultural association, do the Palestinians thereby have a right to custodianship of Muslim holy sites within Israel?" Ask the same question substituting another country and different religious groups.*

4. What effect does or should the fact that archaeology is a "dependable source of patriotic symbols" have on archaeologists working in areas outside of their own cultural or ethnic origins?

5. Can archaeology (and individual archaeologists) function in isolation from modern political concerns?

---

*See also the articles by Meyer, "Who Owns the Spoils of War?", and Scott, "St. Lawrence: Archaeology of a Bering Sea Island."

CHAPTER THIRTEEN
WHO OWNS
THE SPOILS OF WAR?
by Karl E. Meyer

Meyer opens and closes this discussion of the ongoing acrimonious debates over ownership of artworks commandeered as battle spoils during World War II with reference to the theme in Homer's Iliad. *He reviews the relentless "trophy art" collecting of the Third Reich, the subsequent reciprocation of the Soviet Trophy Commission, the mitigating role played by a few archaeologists and journalists, and the articulation of the latest Russian position at a recent New York conference on "The Spoils of War." The battle over ownership and war reparations continues today, with a whole array of political and social implications. Meanwhile, collectors in many countries, including the United States, have taken advantage of the ambiguities about the ownership of "trophy art" and many pieces have "disappeared" from the trophy collections. A supplement summarizes international efforts (and failures), dating back to 1758, to establish the neutrality of works of art in wartime.*

As Germany and Russia spar over the return of wartime booty, historians and legal scholars take a fresh look at what really happened 50 years ago.

What Byron called the "fatal gift of beauty" is again sowing international discord, as it has since the Trojans abducted Helen. The latest dispute concerns a dazzling collection of Old Master and Impressionist paintings, recently exhibited for the first time in half a century in Moscow and St. Petersburg. It also concerns a royal ransom in the decorative arts; several million books, including two or perhaps three Gutenberg Bibles; whole storerooms of manuscripts and archival records; and the celebrated Treasure of Priam, the Bronze Age artifacts unearthed at Troy in 1873 by Heinrich Schliemann, a symbol and metaphor of the entire dispute (see *Archaeology*, November/ December 1993).

Germany claims ownership of most of these prizes, all of which were removed by Russian forces in 1945. At first glance the German case seems airtight. The Soviet Union and Germany agreed in 1990 to exchange all works uprooted from either country during World War II, an agreement confirmed two years later by President Boris Yeltsin of the new Russian Federation. A joint commission was established to compile lists of missing works and to preside over exchanges. But it soon became apparent that under such an agreement far more art would flow from Russia back to Germany than vice versa.

Hesitantly at first, then more boldly, the Russian government took up the refrain of militant nationalists and museum directors such as Irina Antonova of the Pushkin State Museum of Fine Arts in Moscow, whose vaults had hidden the Trojan treasure since 1945. Do not give back a thing, they argued, noting that Russia was still owed reparations for 20 million war dead and 400 looted museums. That Russia had approved a repatriation agreement with Germany, not to mention successive Hague conventions that bar use of cultural treasures as reparations, went unmentioned.

Hence the buzz of anticipation in New York early in 1995 when a dozen Russians turned up at a conference on "The Spoils of War." The three-day event, sponsored by the Bard Graduate Center for Studies in the Decorative Arts, was literally an eye-opener. Delegates from Germany, France, Poland, Hungary, and elsewhere gaped at Russian slides of long-missing Old Master paintings, prints, and drawings seized by Soviet forces. And for the first time at a public forum, Russian cultural officials developed their case for keeping everything. Mark M. Boguslavky of the Institute of State and Law of the Russian Academy of Science, a legal adviser to the Russian Ministry of Culture, claimed that all art removed from Soviet soil during World War II was taken illegally. "On that we all agree," he said, but as for the art removed from Germany by the Red Army, "we cannot agree it was illegal." He reasoned that with Hitler's defeat there was no German state, and since the Soviet Union was the legitimate governing authority in its occupation zone, it had every right to remove cultural property. Besides, in vaguely defined wartime declarations the Allies had accepted the idea of "restitution in kind," and Russia was merely applying that principle to Germany. It had indeed pledged to return what had been illegally removed from Germany, but, since everything was legally removed, Russia was not obliged to return anything.

This demarche was reminiscent of earlier times when Soviet diplomacy consisted of a thump on the table and a tirade in *Pravda*. What was different at the Bard conference, the Cold War being over, was the absence of unanimity among the Russian delegates. Not only did they differ with each other on the need for compromise and an end to secrecy, they differed openly and passionately. Resistance among younger scholars to official orthodoxy was borne home by the presence of Konstantin Akinsha, an art historian and journalist, and Grigorii Kozlov, a former inspector for Russia's Department of Museums and former curator of the Museum of Private Collections affiliated with the Pushkin Museum. Akinsha and Kozlov were the first to disclose, in a 1991 *ARTnews* article, that the Schliemann treasure, along with countless other works missing from German and European collections, had been hidden for decades in Soviet "special depositories." Their report encouraged similar exposés by other young researchers, notably Alexei Rastorgouev, an art historian at Moscow University, whose specialty is the "displaced" art of World War II. Thanks to their combined work, which appeared in Russian and international art journals, it is possible for the first time to piece together what really happened 50 years ago.

Russian passions concerning captured German artworks cannot be understood without recalling the rape of European cultural treasures during the Third Reich. A failed artist himself, Hitler dreamed of building a vast art museum in Linz, near his Austrian birthplace. He recruited a Dresden Museum director, Hans Posse, to gather a collection by whatever means necessary and ordered the Wehrmacht to assist a special trophy unit commanded by Nazi ideologist Alfred Rosenberg. Posse and Rosenberg competed for spoils with the sybaritic Hermann Goering, with Himmler's SS, and with thousands of officers billeted in foreign castles and estates.

In France and the Low Countries art was harvested by seizing works from Jewish collections and state museums, or by forced sales, such as the "purchase" of superb Old Master drawings from Dutch collector Franz Koenigs. In the East, Polish museums were stripped and royal palaces destroyed. Slavs were deemed *Untermenschen,* their history worthless. In his first tour of the Royal Palace in Warsaw, Governor-General Hans Frank set the example by tearing silver eagles from the canopy covering the royal throne and pocketing them. Poland's fate foreshadowed the devastation of the Soviet Union. Within weeks of Hitler's blitzkrieg of June 1941, German forces occupied czarist palaces on the outskirts of Leningrad. At the Palace of Catherine the Great at Tsarskoye Selo, they dismantled the Amber Room, a great chamber whose walls were lined with precious amber, which had been given to Peter the Great by Frederick-William II of Prussia. The walls of the room were taken to Koenigsberg in East Prussia, where they disappeared, removed and hidden by the Germans or unknowingly destroyed in the Russian assault on the city. German depredations over a three-year period are graphically described in Lynn Nicholas' account of World War II plunder, *The Rape of Europa:* "They took anything they could pry loose from the myriad palaces and pavilions around Leningrad, right down to the parquet floors. They opened packed crates and helped themselves to the contents. Mirrors were smashed or machine gunned, brocades and silks ripped from the walls. At Peterhof . . . the gilded bronze statues of Neptune and Samson upon which the waters played were hauled off to the smelting furnace in full view of the distraught townspeople." Not since the Goths and Vandals had Europe witnessed so spiteful an assault on other people's cultural treasures. The ancient cathedral at Novgorod was ravaged, Pushkin's house ransacked, Tolstoy's manuscripts burned, and elsewhere museums, churches, libraries, universities, and scientific institutes were robbed and destroyed. Most of the Nazi plunder has never been recovered.

Small wonder that, as the battlefront shifted toward Germany, Soviet retribution was swift and encompassing. In November 1943 an edict of an Emergency State Committee authorized the removal of state and private libraries and art collections to Russia. A Trophy Commission was formed to comb castles, bunkers, salt mines, and caves in which Germans had hidden their own treasures as well as looted foreign art. In Dresden the Russians removed everything portable, including the jeweled contents of the famous Green Vault in the royal castle and more than 500 drawings from the Koenigs collection, which Hitler's agents had brought from Holland. By then a new vision had taken hold in Moscow: the postwar creation of a great Museum of World Art to be filled with works seized as compensation for Nazi vandalism. In January 1945 Stalin signed a directive authorizing massive removal of cultural property of all kinds, ostensibly for the supermuseum.

Four months later the trophy unit arrived in Berlin, where it seized the Pergamon Altar, with its celebrated Hellenistic frieze depicting the battle of the gods and giants, originally acquired by Germany in Turkish Asia Minor. From a bomb-proof bunker near the Berlin Zoo, it confiscated cases of Trojan gold that Schliemann had found at Hisarlik and presented to his native Germany in 1881. Romantically if erroneously dubbed by its finder the Treasure of Priam, the collection consists of hundreds of gold and silver objects, including a gold-beaded headdress once proudly modeled by Schliemann's young Greek wife, Sophia. The cases were flown to the Pushkin Museum, where a receipt was signed by 28-year-old curator Irina Antonova, a tiny woman with blazing eyes who had grown up in Berlin, where her father had been a Soviet trade official. Antonova has survived six Soviet leadership upheavals and the collapse of communism, and still reigns as Pushkin director and guardian of wartime spoils.

Soviet soldiers needed little encouragement in following the Trophy Commission's lead. General Vassily Chuikoff, having settled in the estate of Otto Krebs outside Weimar, saw to it that 98 Impressionist paintings in the Krebs collection were removed to Leningrad, where they were hidden until this year. Other commanders filled railroad cars with the contents of Prussian estates. At Schloss Karnzow, Lieutenant Victor Baldin came upon soldiers in the cellar shuffling through hundreds of Old Master drawings, placed there for safekeeping by curators of the Bremen Kunsthalle. Baldin crammed into his suitcase 364 drawings, including a Dürer that he acquired in a swap for a pair of boots. Baldin, an art historian, preserved the drawings, and years later tried vainly to have them returned to Bremen. By all these routes, a flood of art reached Russia. Soviet plans for a supermuseum, however, were stalled in good part by the long-forgotten work of a handful of soldiers in the West known as "monuments men." That archaeologists, with an interest in ruins and their preservation, might play a useful military role was not at first obvious to the British War Office. Italy unwittingly caused a change of mind in 1941 when it accused British troops of vandalizing the classical ruins of Leptis Magna, Cyrene, and Sabratha in Libya. Lieutenant Colonel Mortimer Wheeler, the breezily self-assured excavator of Mohenjodaro, who happened to be serving in North Africa, was given the job of safeguarding the sites, which he did with éclat. Wheeler was supported in London by Sir Leonard Woolley, excavator of Ur, who headed the army's Archaeological Adviser's office (consisting of Sir Leonard, Lady Woolley, and a clerk).

When the United States entered the war, influential scholars soon began lobbying for a more ambitious American counterpart to Woolley's office. William Dinsmoor, then president of the Archaeological Institute of America, was among those who met with, and apparently convinced, Chief Justice Harlan Fiske Stone, an ex-officio trustee of the newly formed National Gallery of Art, that an art and monuments unit be formed. Stone sent his recommendations to the White House on December 8, 1942. What probably tipped the scales in favor of the recommendation was Roosevelt and Churchill's decision in January 1943 to invade Sicily, with its vulnerable Greek and Roman ruins and its famous Byzantine churches.

Months later in Sicily, Captain Mason Hammond, a Harvard classics professor acting as art adviser to the Supreme Allied Commander, appropriated a battered vehicle, organized rescue groups, posted off-limits signs, and courted the annoyance of generals. Hammond was the first of several score monuments officers, men and women, most of them scholars and museum curators, who accompanied Allied armies through Italy, France, and Germany. There was

little they could do about wartime devastation: Monte Cassino
was destroyed; Pompeii was bombed, as was a church in Padua with
frescoes by Mantegna. There were devastating aerial assaults on
Dresden, Nürnberg, and other old German cities. Nor could they be
held responsible for thousands of soldiers who pocketed spoils of war.
In one memorable heist, a U.S. Army artillery officer from Texas,
Lieutenant Joe Tom Meador, "liberated" the cathedral treasures of
Quedlinburg in the Harz mountains of north-central Germany. He
mailed home rock-crystal reliquaries, a jewel-encrusted silver casket,
and the priceless *Samuhel Gospels*, written in gold ink and bound in a
jeweled cover, part of a treasure associated with Henry I of Saxony,
who is sometimes described as the founder of Germany. After
Meador's death in 1980, his heirs tried to sell his booty, which to their
astonishment was appraised at tens of millions of dollars. An enter-
prising *New York Times* reporter, William H. Honan, picked up
rumors of the attempted sale, identified Meador, and helped bring
about the repatriation of the Quedlinburg treasures, with the lubrica-
tion of a $3.75 million "finder's fee" to the heirs from the German
Cultural Foundation. The monuments officers were far more successful protecting the quantities of German art and Nazi booty hidden in
castles, caves, and mines. At war's end they learned that senior
American officials, abetted by covetous museum directors, had proposed sequestering German art as war reparations. This idea was
opposed by General Lucius Clay, commander of U.S. Forces in
Germany, who favored the swiftest possible return of all booty to its
rightful owners, though he did suggest that some German masterpieces might be exhibited temporarily in America.

To monuments officers, even that was all too reminiscent of the
Nazi policy of "temporary" removals, purportedly to "protect" other
people's art. They drew up what became known as the Wiesbaden
Manifesto, which soberly warned, "no historical grievance will rankle
so long, or be the cause of so much justified bitterness, as the removal,
for any reason, of a part of the heritage of any nation, even if that
heritage may be interpreted as a prize of war." Signed in November
1945 by 25 officers and supported by five others not present, the
Manifesto came to the attention of Janet Flanner, whose account in

The New Yorker was immediately cited by officials opposing any use of art as reparations.

President Truman rejected the reparation idea but did approve an exhibition of 202 masterpieces from Berlin museums. The National Gallery's first blockbuster show, it drew a million visitors in 1948, then traveled to New York and St. Louis. By then Europe was dividing into East and West, and General Clay was mounting an airlift to encircled West Berlin. Returned in 1955, the Berlin paintings were placed in the new Dahlem Museum in what was then the American sector, and there they remain today. Meanwhile, thanks to the monuments officers, some 500,000 cultural items looted by Nazis in Slavic countries and found in western Germany were repatriated, an unreciprocated restitution that is invariably ignored in Russian reckoning.

All this had its effect on Moscow. Nothing more was said about establishing a Museum of World Art, with its embarrassing resemblance to Hitler's plans for Linz. In 1945, Soviet prosecutors at Nürnberg agreed with Western victors in defining the plunder of art as a war crime. The Soviet Foreign Minister, Vyacheslav Molotov, even joined with Britain in censuring America's temporary removal of German art. But what truly complicated Soviet cultural diplomacy was the division of Germany and the emergence of a comradely ally, the German Democratic Republic. In 1958, as a goodwill gesture and to buttress the legitimacy of the new East German regime, Nikita Krushchev returned the Pergamon Altar to its old home in East Berlin and gave back to Dresden most of its Old Masters and the bejeweled objets d'art from the Green Vault. This wise and realistic gesture was opposed by museum officials such as Irina Antonova, who at the Bard conference in New York was still deploring a decision "dictated by politics." Curators come to believe they own what is in their care. Commenting on the fate of Priam's Treasure in an interview in *Archaeology* (November/December 1993), Valery Kulishov, a member of the Russian State Commission on Restitution, noted: "You must understand the feelings of the Pushkin Museum officials. If you have it, it's part of you. Psychologically, you're so much attached and bound to what you had, even secretly, in your repository. It's very hard now to give it back, regardless of any kind of agreements."

Trophy art, however, is not exhibited or cataloged. Anybody with access to storerooms can steal and sell it. Leakage has been considerable. Of 562 drawings in the Dutch Koenigs collection seized in Dresden, 33 remained in Germany. But in 1957, the Pushkin Museum's unpublished records listed only "337 sheets," and the total today is said to be 308. A similar attrition has taken place in the Krebs collection, which for five decades has been hidden in the Hermitage in St. Petersburg. At the Bard conference, Alexei Rastorgouev showed slides of drawings from Dresden now owned by unidentified Russian private collectors. Dealers in Europe and America routinely check the Koenigs catalog when offered drawings of suspiciously high quality.

Hence the urgent need to display and catalog all of Russia's wartime booty as soon as possible. It was this consideration that prompted the Hermitage director, Mikhail Piotrovski, to arrange the showing this past March of Impressionist and Post-Impressionist paintings from the Krebs and other private collections. A few weeks earlier Irina Antonova, not to be outdone, had quickly organized a comparable show of Old Masters from German and Hungarian collections at the Pushkin. One hopes such competition will be contagious. In Piotrovski's sensible view, it is up to the courts to decide legal title, and up to the museums to make public what they hold. In a wider sense, though, the courts can only settle claims of heirs and museums when and if Russia and Germany reach a political settlement.

In the early 1970s, I delved into the secretive antiquities market and its links with collectors and curators. The results were serialized in *The New Yorker* and published as *The Plundered Past*. If I learned any lesson, it was that on matters of acquiring cultural treasures, no art-consuming nation has truly clean hands. Consider the United States. As Lynn Nicholas recounts in *The Rape of Europa*, in 1939 the Nazis staged a scandalous auction at the Fischer Gallery in Lucerne at which allegedly "degenerate" art by Braque, Picasso, Van Gogh, and others was sold at derisory prices. The pictures had been taken from leading German museums. Among the bidders was a refugee German dealer, Curt Valentin of the Bucholz Gallery in New York, who acquired paintings by Derain, Kirchner, Klee, Lehmbruck, and

Matisse. He was bidding on behalf of the Museum of Modern Art, whose, director, Alfred Barr, exhibited the five works with no hint of their true provenance. No doubt the sale was legal, but it speaks volumes that the entire transaction was secret. By the same token, Harvard's acquisition of a major work by Max Beckmann, sold at the same auction, was also legal. But both institutions were extracting an advantage from a political calamity that befell German museums, a fact not advertised in accession labels.

As for Germany, everyone repudiates the cultural barbarities and wholesale brigandage that marked the Reich. There will be no such unanimity on Germany's legal title to the Schliemann treasure which was spirited from Ottoman Turkey in murky circumstances, provoking a criminal suit and cash settlement at the time, and leading to a formal claim by the present Republic of Turkey. Nor is anyone talking about the controversy surrounding the bust of Queen Nefertiti, Germany's single most celebrated antiquity. Acquired in a division of finds at Amarna in 1914, the statue was hidden for a decade; Egyptians cried foul from the moment it was finally put on display in Berlin. Like other European art-importing countries, Germany has yet to ratify the UNESCO convention barring the illegal importation of cultural property. Purchase of unprovenanced antiquities, many of them clearly smuggled from their country of origin, is widespread, as visitors to German museums can readily see.

As for Russia, it can indeed point to a traumatic past, but even those sympathetic to its cause will wonder whether five decades of concealment attest a confident claim of ownership. Certainly neither Poland nor Holland, Ukraine nor Hungary, ever invaded the Soviet Union, yet their claims for restitution have also gone unanswered. Ironically the Yeltsin government is seeking restitution of real estate and other properties owned by the czarist regime and its subjects in France, Italy, and Israel, appealing to the very norms of law and equity it declines to apply to its own wartime booty.

How sensible if Russia broke the ice by returning a set of rare books taken from Gotha in 1945, an act of restitution urged by a Moscow librarian speaking at the Bard conference. This gesture might be coupled with an offer to submit claims to the World Court for binding adjudication (as Germany has proposed) with the proviso that Turkey's claim also be given a full hearing. And how wise if Germany promoted an international effort to restore Russian museums and churches. Initiatives like these must be taken quickly, for it takes only a modicum of historical memory to know that it is later than the two governments think.

The Russian parliament has already given preliminary approval to legislation that would give Russia full title to all wartime booty. If that legislation is adopted, there will certainly be repercussions. German aid to Russia is reckoned at more than $73 billion since 1990, including $40 billion in loans and $14 billion in direct grants. If Bonn cuts or conditions its aid to Moscow, a likely next move, there will be a Russian outcry over German bullying and a clamor for reprisals in the Russian parliament.

Back in 1945 American monuments officers, in their Wiesbaden declaration, warned that disputes over captured spoils can sow enduring acrimony. That indeed is the theme of Homer's *Iliad*, which begins with Achilles' fury at the prizes of war that Agamemnon greedily bestows on himself. If no progress is made this year toward resolving the quarrel over Russia's wartime booty, positions will harden, and taking a modest step forward will be even more difficult. As evidence, consult the *Iliad*.

LIMITS OF WORLD LAW

Two remarkable people helped write the laws meant to bar warring nations from destroying or looting each other's cultural treasures. One was the German-American soldier and philosopher, Francis Lieber, author of a military code promulgated by Lincoln during the Civil War. The other was Nicholas Roerich, a Russian painter and mystic, who in 1935 persuaded the United States and 20 other countries to approve a treaty asserting the inherent neutrality of works of art in wartime.

The belief that cultural treasures need special treatment was expressed as early as 1758 by Emheric de Vattel, a legal scholar during the Enlightenment, whose treatise *The Law of Nations* spoke to the future: "For whatever cause a country is ravaged, we ought to spare those edifices which do honor to human society, and do not contribute to increase the enemy's strength such as temples, tombs, public buildings and all works of remarkable beauty. . . It is declaring one's self to be an enemy of mankind, thus wantonly to deprive them of these wonders of art." Napoleon, nonetheless, crammed the Louvre with wagonloads of conquered art. At the Congress of Vienna in 1815, the Allies ordered France to return the art, since looting, in the words of the Duke of Wellington, was "contrary to the principles of justice and the rules of modern law."

Yet those laws were unwritten. By chance, this was rectified by Francis Lieber, a Prussian-born soldier who in 1827 emigrated to America. He taught legal philosophy at Columbia College in New York, and during the Civil War President Lincoln asked him to draft a military code. Issued as General Order 100 in 1863, it called among other things for the protection during wartime of "classical works of art, libraries, scientific collections or precious instruments, such as astronomical telescopes."

The Lieber code inspired a similar declaration in 1874 at the Conference of Brussels that was endorsed by the German kaiser. This declaration in turn inspired the Russian czar to promote a more ambitious conference at the Hague. In 1907, some 40 nations approved a series of conventions that expressly forbade the seizure or destruction in wartime of cultural treasures. The Hague codes proved of limited value during World War I, so in 1935 a fresh attempt was made.

This was the work of Nicholas Roerich (1874–1947), a Russian artist who designed the sets for Stravinsky's ballet *Le Sacre du Printemps*. As an explorer, he had led a five-year expedition to central Asia, and had also served as vice-president of the Archaeological Institute of America. A friend of Secretary of Agriculture Henry Wallace, Roerich persuaded the Roosevelt Administration to support a new treaty to protect artistic works, scientific instruments, and historic monuments. He devised a special flag, with three globes in a mystic triad, to mark protected cultural treasures.

Since World War II, insurgents have targeted the great Khmer ruins at Angkor, the walled medieval city of Dubrovnik, and the

Ottoman bridges of Bosnia, as well as thousands of churches, mosques, synagogues, temples, palaces, libraries, and memorials of every kind. Nobody has yet found a way of enforcing civilized aspirations; the worst enemy of humanity's noblest works is still humanity itself.

Karl E. Meyer is a member of the editorial board of The New York Times *and the author of* The Plundered Past *and* The Pleasures of Archaeology.

DISCUSSION QUESTIONS

1. Why are works of art a desirable target during wartime?
2. Should works of art, cultural monuments, and archaeological sites receive special protection and consideration in times of war?
3. After the war, Russia returned the Pergamon Altar to its former home in East Berlin, but its original home was in Pergamon, now in the Republic of Turkey. Priam's Gold is currently in Moscow, carried there during the war from Germany, whence Schliemann had taken it from Troy, in modern Turkey. What is the appropriate modern home for any of these objects? Do modern nation states have legitimate claim to anything that was once found within their territory? What happens if the national boundaries change?
4. The World War II trophy art in Russia has been hidden and kept secret for decades. What purpose, then, did it (and does it) serve? Can useful lessons and new directions for protecting cultural property in wartime be gleaned from the World War II experience?
5. What role did, and do, museum curators, archaeologists, and other scholars play in protecting the cultural heritage in times of war? After the war is over? What should their role be?

6. Should the United States ratify and implement The Hague Convention?*

FURTHER RESEARCH

See also: Lynn H. Nicholas, *The Rape of Europa* (New York: Knopf, 1994); Jeanette Greenfield, *The Return of Cultural Treasures* (New York: Cambridge University Press, 1989); and Kenneth D. Alford, *The Spoils of War* (New York: Carol Publishing, 1994).

---

*See: The Hague Convention (notes in Appendix B).

PART FOUR
AFFECTED PEOPLES

Archaeology studies the human past, but it affects the present and the lives of many people today as well: those who live in areas where archaeologists conduct fieldwork, those who claim descent from the people whose remains we study, those who may be inspired to dig on their own for the riches they assume we are taking, those who hold to a different version of the past than that provided by archaeology. The articles in this section explore some of the effects, both negative and positive, of archaeology on such people.

CHAPTER FOURTEEN
ST. LAWRENCE: ARCHAEOLOGY OF A BERING SEA ISLAND
by Stuart Scott

Scott provides a history of archaeological investigations of the prehistoric Eskimo settlements and ivory carvings, the difficulties of excavating in permafrost, the extensive losses due to coastal erosion and, today, to exploitation of the archaeological resources for income by the native Eskimo population. St. Lawrence shares the pattern of other isolated communities where archaeology has provided inspiration for, and the means to, participate in the twentieth century cash economy.

St. Lawrence, largest island in the Bering Sea, is only slightly larger than Long Island, New York. Barely separated from the nearest Siberian and American land areas, the island lies only 39 miles from Russia's Chukchi Peninsula and 118 miles from the Seward Peninsula of mainland Alaska. The island's mountains must have served as an elevated signpost on the massive continental Bering land bridge when the ancestors of American Indians and Eskimos first crossed from Asia into North America. But unfortunately, no archaeological traces of that earliest migration have yet been found on the island.

Today's island population, numbering approximately 400, is concentrated in two modern villages, Savoonga and Sevookuk, the latter renamed Gambell as a memorial to Mr. and Mrs. V. C. Gambell, American missionary teachers who drowned in 1898 while returning to the island. The newer settlement of Savoonga was established first as a reindeer herding camp in 1917. As would be expected from its geographic position, strong cultural connections exist between St. Lawrence and eastern Siberia. The islanders, in fact, are migrants from Siberia and speakers of Yup'ik, a dialect they share with Siberian Eskimos.

St. Lawrence is a treeless volcanic island that meets all of one's expectations of what Arctic land looks like. Its iron-bound, harborless shoreline and sea cliffs give a stark impression of solemn, stony remoteness. The island's rolling, empty hills are covered only by sparse and shrubby plant life, the seedbed a blanket of weathered volcanic basalt derived from inhospitable cinder cones. Between the dominant mountain ranges are large tracts of marshy tundra with scattered melt-water lakes and ponds. Actually, the melt water has little time to accumulate since for eight months of the year St. Lawrence Island is enclosed by pack ice. The Arctic summer has been described as one crystalline day that lasts for a few glorious weeks. With the disappearance of snow in June, the tundra vegetation blooms with a variety of berry plants, mosses, lichens, and other greens. The leaves from one of these, *Sedum rosea* (in Eskimo, *noonivak*), are stored for fermentation and later mixed with seal oil and eaten as a prized relish to accompany meat, as is seaweed either raw or cooked.

But taken all together, the vegetable products are only a tiny fraction of the native diet. It's the Bering Sea mammal complex, chiefly whale, walrus and seal, that forms the preferred food supply today as well as in the past. Nature seems to have situated St. Lawrence at maximum advantage for intercepting the abnormally rich annual harvest of whale and walrus that migrates north each spring and south each fall between the Bering Sea and the Arctic Ocean. One glance at any of the numerous prehistoric earth mounds on the island's coast is enough to see the success of the ancient sea mammal hunters. The surface of each abandoned settlement is littered with walrus skulls, whale bones, harpoon equipment, boat pieces, paddles, ornaments, lamp fragments, pottery, and the general debris of an ancient maritime way of life.

The ancient residents of St. Lawrence Island were the carriers of a distinct cultural current, one that evolved to provide for life in this universe of harsh polar seas. As recipients of a social heredity with origins in the far past of Asian antiquity, the St. Lawrence Islanders evolved in their own linguistic, racial and geographic direction. Yet even in this adverse setting, they developed an important cultural attribute—an inward vision of art that produced distinctive artistic expressions which are counted among the treasures of antiquity.

One of the imponderables in understanding this art of the distant past is the matter of why the Eskimo cultures of St. Lawrence favored small, portable implements and ornaments. In today's age of intensified admiration of artistically significant objects, the lucrative trade in cultural properties often erases any chance to document archaeologically the sources of art. St. Lawrence Island is no exception. The rich artistic tradition of the island enjoys no real safeguards, resulting in destruction of the sources of the island's renowned art. It seems especially poignant that after the Eskimos' centuries of success in adapting and prospering in one of the world's most inhospitable environments, within the span of a few short years the ruins of their ancient coastal settlements and their contents could be erased.

Perhaps because of its insularity or its obtrusive position in the Bering seaway, the first of many leading figures in prehistoric research were attracted to St. Lawrence Island in the 1920s. This was a period in the growth of American archaeology when typology and classification of artifacts were being more closely related to stratigraphic excavations, out of an immediate need for chronology and culture classifications. During this period, archaeologists were sounding out the essential descriptive time and space questions of their profession— what were the culture forms and how old were they?

While conducting an anthropological survey of Alaskan racial groups in 1926, Ales Hrdlicka, a Czech physician who served for many years as the curator of physical anthropology at the U.S. National Museum, visited the village of Savoonga. There, he purchased some ivory artifacts that had been found at the prehistoric sites of Kookoolik and Kialegak by the St. Lawrence Eskimos. Otto Geist, the German-born naturalist and pioneer archaeologist, was also conducting an archaeological survey on the island in that same year under the auspices of the Alaska Agricultural College and School of Mines (later to become the University of Alaska). Significantly, both Geist and Hrdlicka recognized on the Savoonga ivories a delicate fineline decoration reminiscent of the incised decorative style that the Canadian anthropologist Diamond Jenness found on Little Diomede Island in the Bering Strait and named the Bering Sea Culture.

The discovery on St. Lawrence Island of examples of what was then the earliest specifically Eskimo horizon set the stage for further field investigations. The start of research into this ancient art production also taught the islanders, on a practical level, that the immense repertory of ancient art present in the island's prehistoric mound sites had monetary value. For them, the imagery of ancestral art and the creative process of its manufacture would be overshadowed by its utility as a cash asset.

Between 1927 and 1935, archaeological claims were staked out, with Geist first testing old village sites near Gambell at the Northwest Cape and later turning to the Kookoolik midden near Savoonga. During that same interval, Henry B. Collins, representing the U.S. National Museum, began investigations on Punuk Island and at Kialegak and the Northwest Cape sites. On the basis of this research, he proposed the island's first sequence of archaeological phases. The delicate engraved ornamentation, first noticed outside of archaeological context by Geist and Hrdlicka, became an index of Collins' Old Bering Sea horizon.

Collins' excavations on tiny Punuk Island established that as the type site for the Punuk phase—a cultural stage of Eskimo prehistory marked by the Punuk art style. The Punuk materials were found to be later than the Old Bering Sea horizon. The art was less delicately executed, with the older fineline curvilinear designs replaced by straighter and less refined engraved line decoration. Collins' illuminating study of the Eskimo cultures, together with the findings of other archaeologists, revealed that it was not only the artistically carved objects in human and animal form that flagged the transformations from one prehistoric culture to another. Implements such as detachable harpoon heads, knife handles and winged objects served as benchmarks of their own for each single culture period.

One of the prime motivations among most prehistorians is the search for origins, a search indexed by the finding of successively earlier sites. In the late 1920s to mid-1930s, which Louis Giddings aptly termed a period of "widening horizons," the Punuk stage was gradually recognized as an intermediate period of Eskimo culture. Punuk bone and ivory objects were engraved with more mechanical and elemental designs than those of the Old Bering Sea style, and at the same time Punuk foreshadowed the art of the modern Eskimo. It remained for Otto Geist to uncover proof of yet another distinctive cultural phase, subsequently known as Okvik.

The discovery of Okvik, like so much in archaeology, bore an element of chance. Geist, alone among white investigators of St. Lawrence history, enjoyed a special acceptance among the islanders by his choice of living through several winters with Eskimo families. Living as a participant villager rather than guest observer, Geist had the advantage of gaining firsthand knowledge of a rich source of "fossil" ivory discovered on the outermost Punuk islet by Eskimo ivory diggers. The artifacts cut from the dense walrus ivory are "fossilized" only in the sense that after long contact with organic soil deposits the creamy whiteness darkens into soft deep colors that enhance the objects' appeal to collectors. Geist had noticed on the harpoon heads and other items brought back to Savoonga curious and unfamiliar designs which he thought "seemed to represent a somewhat different culture from those found on St. Lawrence Island, probably due to specialization."

Alarmed by the volume of ivory being brought from the Punuk site and sold to ships' crews or exported through local cooperative stores, Geist concluded his 1934 fieldwork at Kookoolik and with a small crew began a short salvage excavation at the Punuk site in August and September of that year. The art and artifacts they found there, together with other pieces purchased from the ivory-carving trade, attracted a great deal of attention not only because the material represented an early phase of the marine-oriented Eskimo culture, but also because of its aesthetic quality, particularly that of the Okvik sculptural art.

Archaeology is a game of inches, intellectually and operationally. Understanding mound fill stratification on St. Lawrence Island, however, was particularly slow and tedious because of the Arctic soil conditions. Excavators have described in vivid terms the difficulties of controlled digging in the shallow upper zone of permanently frozen ground where slow natural thawing often produces a morass of driftwood, bones and blubber-soaked black earth. In 1931, the east or main midden of Kookoolik had become the target during the brief summer excavation season. There, a 30-foot-wide test cut was started as the primary means to extract physical evidence from the mound—its architecture, features and objects.

Working backward in time, Geist began with the excavation of a recent Eskimo house framed with driftwood timbers and covered with sand and dirt. Bottles, iron knives and porcelain testified to the relatively modern age of this structure, as indeed was obvious from its position near the top of the mound. In the following season the first house was completely removed, revealing a second house frame. Although the second house was smaller than the overlying structure, both were judged to belong to the same general occupation period on the basis of a nearly identical assemblage of household items—wooden bowls, plates, knives, harpoon heads and arrows, iron, and so on. The continued deepening of the large trench brought to light the logs from a series of earlier and successively smaller dwellings.

The data on Kookoolik's prehistory were not limited to the sequence of superimposed houses. Meat caches, considerably smaller than the dwellings, were usually constructed as deep pits walled with stone and bone, with wooden roofs covered in sod and dirt. Together with the houses, these features produced the great majority of the artifactual refuse. Skeletal remains of the mound dwellers themselves provided some information on mortuary practices. In the case of the uppermost house in the test cut, human remains were found in a scattered, disordered state. These were thought to be the remains of the last inhabitants of Kookoolik, who died as victims of a recorded famine during the winter of 1878–79. In lower levels, however, more deliberate burials were found covered with hewn planks.

In the 1930s, radiocarbon dating did not yet exist as an aid in constructing cultural chronologies. Archaeologist Geist and his coworkers relied on observable stratigraphic phenomena such as buried humus lines. These layers of compressed sod were found to be evidence of those periods in the long discontinuous history of Kookoolik when the mound village was not occupied and grass could grow into layers of sod before being covered by later occupations.

Although the sod lines helped to distinguish various substrata, it was the ornamental art and artifacts that painted a more vivid profile of the growth of Kookoolik. The digging produced items of stone, pottery, wood, baleen, bone, ivory, and iron that could unmistakably be classed as utilitarian in the sense that they were implements used in the routine mechanical activities of living. Among these are such serviceable tools as lamp fragments, adze blades, sled runners, line sinkers, root picks, whetstones, oar locks, and many more. Among the portable artifacts, artistry versus utility is sometimes a blurred distinction. As the anthropologist Edmund Carpenter has observed, life in the Arctic is reduced to its barest essentials, yet art turns out to be among those essentials. Decorative art was applied to detachable harpoon heads as well as to images in animal, human and abstract shapes. Whatever their mystical or subjective purpose, the changing art forms serve as time indicators to discriminate between cultural ages—in Kookoolik's case, a span from Old Bering Sea through the Punuk period to nineteenth-century Eskimo.

Geist, Rainey, Jenness, Hrdlicka, and Collins were followed by others whose detailed investigations on St. Lawrence Island have added to our knowledge of western Arctic prehistory. In 1939, James L. Giddings conducted new excavations at the Hillside Site, discovered earlier by Collins on the slope of Mt. Sevookuk near the present village of Gambell. At Hillside, Giddings found and excavated a round house presumed to be of the Okvik period. With the passing of time, aspects of St. Lawrence Island prehistory had broadened considerably to include other questions in Arctic anthropology. For example, when did the Eskimo first appear in the Bering Sea region? What is the origin of the specialized sea mammal hunting cultures? What role was played by external stimuli, either from the Asiatic or

American mainlands, in developing the strong artistic tradition of the Bering Sea cultures? Despite these lingering basic questions, no extensive archaeological investigations were conducted on St. Lawrence Island for nearly 20 years following Giddings' work at Gambell.

Then, in 1958, Robert Ackerman of Washington State University circumnavigated the island in a lengthy archaeological reconnaissance that included additional excavation of Punuk Stage sites. Subsequent descriptive and chronological work was carried forward in the 1960s by Hans-Georg Bandi, a Danish archaeologist, who continued survey studies along the western and southern coasts and excavated Old Bering Sea and Punuk burials.

In the 1970s, a team of archaeologists from the University of Alaska conducted survey and excavations of a refuse midden complex at Kialegak Point on the island's Southeast Cape. This most recent work was brought about by the accidental discovery of a 1,600-year-old frozen, naturally mummified and tattooed Eskimo woman who appears to have died in a landslide or earthquake. With permission of the island residents, the body was brought to the Arctic Health Research Center in Fairbanks for further study. Based on the postmortem examination, this elderly Eskimo woman was found to have been burdened in life with hardened arteries, emphysema and other afflictions before her death by accidental inhumation and asphyxiation. Tattooing on both forearms and several fingers had been executed in artistic motifs comparable to the Old Bering Sea style of artifact ornamentation, offering a rare glimpse of an actual individual of the Old Bering Sea phase of Alaskan prehistory. Following the clinical examination of this unusual prehistoric find, the body was returned to the discovery site for reburial in 1977.

Apart from the unique opportunity to study, in both literal and figurative terms, a point frozen in time, Kialegak provided the investigators with the chance to evaluate the archaeological resources of that area. Measurements and observations were made on additional human skeletal material believed to belong to the 1878–79 period of starvation and epidemic. Items from both the surface, and to a lesser extent from stratification of refuse deposits, comprised a rich cultural content of net sinkers, harpoon heads, adzes, sled runners, knife blades, and awls in the usual media of ivory, bone, wood, baleen, and pottery. The University of Alaska findings showed Kialegak Point to be one of the most extensive archaeological zones in the Bering Sea region, perhaps spanning the entire Eskimo culture history of St. Lawrence.

The prehistory of St. Lawrence Island is a story of advanced hunters confronted by exceptional natural circumstances. Fortunately, their equally exceptional art, particularly the evolution of design elements in that art, has allowed us to document the developmental changes in culture over a 2,000 year period of island life. There remains, however, the troublesome question of the long-term preservation of such prehistoric seaside villages as Kookoolik. Many sites have suffered heavily from erosion. For example, an unquestionably major and unknown portion of the ancient Okvik type site has been swept into the sea by storm waves and pack ice. But another aspect of the island scene is just as damaging to the preservation of the sites and the artifacts they contain.

We've seen how a materialistically oriented archaeology was applied, beginning in the 1920s, to the problem of understanding St. Lawrence and the Bering Sea phases of ancient Alaska's history. Each researcher has noted the sad fact that to the list of extractive industries in Alaska's economy—fur, seal, gold, whaling, and petroleum—we can now add a smaller but comparatively destructive trade in ancient Eskimo artifacts. When archaeologists began to study the island, the styles and substyles of ivory art were valued first for their service to prehistoric research, and then for the appeal of their beauty to both museums and private collectors. The Eskimo were quick to realize that their ancestors had left them a large stock of a valuable commodity. During any given summer it is probable that archaeological sites provide about 80 percent of the income of the people of Savoonga.

Father Sebastian Englert, for many years the Capuchin parish priest and historian of Easter Island, another island endowed with a wealth of ancient art and artifacts, penned a rather despondent version of the modern gospel of progress. "For the islanders," he wrote, "increased contact with the new and exciting world is drawing a veil over the past as a winding sheet is drawn over a corpse." His words might well have described a modern scene on Nome's Front Street, where a St. Lawrence Islander, lacking the price of a hotel room, nevertheless carries a pocket full of thousand-year-old carvings to be sold to the highest bidder.

The spectacle of prehistoric mounds being rapidly obliterated by artifact hunters is somewhat indigestible to archaeologists or anyone else concerned with preserving the past. St. Lawrence, however, shares the pattern of many isolated locations where the twentieth century brought a cash economy to an environment that provides little opportunity to earn money. Who can deny the islanders their share of the satisfactions of modern economic life? The Eskimo are free to administer their historic resources since the Native Corporation was granted patent title to St. Lawrence Island in 1971 under a provision of the Alaska Native Claims Settlement Act. The dilemma of conservation versus consumption is never easily solved, but on St. Lawrence Island a practical and enlightened eye might see that to fashion a life of the present should not, and need not, tragically erase our chances to glimpse the human condition of the past.

Stuart Scott teaches archaeology at the State University of New York, Buffalo, and has extensive archaeological field experience in both the Old and New Worlds.

DISCUSSION QUESTIONS

1. How does archaeological interest create a market for local antiquities? Can archaeologists avoid this outcome?
2. Should the St. Lawrence Islanders have the right to sell their own heritage if they choose to? If so, should others (everyone, or just some groups?) be able to claim the same right?
3. What options other than selling their ancestral antiquities do the natives have for access to the cash economy?

4. Some legal scholars, art dealers, and collectors have called for an open, free, legal international market in antiquities, arguing that only such a market will eliminate looting.* Does (or could) the St. Lawrence example support their view or offer insights into solutions to the problems of looting?

FURTHER RESEARCH

For a more detailed account of "subsistence digging," see David P. Staley, "St. Lawrence Island's Subsistence Diggers: New Perspective on Human Effects on Archaeological Sites," in "The Antiquities Market," *Journal of Field Archaeology* 20 (1993): 347–55.

For the archaeologist's role in creating a market interest, see K.D. Vitelli, "The International Traffic in Antiquities: Archaeological Ethics and the Archaeologist's Responsibility," in *Ethics and Values in Archaeology*, ed. E. L. Green (New York: The Free Press, 1984), 143–55.

---

*See: Joseph Veach Noble, "A Plea for Sense in Regard to Trade in Antiquities," *Archaeology* (April 1972):144–45; and papers by John Merryman, Clemency Coggins, and others, on the pros and cons of establishing a legal trade in antiquities, in the *Proceedings of the Fifth Symposium on Legal Aspects of the International Art Trade: Licit Trade in Works of Art. Vienna, 28–30 September, 1994* [forthcoming] (International Chamber of Commerce Publication).

CHAPTER FIFTEEN

THE RAPE OF MALI

by Michel Brent

In this compelling case study, Brent covers the issues—including a number not touched on elsewhere—related to looting and the market. The pillaging of Mali's past by peasant looters serving local dealers, and ultimately wealthy European collectors, is out of control. One of the world's five poorest countries, Mali has few means to enforce antiquities laws. Dealers organize teams of farmers that work as much as 24 hours a day, digging for antiquities. In return, the ex-farmers receive food, caffeine-laden cola nuts, and the chance to earn up to 20 times their annual pay as farmers with a single find, while their fields remain unfarmed and the agricultural economy suffers. Dealers, museum curators and trustees, conservators, forgers, graduate students, analytical laboratories, and others, are implicated in the massive destruction of one of Africa's great archaeological cultures before even a fraction of it has been studied scientifically.

European dealers and collectors have systematically plundered the heritage of one of the world's poorest countries. "You absolutely must take this message to our friends in Europe and America: If we catch them in the act, we will make sacrifices and offerings with the blood of those who still come to steal our fetishes. And even if the officials in Bamako come to question us, I assure you that they will find no proof, not the least trace, and they will have to return to Bamako empty-handed." Sitting in a hut in the company of two other patriarchs, Barassor Mariko, the guardian of a sanctuary in the village of Denie Koro, spoke again and again of the disaster that had befallen his Bambara people. Four of the most important fetishes had been stolen from his village in less than ten years and the life of the village had been severely disrupted. Townspeople had become lazy, births had declined, and the harvests had been poor. To make matters worse, religious sacrifices could no longer be performed. "Do you realize," said the old man, "that by stealing our fetishes those impious ones have stolen our very gods? These fetishes have been at Denie Koro since the very beginning of the village several hundred years ago. When you tell me that the gods they stole from us are probably in the house of a man who does not even know our religion, I am deeply hurt. To us, this is a crime."

The government of Mali also considers it a crime, but can do little about it. The pillaging of the country's past by peasant looters serving local dealers, and ultimately wealthy European collectors, is today out of control. Not since the wholesale rape of Egypt's archaeological treasures in the first half of the nineteenth century has a country been so methodically stripped of its national heritage. Unlike most African countries, Mali is a source of both finely crafted ethnographic objects such as masks and fetishes, and artifacts such as bronze sculptures and terra-cotta statues. The latter are believed to represent the spirits of people who flourished here for some 2,000 years. Prized by collectors the world over, they have sold at auction for as much as $275,000. Hundreds of known archaeological sites on Mali's Inland Niger Delta have been looted. Work parties organized by Malian antiquities dealers comb the earth for marketable items. Meanwhile, European dealers crisscross the Malian outback in Land Rovers, their trunks filled with bundles of French francs for the purchase of newly found antiquities.

Mali is one of the world's five poorest countries. Life, expectancy here is only 44 years, caloric intake is 30 percent below the minimal requirement, and only ten percent of the population is literate. It is a large country (744,000 square miles), and its borders go largely unpatrolled. Laws prohibiting the export of antiquities were passed in 1985 and 1986, but there is little means to enforce them. Furthermore, only five major art-importing nations—Italy, Argentina, the United States, Canada, and Australia—have implemented the 1970 UNESCO Convention on cultural property, a treaty that sets guidelines for the return of illegally exported artifacts.

How Malian antiquities have been looted and spirited out of the country is a story of the skewed relationship between First and Third World countries and how poverty, bribery, and unbridled acquisitiveness have decimated the archaeological record of one of Africa's great civilizations before even a fraction of it has been studied scientifically.

Fueled by the public's interest in the primitivism of Braque and Picasso, art dealers earlier in this century began encouraging European colonials in Africa to collect tribal art. By the 1970s, trafficking in Malian antiquities had become an extremely lucrative business. One of the world's finest private collections was assembled by the Belgian Count Baudouin de Grunne. Mayor of Wezembeek-Oppem, a suburb of Brussels, de Grunne was introduced to Malian ceramics by a collector friend in the 1960s. The friend traded a few Malian terracotta heads for a Batcham mask from Cameroon that the Count had in his collection. De Grunne fell in love with the terra cottas and soon began to acquire similar pieces from Mali with the help of antiquities dealer friends—Philippe Guimiot and Emile Deletaille in Brussels and Alain de Monbrison in Paris. One Malian antiquities dealer, Boubou Diarra, eventually named one of his sons "Emile" in honor of his profitable business dealings with Deletaille.

Terra-cotta statuettes were dug from the Niger Delta by farmers working in teams, sometimes 24 hours a day. Hired by local antiquities dealers who gave them food and caffeine-laden kola nuts, these peasants raked the earth with *dabas* (hoes), hoping to find a fine piece that would net them a sum equal to ten or 20 times their annual pay as farmers. In the beginning, such clandestine digs were poorly organized. As market demand grew, more and more peasants were diverted from traditional farming, thus destabilizing the local economy. Even modest local dealers began forming their own crews. More than a thousand peasants were soon engaged in looting year-round within a 100-mile radius of Mopti, a town at the confluence of the Niger and Bani rivers.

What left Mali was rarely intact. Broken pieces had to be reassembled by craftsmen in Brussels and Paris. Restorers had to guess which head went with which torso, which foreleg belonged to which horse, which arm would best fit a shoulder. When missing pieces could not be found, restorers simply created them by grinding up stray fragments to make a mortar that would stick to any form—and fool any expert. De Grunne and his dealer friends were so single-minded in their quest, and so refined in their taste, that even today de Grunne's collection of Malian terra cottas is considered the finest in the world.

The venerable appearance of Belgium's Tervuren Museum, which houses a 450,000-piece collection of African art, is belied by its links with the illicit artifact trade. In the 1970s the museum decided to improve its collection of West African art. Its curators had two options—they could buy from antiquities dealers or they could organize scientific excavations in West Africa and collect in the field. Their decision to buy from dealers was prompted by the presence of antiquities dealers like the "Friends of the Museum" committee. Like many European museums, the Tervuren is influenced by organizations like Friends of the Museum, a nonprofit group whose board of directors consists of art collectors, influential people from the world of politics or business, as well as antiquities dealers. Friends of the Museum runs a small gift shop within the Tervuren. In exchange for the right to run the shop, the group is expected to make donations to the museum. A dealer in a position to choose what is to be given to the museum picks an item that is part of a group or series of objects. The rest of the series, for sale in his or her gallery, can then be valued much higher. The fact that one object from the group is on display at a prestigious museum is proof of its high quality. This cozy arrangement has worked for 20-odd years, with the full complicity of the Tervuren's ethnography department. And in a similar arrangement, the department has ensured that the museum takes on loan a number of items belonging to merchant friends, which raises the value of their other pieces.

Museums shouldn't necessarily be lumped with private dealers and collectors. What goes into a museum becomes accessible to the public and is available for research; objects in private collections are often inaccessible. But museums have contributed to the expansion of the trade in illicit artifacts. During my research, I called Sylvia Williams, director of the National Museum of African Art at the Smithsonian Institution. I wanted to check on the museum's 1983 purchase of several African objects from Emile Deletaille. The museum reportedly paid $1.5 million for the objects. Williams was at first extremely guarded, and asked repeatedly why I needed to have this information. Eventually, she admitted that the Smithsonian had bought a "few" items from Deletaille. There is little doubt that the objects purchased by the Smithsonian were exported illegally.

Meanwhile, the looting in Mali goes on, unabated. "Whether it is around the region of Jenne, or the valley of Tilemsi near Gao, at Timbuktu, or in the cliffs of the Bandiagara, to the south in the region of Bougouni, or in the region of Mema," says Téréba Togola, an archaeologist from the Institute of Human Sciences in Bamako, "we hear reports of pillaging from everywhere." Between 1989 and 1991, a team of scientists directed by the Dutch archaeologist Diderik van der Waals surveyed a 125-square-mile area between the Bandiagara plateau and the city of Diafarabé, inventorying plundered sites. Out of 834 catalogued sites, 45 percent had been looted. "On several occasions, we even encountered the looters at work," says van der Waals. "They were either isolated individuals or well organized groups who worked for their own account or were employed by a local merchant." If one of these diggers had not perished, buried in a tunnel that collapsed in February 1990, the authorities in Bamako may never have known about the looting of a site about an hour by foot from the village of Thial. "I tried to count the pillage holes," says Mamadi Dembélé, the chief archaeologist on a government team sent to investigate the site three months later, "but I had to rapidly abandon that because there were so many. These holes were spread out over many acres. It was a real carnage! The state of the site suggested that these digs had begun at least two months before the accident happened, and that many ceramic objects had been removed. Of course, the digs had stopped. But to see the remains of the campfires on these sites, one could only conclude that, among the 200 looters who had been digging there, many had probably been permanently camping on the site." Instead of being transported to the storage rooms of the National Museum in Bamako many statuettes found during the investigation at Thial were stored in Mopti, then sold by corrupt officials to an art gallery in Paris three months later.

It is not only ceramics and other archaeological pieces that leave Mali clandestinely. Ethnographic objects such as fetishes, sculptures, the canes of ancestors, amulets, and ritual jewelry have for years been the prey of antiquities dealers. And they are still being smuggled out of the country, despite the fact that, according to specialists in ethnographic art, "good pieces" are becoming increasingly rare. In the Dogon region along the Niger River the thefts have reached such proportions that exasperated village people have even mutilated or destroyed their own sculptures to discourage thieves from sacking the villages. "Where we live, we are always on the alert. In many villages, such as Kerigamana, Tireli, Dono Sogu, or Komboro Pei, to name only a few, the people have destroyed their Toguna bas-reliefs," says Apomi Saye, a Dogon who lives in the village of Tireli. Toguna are carved wood pillars, much appreciated by collectors, that support the straw roofs of meeting halls used by the men. "They are sick of the youths who come to steal them to sell in Mopti where they find antique dealers who receive stolen goods and will give them two or three hundred dollars for our works of art," he says. "There are also the famous Dogon doors that everyone in the West knows of. These no longer, alas, decorate the houses of our villages for the good and simple reason that they have all been sold, stolen, or taken away by the dealers. Do you ever ask the question, you who live in the West, if the important collection of Dogon objects at The Metropolitan Museum in New York, for example, has all its export licenses in good order?"

No government money is currently earmarked for the fight against looting. The paltry salaries of ministers contribute to corruption, which exists at every level of authority. In 1992, Eric Huysecom, an archaeologist at the University of Geneva, was on a mission to Mali accompanied by a Malian colleague from the Institute of Human Sciences at Bamako. In a stopover at Sofara, a town 35 miles southwest of Mopti, they found illegally excavated ceramics for sale in the local market. "After we notified the director of the Institute," said Huysecom, "we decided to ask the authorities in Mopti, the Regional Department of Youth, Sports, Art, and Culture that also administers Sofara, to intervene. We wanted to wait until the following Tuesday, the day of the weekly market, to do so. One week later, not one ceramic was for sale in the market of Sofara, and an employee of the Regional Department who was supposed to have joined us, arrived at our rendezvous six hours late on a motor scooter. Who had warned the local merchants?"

Important merchants like Bonbon Diarra of Sevaré, or Youssouf Cissé of Mopti have for years exported authentic pieces in great quantities without the least trouble. They have accomplished this with the complicity of various public and private organizations in Bamako. Gifts have been showered on the directors of airline companies and local customs officials, many of whom are unable to differentiate between tourist curios and genuine artifacts. Furthermore, Malian antiquities dealers have a very articulate spokesman and advocate in Mamadou Kaba Diane, a man of great learning and one of many highly sophisticated "facilitators" who know how to defend the profession and use political influence to maintain the status quo.

Once artifacts leave Mali, it is hard to get them back. On November 27, 1991, a cargo of art objects from Bamako was seized by American customs authorities in New Orleans. Examination of the cargo by a specialist revealed that it consisted of eighteenth-century artifacts of great value, and that the shipment violated Mali's 1985 law forbidding the exportation of antiquities. The personalities in this transaction were well known. The exporter was Samba Kamissoko, a Malian antiquities dealer from Bamako who had been imprisoned for a year for illegal trafficking in art objects. The shipment was addressed to Charles Davis, the owner of the Davis Gallery of New Orleans, an important commercial gallery selling ethnographic art in the United States. I obtained documents detailing the pieces in the cargo and their price tags. The shipment (by air freight) contained 22 door locks valued at $85 each, five canes at $680 each, three Bambara doors at $1,300 each, a Dogon door valued at $5,000, a puppet valued at $40,000, two masks at $2,500 each, and a Bambara figure in iron valued at $8,300. The invoice totaled $67,000. Two months after the objects were seized, Clark W. Settles, the customs officer assigned to the case, notified Malian ambassador Mohammed Alhousseyni Toure that the pieces could not remain under seizure much longer and that, if measures were not taken rapidly by Mali to recoup these objects, they would be handed over to the Davis Gallery. Settles pointed out that no crime had been committed under American law. The ambassador appealed to Malian authorities to expedite the return, but nothing happened. Since legal action was too costly, no effort was made to reclaim the cargo. A few weeks later, Charles Davis took possession of the shipment. In September 1993 the United States enacted an emergency import ban on Malian antiquities. The action, requested by Mali, was taken under the terms of the UNESCO Convention. Since then, direct shipments to the United States have ceased. More circuitous routes through Europe are now being utilized.

European antiquities dealers have various sources of supply. Some still buy directly from African dealers, but this practice seems to be less widespread now than it was ten or 15 years ago. I was told by dealers in Germany, France, and Belgium that 20 percent of their purchases are through public auctions, 20 percent in the countries of origin, 10 percent from private African citizens who bring objects to Europe, 10 percent from fellow dealers, and 40 percent from former colonials. Diplomatic pouches are also suspected of being used to transport objects. An archaeologist, who asked to remain nameless, told me: "You only need walk around the more affluent neighborhoods of African cities to perceive the extent of the traffic that goes on."

A recent trend in Europe resulting from the illicit trade involves students, and is giving archaeologists serious cause for concern. Antiquities dealers know very well that most students of art history and archaeology want to work in the field. They also know that there are a few scholarships and that most parents are hard pressed to finance a stay of a few months in the bush. Traders have therefore taken on the guise of patrons, sometimes through pseudo-cultural foundations created to finance fieldwork. But the grants come with strings attached: the donor either asks to be rewarded in objects, or with photographs and information about sites where it still is possible to find objects. When I asked a few such students if they didn't fear the possibility of being corrupted, they told me, matter-of-factly, that the illegal aspect of the trade was not their problem.

Another trend involves traders who behave as if they were scholars of art. They write articles and publish magazines and books about ethnic groups or about a given aspect of African art. If a spate of books or articles suddenly appears about, say, the art of Tanzania, it is sometimes because traders have just found a new source of objects in that country, and publication is the best way of advertising their wares and inflating their value.

In the antiquities business, dated and authenticated pieces are worth considerably more than those without pedigrees. Until a few years ago, the Oxford University Research Laboratory for Archaeology and the History of Art performed thermoluminescence tests on ceramics from Mali, dating and authenticating them. While making a film in 1990, dealing with the traffic of ceramics between Mali and Europe, the Dutch anthropologist Wouter Van Beek asked Michael Tite, director of the lab, why he was authenticating Malian artifacts in view of the country's looting problem. Tite replied that the authenticating business paid for scholarly work, and that if the Oxford lab did not do the work, someone else would. Since then, Tite has said he never had the slightest suspicion that the objects were being smuggled out of Africa and has ceased dating objects originating from West Africa. He also categorically refuses to be interviewed.

The Oxford lab authenticated the majority of pieces in the de Grunne collection, which was recently sold to the Dapper Foundation in Paris for some $10 million. The Foundation, actually the private collection of French millionaire businessman Michel Leveau, has in recent years spent some $25 million for African art, including the de Grunne collection. De Grunne paid between $15,000 and $150,000 for each of the 50 pieces in his collection. It is estimated that he realized at least $4 million in profit from the sale. On July 12, 1990, before the pieces left Brussels, Mali's Minister of Culture, Bakary Traore, sent a letter to de Grunne informing him that Mali was interested in bidding for its purchase and requesting a catalog. Since negotiations were already under way with the Foundation, de Grunne's secretary politely turned down the Malians, writing that the Count was on vacation in another country and that he would answer them on his return. De Grunne never responded, and the Foundation purchased the objects. It has asked scholars such as Samuel Sidibe, director of Mali's National Museum, to assist in assembling an exhibition of Malian ceramics, all of which were most likely illegally exported from his own country. Sidibe, needless to say, has refused to cooperate. In the meantime, the collection appears to be off-limits to scholars, despite the Foundation's statements to the contrary. Jacqueline Evrard, who in 1977 was the first art historian to study de Grunne's ceramics, wrote to the Foundation requesting to view the collection again in the company of a few interested friends. She never received a response. And an ethnology student at the University of Sapienza in Rome was categorically refused permission to view the collection.

The European community must address several questions concerning the trade in African art. Why, for instance, of the 78 countries that signed the UNESCO Convention, have only the poorest European countries or those experiencing the most looting—Italy, Greece, Spain, and Portugal—ratified it? The exportation of works of art may be forbidden in Africa, but their importation into Europe is not. In Belgium, for example, possession of a stolen object can be redressed by law only if a complaint is lodged within three years of the date of the theft. As a result, my country has become a hub of the illicit trade not only in African objects, but in antiquities from around the world. Legislation would perhaps not halt the traffic, but would no doubt do much toward diminishing it.

Blame for the current state of affairs is difficult to assign; not all of the players in the illicit trade fit easily into "white hat-black hat" categories. After all, is there a strong ethical reason for preventing an African family, or ethnic group, from selling things that are their own property if they wish to do so? Should we feel indignant that museums go on buying objects without proper export authorizations, or should we be thankful that these objects do not end up hidden away in private collections or bank vaults? How should we define a cultural heritage, a patrimony, and to what extent? Should it include every small object from the past?

One thing is certain: Rich and powerful Europeans have focused their attention on African art and intend to possess it. They are buying the history of Mali.

PLIGHT OF ANCIENT JENNE
by Roderick J. McIntosh

Michel Brent used our house in Jenne as a pied-à-terre while he dashed about the vast Inland Delta of the Niger River, searching for more pillaged sites and more villains in the sad melodrama of Mali's plundered heritage. Now, after several weeks of peripatetic investigation, he was preparing to leave for the capital to catch his return flight to Brussels. But my Malian colleague, Téréba Togola from the Institute of Human Sciences in Bamako, and I had one last horror to show him.

It was an odd going-away gift from two archaeologists to a journalist: a visit to what Téréba considered to be the most thoroughly plundered archaeological site in his country. We drove 20 jarring miles west to the village of Mounya.

Outside of Egypt, Mali is the African country most richly endowed with archaeological sites. The richest part of Mali and unquestionably the most plundered surrounds the city of Jenne. Here, my wife and I have investigated early urban sites since the late 1970s (*Archaeology*, January/February 1980). Téréba and I recently returned to Jenne-jeno, which the inhabitants of modern Jenne claim as their ancestral settlement. We were interested in the prehistory, demography, and diversity of the region. How large was the population of Jenne-jeno—and what was its occupational and ethnic make up?

The first permanent settlement at Jenne-jeno was established in the second or third century B.C. The community was large even then, occupying about 25 acres. Most interesting was the evidence of long-distance trade in the form of grindstones and stone ornaments, and of iron-forging activities. By the mid-first millennium A.D., trade had expanded hundreds of miles into the Sahara and Jenne-jeno had grown in size to some 70 acres. Its growth was accompanied by the emergence of satellite communities, 65 of which we have inventoried. Our investigations suggest that most were occupied throughout the greater part of the first millennium A.D.

Did all of the sites clustered around Jenne-jeno function as part of a larger urban network, uniting a great diversity of specialists (fishers, millet farmers, pastoralists) and artisans (blacksmiths and goldsmiths, weavers and leatherworkers, potters and boatmakers)? The picture is complex: a blacksmith, for instance, might be a farmer for most of the year. Until we can demonstrate that the various satellites were occupied contemporaneously, we won't fully understand the course of urbanism here.

Early in 1994 our Senegalese-American crew laboriously recorded surface features at Jenne-jeno and at all of the satellite mounds. Our Malian-Swedish team experimented with a portable coring ring, sampling deposits at both the satellite clusters as well as the modern town of Jenne, much of which was also inhabited in prehistory. By the time Michel Brent visited us, this work had already shown that Jenne-jeno was even more populous than we had believed. Our impression of the diversity of occupations was also reinforced at the satellite mounds. But so, too, was our frustration indeed—rage—at the increase since the early 1990s of illegal digging at the Jenne-jeno satellites and at more distant mounds. Looters were ripping from the earth the very evidence we would need to study conclusively the development of diversity within the urban community.

Surface survey and test coring are important, but they can only shed light on later occupational periods. Extensive and costly excavation of these deeply stratified mounds is required if we are to understand the 1,600-year history of the site. Our previous excavations at Jenne-jeno and two satellites had clearly demonstrated how critical the terra cottas would be for a final appreciation of community diversity; we presume that terra-cotta statues created by a heterogenous population would reflect a diversity of beliefs and rituals. We had found 30 examples of terra-cotta statuary and appliqué art. Of the hundreds, if not thousands, of terra cottas and ceramics that have been removed from Inland Niger Delta archaeological sites, these were the first and, as yet, only pieces to come from a scientifically excavated, dated, and carefully documented context. The different contexts (statuettes placed in a niche within the wall of a blacksmith's house, in the floor of a ritual structure, deconsecrated and tossed in a rubbish mound, etc.) and the many styles of this art indicate a great diversity of belief systems among the inhabitants of cosmopolitan Jenne-jeno.

To archaeologists, evidence of such diversity is precious, from the most minute lump of copper to the most spectacular terra-cotta figurine.

No sooner had we arrived at Mounya than Michel bounded ahead of Téréba and me, leaping over the trenches left by looters who had already plundered 90 percent of the site. Then, Michel ran to a particularly deep hole at the edge of the site and waved frantically to us to join him. As we approached, we saw clouds of dust. Then heads emerged from the hole. Michel had discovered three looters at work.

These were the poorest of the local peasants, with the wasted muscles and tattered clothes one sees all too often in rural Mali. Michel and Téréba insisted that I take the truck to the nearest village to find authorities who could imprison them. When I returned after an unsuccessful search, we questioned the men about their employers. As afraid as they were of prison, they were even more afraid to divulge the name of the wealthy antiquities dealers for whom they worked. We accomplished nothing at Mounya. Our anger and frustration made each of us resolve to work harder to expose the greed of international merchants, to push for local history interpretation programs and stricter enforcement of Malian heritage legislation, and to make art professionals and academics confront their own considerable contribution to the plunder.

Michel Brent, trained in the law, is a career journalist who writes for Le Vif-L'Express, *a Belgian news magazine.*

Roderick J. McIntosh teaches archaeology at Rice University and has worked in Mali.

DISCUSSION QUESTIONS

1. Interest in the "primitivism" of modern art is said to have fueled the illicit traffic in African tribal art. Compare the situation with that described by Elia in the earlier article, "A Seductive and Troubling Work." Are there new trends in art fashion that could have a similar effect on archaeological sites and materials?

2. What repercussions on the local economy and social organization follow from local participation in the illicit antiquities market? Do these suggest ways that efforts to combat looting and save the heritage might be redirected and made more effective?

3. What are the chances of detecting fakes made from ground-up stray fragments of original materials? What difference does it make whether such fakes are detected or not?

4. To what extent do (or should) dealers play an advisory role for museum acquisition committees? (Ask your local museum.)

5. What is the nature of the relationship between museums and dealers? How do museums learn about what is on the market and where it has come from?

6. The Metropolitan Museum in New York City and the Smithsonian's National Museum of African Art are cited as being among the U.S. museums that include illegally exported materials from Mali in their collections. Would anything be gained by calling for a return of those materials to Mali? Does the fact that no U.S. law was broken (since the acquisitions predate invocation of the UNESCO emergency clause*) in acquiring the pieces mean there is no obligation to do anything about their presence in U.S. museums?

7. How do museums contribute to increasing the value of objects on the market and in private collections? Is it in their own best interest for museums to do this?

8. Whose responsibility is it to determine whether ethnographic objects, offered for sale, are significant religious items needed for current practices?

---

*For a discussion of the imposition of an emergency ban on Malian imports under the Cultural Property Implementation Act, see Katherine Biers, "Mali Import Restrictions," *Archaeology* (Jan/Feb 1994): 20.

9. If U.S. Customs officers do not recognize Malian antiquities unless they are coming directly from Mali, and diplomatic pouches (exempt from Customs inspections) are used by government officials to remove art works illegally, it would seem that U.S. government personnel are poorly educated on the values of cultural property. What training in this area do U.S. government officials and representatives receive? Are there opportunities here for archaeologists?

10. How would you respond if you discovered that a grant you received (and badly needed) for field research was funded by a dealer-patron who expected, in exchange, information about sites and available art works?

11. Have you seen any "scholarly" articles written by dealers? If legitimate archaeological publications can stimulate, unwittingly, market demand for antiquities, are archaeologists in a position to criticize dealers for doing the same thing, if intentionally?

12. If you could have radiocarbon dating and other analytical work on materials from your field projects done free of charge by your university research labs because they make money by charging dealers for authentication work, would you support the lab's policy?** (Think of other comparable arrangements that affect archaeological work.)

13. Should African families, or members of any ethnic group, be forbidden from selling their own heritage if they choose to? Is the Malian case different from that of the St. Lawrence Islanders described in the article by Scott ("St. Lawrence: Archaeology of a Bering Sea Island")?

**For the new policy on authenticating unprovenienced materials of the Oxford University Research Laboratory for Archaeology and Art History, see R.R. Inskeep, "Making an Honest Man of Oxford: Good News for Mali," *Antiquity* 66 (1992): 114.

CHAPTER SIXTEEN

CHAMPION OF ABORIGINAL ART
by Denis D. Gray

Percy Trezize works closely with Aboriginal tribal elders on prehistoric Australian rock art. He is driven by his commitment to bring justice to the Aborigines, convinced that academic interest in the Aboriginal past will restore pride to a much maligned people. His careful excavations have led to an outline of environmental and cultural changes over the millennia and pushed back the dates for the earliest rock art. His book, Dream Road, *fulfills his promise to the last of the old initiated men of publishing their material so it will be available to their descendants when they become interested in their ancient traditions once again.*

"Yooo . . . .Yooo," he calls out in sharp, full-throated bursts as we near a snake-shaped outcrop deep in the Australian bush. "Politeness," explains Percy Trezise, "lets the spirits know we are coming . . ." The lean, 67-year-old Trezise pushes ahead with a vigorous stride, dressed in green shorts, a kepi, and leggings to protect against thorny undergrowth. He is at ease in this rugged land, already shimmering with heat and buzzing with insects although it is hardly past mid-morning.

Rainbow Serpent Shelter, which bears a remarkable resemblance to an overfed python, is sacred Aboriginal ground soaked in ancestral myths—and it's a very special place for Trezise. Here, in a shallow cave engraved with barely discernible geometric patterns, he is conducting research, convinced he will prove Aboriginal tribes lived and created art on the Australian continent longer than has generally been believed.

And this, he says with crusading ardor, will not only spur greater academic interest in the Aboriginal past but help restore pride to a people still maligned and once massacred by invading Europeans who regarded them as capable of little more than infantile scribblings on cave walls.

Rainbow Serpent Shelter is near the tiny town of Laura on the Cape York Peninsula, an England-sized area of trackless forests and untamed seacoasts that is Australia's last great wilderness. The shelter is just a single exhibit in what Trezise describes as one of the world's largest galleries of rock and prehistoric art. For 30 years he has explored this region, finding, cataloging, and analyzing hundreds of sites. Along the way he has also championed Aboriginal causes and recorded tribal legends, many woven into 19 highly popular children's books he has written and illustrated. These, he believes, are helping to change attitudes toward the "first Australians."

Trezise dates his involvement in such matters to 1939, when he won a book about the Aborigines as a high school prize. Nineteen years later, a blinding rainstorm forced Trezise—then a professional pilot who had served in World War II—to land at Laura. It would become his second home and the focus of his life.

Aboriginal rock art had long been studied across Australia, from Arnhem Land in the Northern Territory to the Flinder's Ranges of South Australia, from the Kimberly and Pilbara areas of the west to Sydney in the southeast. But the first significant discovery in Cape York wasn't made until 1959 when road-construction crews near Laura came upon what was later to be called the Split Rock Galleries.

Trezise saw these galleries the same year, was overwhelmed by their richness and convinced they could not be the only site in the area. Fortunately, his flight routes took him over the area almost daily. He used the opportunity to conduct aerial surveys, swooping down low to the consternation of both passengers and wildlife on the ground, to pinpoint extensive sandstone escarpments that might enfold the art he sensed was spread out below.

At the same time, Trezise set out to befriend normally reticent Aboriginal elders who possessed knowledge of vanishing tribal lore and could thus help decode the art's meaning. Dick Roughsey, a talented artist of the Lardil Aboriginal group, became a close friend to whom Trezise was designated "brother" in the kinship system of the tribe. Proudly, Trezise recalls being given the name of Warrenby, a legendary Lardil leader.

With Roughsey and other mentors, like Caesar Le Choo, Willy Long, George Pegus, and Harry Mole, Trezise entered what he described in his 1969 book *Quinkan Country* as "a land where legend still overshadowed reality—a living land whose rocks and trees possessed spirits to murmur secrets to those who wished to hear them."

Viewed through the psyches of his guides, the Cape York bush became a continuum of the Dreamtime, when ancestral spirits came down from the sky and up from the earth to create the world and then assumed the shapes of trees and hills and pools. What was to Trezise a geologically and aesthetically interesting granite hilltop was to Roughsey and the others the terrifying spot where Gidja the Moon Man cooked and ate his two grandsons; the inconspicuous matchwood tree, the font of life and death whose trunks are inverted into graves so souls can slide up through the magic wood and onward to Woolunda, the Aboriginal heaven.

Blistering heat, venomous snakes, and stinging insects assaulted Trezise and his companions during their numerous expeditions. But Trezise's recollections are mostly happy ones: of days coming upon exciting rock-art discoveries; evening meals of wallabies, plain turkeys, and barramundi fish; and settling in around a campfire to tape legends of millennia past over rum and river water. At nighttime, Trezise's companions would nestle close to the fire for protection against the Quinkans, malevolent spirits said to haunt the Laura region and often portrayed in rock-art paintings as creatures with grotesquely outstretched legs and arms, bouncing across the land with the aid of their powerful penises.

During 15 years Trezise probably discovered more rock-art sites in the region than anyone else. He is a skilled artist and photographer. Thousands of his quarter-scale drawings, all produced on-site, now form an invaluable database at the Australian Institute of Aboriginal and Torres Strait Islander Studies in Canberra.

Sometimes his treks became family affairs with sons Matthew and Stephen, daughters Victoria and Anna, and Trezise's wife Beverley helping to scour the bush. In the early 1960s the family bought the quaint Laura Hotel, which Matthew runs, and paid out another 18,000 Australian dollars for 25 square miles of rock-art-rich land. On it they built a pleasantly ramshackle homestead and the Jowalbinna Bush Camp, a riverside camping ground from which Stephen guides small groups of tourists into the surrounding galleries. Adjacent to their land is the 400-square-mile Quinkan Reserve, established in 1977 after a Trezise-led campaign to place under protection as much of the Laura country as possible. The reserve is administered by the Ang-gnarra Aboriginal Corporation.

With Jowalbinna Bush Camp as our base and Steve as our guide, we dipped into forested gorges, hiked up escarpments, and clambered into overhanging shelters to a magnificent museum-in-the-wild. At Split Rock: a female ancestral being of elongated shape, elaborate headdress and serene, Madonna-like expression. At Giant Wallaroo: hunting action as packs of dingoes track down mountain kangaroos. At Emu Dreaming Gallery: a row of equidistant oval-shaped pits in the cave wall.

Trezise is the acknowledged authority in explaining the forces that inspired Cape York rock art, its meanings, and the chronological sequence of art styles that span several thousand years. But inevitably his detective work has gaps and dead ends; the arrival of Europeans led to rapid detribalization of the Aborigines during which links with the past—earlier maintained through oral tradition—were severed. Trezise's old Aboriginal friends could identify or make reasonable deductions about some of what they saw on the cave walls: mythical heroes, totemic ancestors, and spirits; hunts, sorcery, and love magic. But many depictions drew a blank. Were the oval-shaped pits at Emu Dreaming eggs of the emu, or were they used for counting the seasons?

Such engravings belong to what Trezise categorizes as the earliest rock-art style, featuring geometric shapes, bird and animal tracks, and linear designs resembling mazes. From this presumably symbolic beginning evolved engravings of human beings, animals, and plants followed by stencils of hands and weapons, then simple linear drawings in monochrome. In time, the Aborigines drew large poly-chrome figures in red and yellow ochres, decorated with white or cream pipeclay.

The last stage of what Trezise calls "one of the most continuous art forms in the world" was a tragic one. It came as gold was discovered on the Cape in the early 1870s, sparking a rush by tens of thousands of Europeans and Chinese. The Aborigines in their path were deci-mated by firepower and disease. The survivors retreated to their cave dwellings in the high country to hide from the bullets and to paint.

One of their works was of a horse, more than 17 feet long and ten feet high, in yellow red ochre with a white outline. Trezise surmises that at first the tribes must have been terrified of this animal import, never having seen any fauna bigger than a red kangaroo until they spotted the gun-yielding Europeans on horseback. The Aborigines tried to stem the incursion, and when their spears proved useless, they attempted to kill the invaders with black magic. In both the Emu Dreaming and Pig galleries a half dozen white men with rifles are depicted. In the Pig Gallery, birds are shown standing atop the bodies of two of the men, beaks thrust into their armpits.

"The Aborigines are bloody good blokes," says Trezise. He is sitting on the verandah of his homestead under a star-studded sky, sipping whiskey and water. His stories of vanished Aboriginal society are both graphic and sometimes idealized. He takes us on an imaginary hunt for kangaroo, imitating the stalking stance and calls of the trackers as they close in on a targeted animal with spears and boomer-angs. Trezise describes the nomadic tribes as careful "land managers," never taking from the natural environment more than was needed to sustain them. He pictures them in their last strongholds, executing the large sorcery paintings and sensing that their race and way of life are doomed. "I am passionately committed to bringing justice to the Aborigines, to telling the world they have the world's oldest art," Trezise says. "Even today, there is an abysmal ignorance about them. Most white Australians haven't had a single conversation with an Aborigine in their lives."

The next morning, Trezise takes us by Landrover and foot to Rainbow Serpent Shelter. He and several archaeologists have worked there for years, excavating the cave floor and attempting to date the residues of human habitation. In 1960, when Trezise began his Laura treks, evidence for the earliest peopling of Australia was less than 10,000 years. Since then, he and others have steadily been pushing back this date. The research at Rainbow Serpent Shelter, he says, indicates it was a living site from some 13,000 years ago to early in this century. But the first visitors came here more than 40,000 years ago. Initially, Trezise exposed a boulder rising from the cave floor and found it was entirely covered with engravings, some overlaid with silica. Scientists at Australia's James Cook University, who studied the samples said anything under the silica would be more than 18,000 years old. Excavations of the cave floor yielded occupational debris, stone tools, a stone ax, utilized quartz crystals, and charcoal. From this and associated data, Trezise has constructed a tentative profile of environmental and life-style changes in the Laura area over the millennia. He is certain that dating tests now in their final phase will confirm the great antiquity of aboriginal culture in Australia.

Trezise hopes the last stage of his life will be a further refinement and synthesis of material gathered over the past three decades. He co-chaired the Second Australian Rock Art Association Congress summer in 1992 in the tropical resort of Cairns in northern Queensland. More than 350 delegates from around the world attended, making it the biggest rock-art congress ever held. The main item of news from the Congress was the announcement by the Ang-gnarra Aboriginal Corporation, custodians of many decorated sites around Laura, that an Australian geologist named Alan Watchman had dated paint on the wall of a shelter to 24,600 years ago, making it among the oldest dated painted sites in the world.

Meanwhile Trezise has written another book, titled *Dream Road.* "I made a promise to the last of the old initiated men," Trezise says. "I told them I would publish all their material in a book which will become available to their descendants when they again became interested in the ancient traditions and history."

Dick Roughsey and Caesar Le Choo and almost all his other companions have already made their way up the matchwood trees to Woolunda. And while professing non-belief in the hereafter, Trezise says that, somehow, he feels their spirits hovering around when he visits the sacred sites and galleries of Quinkan.

Denis D. Gray is Associated Press bureau chief in Bangkok, Thailand.

DISCUSSION QUESTIONS

1. The effect of European colonization on the lives and culture of Aboriginal Australians provides many parallels with those of the European colonization of the Americas. Explore these.* Where else have Europeans and other colonial powers left a similar legacy?
2. How have the responses of archaeologists to Aborigines' concerns in Australia differed from similar situations in North America?
3. What are the pros and cons of archaeologists working closely with descendants of the people they study?
4. Why should native peoples with their own understanding of their history care about the work of archaeologists?
5. What, if any, differences exist in the relationship of contemporary Greeks to the archaeological past of Greece, and that of Australian Aborigines to the archaeological past of Australia? (You might compare other contemporary peoples' relationships with their pasts and that of the Aborigines.)

FURTHER RESEARCH

See also: Eric Willmot, "The Dragon Principle," in *Who Owns the Past?*, ed. Isabel McBryde (Melbourne: Oxford University Press, 1985), 41–48, for a comment on ownership of the past by an Australian Aboriginal scholar; Peter Ucko, "Australian Academic Archaeology: Aboriginal Transformations of its Aims and Practices," *Australian Archaeology* 16 (1987): 11–26; and the World Archaeological Congress' WorldWideWeb page at http://wac.soton.ac.uk/wac/.

---

* For another parallel between archaeological issues in Australia and North America, see R. Lewin, "Extinction Threatens Australian Anthropology: Moves by Aborigines to Impound and Rebury Skeletal Remains in Universities and Museums Could End Physical Anthropology in Australia," *Science* 225 (1984): 393–94.

CHAPTER SEVENTEEN
PEOPLE
WITHOUT HISTORY
by Roderick J. McIntosh
Susan Keech McIntosh
and Téréba Togola

*"The nature of archaeology in the twenty-first century depends on the
outcome of debates currently raging in the discipline, as 'people without
history' strive to reclaim their pasts" and question traditional Western
assertions about such fundamental issues as the economic basis of complex
societies, or the evolution of societies from hunter-gatherers to civilization. The authors see two choices for the future: "a narrowly provincial
archaeology that elaborates the current nationalistic polemic," or an
archaeology that transcends polemics "to reveal the complexity of the
human experience." The authors provide many examples of how the
latter choice will contribute to a richer discipline and more significant
contributions to the modern world.*

Quick—what do Native Americans, Turks, and Nigerians
have in common? Answer: the finest artifacts of their
most brilliant civilizations have been looted and sold to
the highest Western bidders. The issue of who owns the past is an
emotional one, having as much to do with the politics of the present
as the conservation of the past. The fact that Nigerians, for example,
must travel to the British Museum to see the finest Benin bronzes,
while Britain mounts huge funding drives to prevent the sale of
venerated items of its own cultural patrimony to non-Western buyers,
speaks volumes about the relative wealth and power of these two
countries. As archaeologists become increasingly concerned about

185

hidden political and ideological agendas in their quest for the past, the way they recover, interpret, and conserve the past is changing. The nature of archaeology in the twenty-first century depends on the outcome of debates currently raging in the discipline, as "people without history" strive to reclaim their pasts.

People without history are those, according to Eric Wolf in his influential book *Europe and the People Without History*, to whom a history has been denied by those who have claimed history as their own. As Western civilization expanded through conquest, colonization, and commerce, the primitive groups it encountered were displaced, subjugated, or exploited. And since those in power write histories and feature themselves prominently therein, it is not surprising to find non-Western peoples depicted in conventional Western histories as passive recipients of change inaugurated by Western culture-bearers. Furthermore, the historical depiction of non-Western peoples as primitive or savage has served to justify their subjugation by the West, regardless of the human misery and suffering involved. During the past two decades, there has been a great debate over the historical conventions, including categories (such as Western and non-Western), interpretive models, and research agendas, that together restrict our ability to reconstruct the past of people without history.

In recent decades, many Third World archaeologists have angrily rejected Western concepts and models that relegate their own past to inferior or peripheral status merely because it does not replicate the prehistory of Europe and the Near East. Traditional Western assertions—that complex society is always built upon an agricultural base, that social stratification is economically based, that all states are expansionist, or that societies evolve in a linear manner, in stages, from hunter-gatherers to civilization—have at times taken the form not of hypotheses to be tested but of judgmental statements about the ranking of human experience. The hidden message is that non-Western prehistories are derived, shadowlike manifestations of sequences already brilliantly experienced in the Near East or Europe. Or worse, that they represent truncated, failed, or retarded examples of human cultural evolution. Third World archaeologists understand how their national prehistories are thus demeaned; it is scarcely surprising that emotions run high, and debate degenerates into polemic. Many Third World archaeologists, among others, see clearly that the ability to name things, to create the categories of analysis through which we perceive reality, is a source of power. Pitted against each other are archaeologists who claim that archaeology's scientific authority elevates it above the cultural biases of individual practitioners and those who doubt that objectivity is possible. The outcome of the debate will determine how archaeology in these countries will develop in the future.

Global archaeology in 2050 may take one of two courses. One possibility is a narrowly provincial archaeology that elaborates the current nationalist polemic. In this scenario, individual nations would pursue their past in isolation, limiting investigation to a restricted set of questions and rejecting cross-cultural studies as irrelevant. Alternatively, archaeology may transcend the current polemics to reveal the complexity of the human experience without conferring privilege on any particular people or place. At the heart of this scenario is genuinely collaborative international research, conducted in an atmosphere of mutual respect among nations. Such an archaeology could contribute to a world order that ennobles all peoples. The debate that will lead archaeology in one of these directions or the other is in full swing, and we can expect it to continue through the final decade of this century. Let us look more closely at some of the current issues that are relevant to these two very different visions of archaeology in the future.

All nations commit to their collective memory selected episodes from the past, be they Israel's veneration of Masada or the Danes' embrace of their Viking heritage. Rather than being literal, objective accounts of past reality, national prehistories can be seen as statements to the world about how a people see themselves and would like to be seen by others. A nation's emphasis or lack of emphasis on certain aspects of its past reflects important social or political priorities. For example, in choosing a name, Zimbabwe focused on its most prominent archaeological site, Great Zimbabwe. By this one stroke, Zimbabwe not only reclaimed its heritage from the outgoing white regime (which had long insisted on the non-African origins of the site), but it also promoted unity by allowing all its multiple ethnic groups to claim a common glorious past. In the United States prior to the 1970s, the research vacuum on the archaeology of slavery reflected the near invisibility of American blacks in the national political agenda.

Clearly, nationalist archaeologies enable Third World nations to reclaim a past previously reliant on history recorded by Westerners. Mexico's National Museum of Anthropology, for example, brilliantly displays an intensely nationalistic archaeology that aggressively emphasizes pre-Hispanic cultures, as evidence of the spirit of the nation's Indian majority. There is always the danger, however, that nationalist archaeologies will devolve into provincialism. Indeed, there is currently a debate in Mexico over whether the exclusion of North American researchers, with their larger field budgets and vigorous theoretical debates, may have accelerated a provincialization of Mexican archaeology. According to Jaime King's article "Mesoamerica: Events and Processes, the Last 50 Years" *(American Antiquity,* 1985), Mexican archaeology has become the "mouthpiece of . . . demagogic politicians and generations of students trained in sloganeering."

National agendas in archaeology may be not merely provincial but downright unsavory, as when they serve to devalue certain groups within the society. Guatemala's discouragement of Maya research, for example, is part of a policy to devalue the traditions of an Indian majority that is held to be racially inferior. And what if a national agenda demands destruction of archaeological sites? Few modern instances can match the intensity of the Spanish obliteration of Aztec temples and idols during the first centuries of Conquest. But beginning in 1966 and continuing for the ten years of the Cultural Revolution, Chinese sites were considered by the Red Guard to be reactionary monuments of old thought, the last vestiges of feudal ideals to be duly obliterated. Similarly, from 1975 to 1979, the Khmer Rouge engaged in purposeful dynamiting and defacing of Angkor Wat and other sites. Is there any place for the argument that certain sites are part of the world cultural inheritance, with international claims having priority over those based on national agendas?

We see, then, how nationalist archaeologies can liberate prehistory from Western interpretive constructs. In the process, however, the limitations imposed by Western interpretations can be replaced by those imposed by nationalist ideologies. How much progress can be claimed if all we have accomplished is the exchange of one set of limiting conditions for another? Surely an archaeological community wishing to be freed of a received canon of priorities and interpretations should actively encourage local archaeologists to feel unconstrained and un-self-conscious in exploring their own.

At the moment, narrow sectional interpretations encourage hatred, as when Israeli fundamentalists in 1983 attempted to blow up Jerusalem's Dome of the Rock mosque on Haram Ash-Sharif in preparation for building the Third Temple. Archaeology's moral imperative is to demonstrate the equal claims of Israelis and Palestinians to Haram Ash-Sharif/Temple Mount. If only the combatants could see that the Holy Land is not the repository of some mystical vitalism to be jealously possessed. Rather, archaeology and history show us that it has always been a crossroads for many peoples possessing many different beliefs. It is no coincidence that the great religious systems born in the Holy Land accommodated and transcended the diverse histories of all by appealing to the universal themes of our humanity.

An archaeology tolerant of local potentialities can thrive only in an atmosphere of mutual respect among nations for the cultural priorities and beliefs of others. This will require that we lower the banner of objective science, under which archaeologists have felt justified in profaning the most cherished and sacred aspects of others' pasts. Particularly intense emotion has focused on ritual art, human burials, and the repatriation of national cultural treasures. Ritual art is frequently viewed by the society that created it as the repository for powerful spirits whose propitiation involves the observation of specific rituals. For example, the Hopi view of the world as a living spirit includes the obligation of an initiated few to provide continuous care for living spirits (Kachinas) represented by (or residing in) the well-known Kachina dolls. Without proper care of the Kachinas, the cosmological order is upset, and the world is at risk. Hopis have demanded the return of Kachinas from museums, calling them trapped friends unable to come home. By what right does the uninitiated scholar or curator disturb the Hopi cosmos by the profanity of manipulating Kachinas? It is not surprising that non-Hopi do not regard Kachinas with the same awe or emotion as Hopi. The problem, non-Westerners argue, arises when Western archaeologists or art historians invoke the authority of science and the advancement of knowledge to justify profaning what another culture considers sacred. For the Hopi, the presence of Kachinas in museums exemplifies how the world view of the powerful has triumphed over that of the powerless.

The same conflict underlies the charged issue of the repatriation of antiquities. Foreign governments view their right to control their own cultural heritage very seriously. They resent it when cherished aspects of their past are treated as commodities in Western-dominated art markets. How else could Mexico interpret the theft on Christmas Eve, 1985, of 140 of its most important pieces of prehistoric gold, jade, obsidian, and turquoise from the National Museum of Anthropology? How else should they view the wholesale destruction of entire categories of archaeological sites by plunderers whose only goal is profit? Archaeologists and art historians who authenticate, date, or appraise antiques that lack proper export papers have long been unwitting, or uncaring, accomplices in this illicit activity. The continued failure of archaeologists to address this issue can only increase the atmosphere of hostility and suspicion in which various governments, including Italy, refuse to allow any antiquities to leave the country for even temporary study. Lest we think that these issues are confined to arcane political debates among governments and scholars, consider how the entire population of Irakleon, Crete, stopped the shipment of a Minoan exhibit to England and the United States in the mid-1970s by bodily blocking its progress to the docks.

To comprehend how the fear of losing venerated aspects of one's national heritage can provoke popular uprisings, we need only imagine the groundswell of sentiment that would attend the announcement that the original copies of the Declaration of Independence and the United States Constitution would be sold to the highest bidder in order to reduce the federal deficit. If it is nearly impossible for us to imagine the sale of these objects ever taking place, it is only because of our currently strong position of world power. For many other countries, similar sales are routine and have been for some time. This, too, says much about their relative geopolitical position. Perhaps we can see why the Greeks are so tenacious and emotional about the repatriation of the Elgin Marbles from the British Museum. Once again, it is clear why the current polemic about who controls the past is firmly rooted in the politics of the present.

On other difficult issues, such as reburial of ancient human remains, significant progress has been made, giving hope that a new dialogue of respect between nations is in its formative stages. The subjects of the reburial debate are the hundreds of thousands of aboriginal skeletons from the United States and Australia that are currently stored or displayed in museums or that will be disinterred by future excavation. Aboriginal populations argue that their religious freedom is abridged when sacred burial grounds are desecrated, and their ancestors' journey through life (of which death is but a part) is interrupted by removing their bones from the ground. Archaeologists and physical anthropologists, on the other hand, assert that the scientific knowledge of adaptation and disease patterns gained from permanent museum access to skeletal material exerts prior claim over religious freedom. The outcome of this lengthy and often polemical debate has been promising. Some Native American groups and Australian Aborigines now admit the potential of archaeological studies to provide information on the cultural practices and life-style of their ancestors before contact with Europeans. Rather than the wholesale and immediate reburial they originally demanded, they will—after consideration on a case-by-case basis—accept study of new finds and of material already in storage, followed by reburial with appropriate rites. Archaeologists and physical anthropologists, in their turn, have agreed to consider ancestral remains as sacred and venerated objects, and the two sides will work together to stop looting of sites and draft ethical agreements on the treatment of artifacts and human remains. The resolution of the debate in Australia has been complicated by Aboriginal claims to land rights over sacred burial grounds, and by a legal system that permits desecration of even recent Aboriginal cemeteries while prohibiting excavation of white graves. However, the American experience is an encouraging sign that even seemingly intractable differences can lead us to new levels of tolerance and mutual respect.

We take the hopeful view that archaeology in the twenty-first century will build on a foundation of mutual respect among nations. We believe that the issues raised by the current polemics in archaeology will be seriously discussed and, ultimately, resolved. If this happens, then we likely will escape an archaeology of the future that is defined by narrow, nationalist agendas. The alternative, an international archaeology committed to pluralistic research that does not privilege any particular people or place, will embark on research paths scarcely imaginable today.

To do this, we must first attack the consequences of unequal distribution of resources. Archaeology's vitality is greatest in richer nations, where existing resources for research are not exhausted by basic inventory and salvage activities. In the future, increasingly sophisticated and inexpensive technology can lessen the disparities among nations by fulfilling various labor-intensive aspects of archaeology. Site detection, for example, today accomplished mainly by foot survey, could be revolutionized by declassification of spy satellite imagery.

Hand-recording and drawing of artifacts could be made largely obsolete by the widespread availability of an optical-scanning computer catalog system. In this system, several digitized perspective images of each object, as well as a multitude of the object's attributes, would be automatically recorded and directly fed into computerized data bases, early generations of which are already used by archaeologists. Beyond this, a proliferation of inexpensive, flexible data bases should counter the inherent threat of rigid standardization of categories. Lastly, if one can overcome some governments' distrust of open telecommunications systems, we may envision a day when archaeologists everywhere are linked in a global computer mail system. With the development of simultaneous multi-language computer translation capability, a globally interactive archaeology will become possible.

Despite all the potential offered by technology, the most significant remedies to uneven resource distribution, will come from human agencies. Centralized committees such as UNESCO have led spectacular successes in the salvage and museum-conservation arena, but much more can be done to provide archaeologists from poor nations (or minorities or nonconformists from richer ones) access to expensive dating techniques, travel funds for conferences, or exchange visits to ongoing research elsewhere. Particularly important will be a greater commitment by individual archaeologists and national funding bodies to balanced international collaboration. We would like to see funding preference given to research projects with an explicitly comparative problem orientation and multinational representation among principal investigators and site supervisors. Imagine how different the past might begin to look if, for example, the members of a Senegalese-Chinese team were to spend six months in each other's countries, lending their different perspectives on tumulus burials, or if a research team of Native Americans, Kung Bushmen, and Australian Aborigines collaborated on meaning in rock art.

At a time when some assert that all cross-cultural studies are bogus and that all cultures traveled along unique and non- comparable paths, we believe that balanced international collaborative strategies are particularly important, not just to prove or disprove that claim but to transcend the limits of entrenched traditional interpretations. Archaeology has already shown that the experience of world prehistory is much more diverse than traditional models would allow. Take, for example, the expectation that past hunting and gathering societies were largely egalitarian, mobile, and smallscale. Instances are now known from Australian prehistory of nonagricultural groups living in sizable, semi-sedentary settlements, with rudimentary social hierarchies in which a small group directed the labor of others toward the expansion of settlements and redistribution networks. The complexity of hunting-gathering society appears even more developed among the Chumash of California, whose society included craft specialists serving emerging elites. More than 10,000 years ago, the Jomon period in Japan witnessed hunting-gathering societies living in dense, sedentary settlements.

Urbanism is another case in which traditional models have proven inadequate. The Western conception of early cities possessing palatial architecture with encircling walls symbolically reinforcing a despotic social structure is not useful in the study of other cultures. Early Bronze Age cities of China are clusters of hamlets—for specialists, nobles, and royalty—spread over many square kilometers. Other assaults on the idea that palatial or monumental architecture are requisites for urban life come from places as disparate as the Middle Niger of West Africa and Cahokia on the Mississippi. Traditional models of states are under siege, too. In the Near Eastern model, the state is marked by elite control of large-scale foreign trade and economic centralization. The state is also intent upon perpetual territorial expansion as a source for new wealth and subjugated labor. This model is challenged by alternative cases in which the prime concern of the state is the maintenance of cosmic order. This is most dramatically illustrated by the Aztec empire. While certainly militarist and despotic, the empire took on a form of federalism in that local chiefdoms or communities had great autonomy as long as tribute and, especially, human sacrifices required by the gods continued to flow to the center. While the state's function as a tribute-gathering machine was maintained by terror, the ultimate purpose was cosmological rather than expansionist.

We need not multiply the examples to show that no single paradigm or interpretive tradition can do justice to the real complexity of the human prehistoric experience. The archaeology of the twenty-first century must probe that complexity with new research strategies grounded in methodological and interpretive pluralism. This pluralism need not devolve into a thousand national or local prehistories, all spinning separate tales and ignorant of developments elsewhere. As the people without history reclaim their past through the polemical posturing of the current decade, it will be natural for them to ask if insights into their own prehistories have a larger lesson for developments elsewhere. If a truly collaborative dialogue among nations can be established, archaeology will enter new interpretive fields.

It would, however, be naive to think the path will be easy. Those heavily invested in traditional approaches will retrench petulantly, and on the other side of the coin, the danger of national prehistories becoming militantly isolationist is real. Neither approach will promote the liberal exchange of ideas. Particularly destructive is the radical reductionist position, taken by some Western archaeologists, that prehistory and history can never be more than stories about the *present*, written to obscure or legitimate present values, practices, and social inequities.

This argument has been used to discourage new research, by the logic that discoveries are usually made by archaeologists of wealthy nations, who then create prehistories for non-Western peoples that reflect, and thus legitimate, inequalities in the world power structure.

Such concern is noble on one level, but Third World archaeologists have been quick to label such thinking a new form of Western paternalism. With their limited resources, they depend on Western financing to excavate and document sites threatened by urban or agricultural expansion, desertification, or dam projects. They are thus wary of the extremist position that would discourage such financing, resulting in the loss of significant segments of their past forever. Further, Western proponents of this extreme view—that the past is unknowable—seem to imply that Third World people are intellectually passive and accept any externally given version of their past. If this radical view prevails and discovery is forbidden, then Third World people will forever be consigned to being people without history, with a past always derived from, and lesser than, that of nations with vigorous research traditions.

For the year 2050, balanced international collaboration and research pluralism in an atmosphere of mutual respect among nations will be the antidotes to Western paternalism in its many forms. We look forward to a vision of archaeological humanism that would actively promote mutual respect among nations and mutual intelligibility among cultures. If successful, archaeologists of the future will be in a privileged position to contribute to the enterprise of defining universal standards of human rights.

Roderick J. and Susan Keech McIntosh teach anthropology and archae-ology at Rice University and have done fieldwork in Mali.

Téréba Togola is a researcher at the Institut des Sciences Humaines in Mali.

DISCUSSION QUESTIONS

1. If owning the past and the ability to name things is about political power, do archaeologists have great political power?
2. Is the scientific integrity of archaeology put at risk if archaeologists accept restrictions on how they may go about reconstructing the past?
3. Does, in fact, archaeology's scientific authority elevate it above the cultural biases of individual observers?
4. Is it possible both to respect the rights of descendant communities and claim that the cultural heritage belongs to the entire international community?
5. What are the pros and cons of "lowering the banner of objective science" to achieve a more tolerant and respectful archaeology?
6. Are all archaeologists and art historians who authenticate, date, or appraise antiquities accomplices in an illicit and destructive activity?
7. Do scholars have a right to study and make public aspects of sacred beliefs and rituals that descendant communities consider the sacred preserve of the initiated few?
8. How would Americans respond to an announcement that the original copies of the Declaration of Independence had been sold overseas to reduce the federal deficit? (Consider the recent debates in Congress and elsewhere concerning the appropriate and legal uses of the American flag.)
9. How is the Internet affecting the world community of archaeologists?
10. How many field projects directed by non-U.S. citizens are taking place in the United States?

11. Think of some particularly compelling issues in current archaeology, and design cross-cultural teams (e.g., a research team of Native Americans, Kung Bushmen, and Australian Aborigines collaborating on meaning in rock art) that might effectively and innovatively pursue those issues.

FURTHER RESEARCH

See also: Robert Layton, ed., *Conflict in the Archaeology of Living Traditions, One World Archaeology*, Vol. 8 (London: Unwin Hyman, 1989); Eric Wolf, *Europe and the People Without History* (Berkeley: University of California Press, 1982); and Richard Wilk, "The Ancient Maya and the Political Present," *Journal of Anthropological Research* 41 (1985): 307–26.

PART FIVE
REBURIAL
AND REPATRIATION

One aspect of archaeology's effect on living peoples that has received a great deal of attention in North America recently is the question of the appropriate treatment of sacred and human remains. The respect accorded to the graves of white immigrant ancestors has not generally been extended to others. The many questions raised by the articles in the previous section, "Affected Peoples," are brought into focus in the emotional debates about repatriation and reburial as they are playing out in North America. The issues, as manifested in particular instances, raise both local and universal questions for archaeologists.

CHAPTER EIGHTEEN
REBURIAL: IS
IT REASONABLE?
by Duane Anderson

Archaeologists attracted little attention from the Native American community until the general activism of the 1960s and 1970s. This is the story of how the situation developed in Iowa (before NAGPRA, passed November 16, 1990), including successful cooperative ventures between Native Americans and archaeologists: at the Little Maquoketa Mound site near Dubuque; several conferences featuring both archaeologists and Indian leaders, who, in spite of legitimate differences, nevertheless were able to join forces against looting and for preservation; a Native American farm in the Living History Farm program; and reconstruction of a portion of a Mesquakie Indian village in the Iowa Museum of Natural History.

For many years archaeologists and anthropologists in the United States went about their business of studying and preserving the past without attracting much attention from the Native American community. But in the activist climate of the 1960s and 1970s American Indians became vocally concerned over archaeological excavation of ancient cemetery areas and the public display of human remains in museums and related institutions. Controversies in many Western and Midwestern states pitting the scientific community against the Indian community (the latter with wide political support) were paralleled by demands of Orthodox Jews in Israel, Aboriginals in Australia, and the late President Sadat's desire to rebury the pharaohs in Egypt. In the State of Iowa within the last decade the conflict has resulted in legislation providing for disinterment and reburial under strictly controlled conditions and in a variety of cooperative projects.

Standard archaeological procedures were first publicly questioned in Iowa in 1971, when an Indian activist, Running Moccasins, publicized the fact that the remains of a young Indian female discovered by highway construction workers had been taken to the University of Iowa for study, and demanded that they be returned for proper Indian burial. Pressure from Indians, churches and students finally forced the State Archaeologist, whose office was legally entrusted with articles of historical significance, to announce that the bones had been shown to have no historical or scientific significance and had been returned for reburial. The incident brought to light the inadequacies of the Iowa legal code for dealing with such situations, and left archaeologists without a procedure for conducting investigations of aboriginal remains.

A similar incident at a Sioux City sand and gravel pit resulted in violence, legal tangles and an injunction halting excavation at the site. In 1972, a salvage excavation project conducted by the Sanford Museum at the request of the landowner resulted in recovery of 27 individuals from a Late Prehistoric ossuary; only later did the investigating archaeologists learn that violation-of-sepulchre laws were now being interpreted to include aboriginal remains. In response to this situation and to mounting demands from Indians and the general public that museums stop exhibiting the bones of Indians "as though they were some sort of tourist attraction," archaeologists continued to insist on the scientific value of examining skeletal remains.

Between 1972 and 1975 numerous accidental discoveries of human remains were made by scientists, construction workers and others, but scientific investigation of the bones remained at a standstill. Museums and archaeologists refused to have anything to do with the question, pending clarification of the laws and cessation of Indian opposition. No progress was made in the understanding of prehistoric cultures from a biological standpoint, but pot-hunters and curiosity seekers continued to loot and disturb cemetery areas. Then two events of 1975 proved to be a turning point toward a solution of the impasse. First, professional archaeologists at a conference on "The Future of

Iowa Archaeology" resolved to seek an understanding with Indian leaders and began a series of discussions with them. Soon afterwards several state officials, including the author, who had been appointed State Archaeologist, took a strong position on the desirability of scientific investigation of an ossuary uncovered at a construction site on the grounds of Lewis Central School, near Council Bluffs.

The author requested the cooperation of Running Moccasins in persuading Indians of the desirability of archaeological investigation of the site. The activist agreed after learning that the undertaker engaged as a result of Indian demands for immediate reburial intended to remove the remains from the ossuary with a bulldozer. Running Moccasins advised the Indian community that recovery with hand tools and archaeological techniques was a preferable method of disinterment, and joined the author in a successful request for state funding of the project. Excavation and study proceeded rapidly with the help of local agencies, and within nine days both the artifactual and osteological material were placed in a casket and then reburied in a local cemetery.

Encouraged by this cooperative venture, the participants joined forces to find a solution to Iowa's "burial problems." The State Archaeologist, the State Historic Preservation Officer, and the Assistant Attorney General sent a list of proposed changes in the Iowa Code to the Legislative Service Bureau for drafting. An informal Indian committee with Running Moccasins as its spokesperson sent a petition to the Governor that contained a number of requests closely paralleling the suggestions of the state officials. A draft of the proposed legislation was circulated among members of the Association of Iowa Archaeologists and approved with minor changes; similar results were obtained from a telephone poll of the Indians. Identical bills were introduced simultaneously in each house of the legislature and the law was passed in May 1976, with the endorsement of professional archaeologists, the State Historical Board and the Iowa Archeological Society.

Basically, this statute does four things: 1) provides a contingency fund to pay for the recovery of human skeletal remains; 2) clarifies the primary responsibility of the State Archaeologist in coordinating investigations; 3) establishes a state cemetery for the reinterment of "ancient" (more than 150 years old) human skeletal remains; and 4) clarifies the section of the legal code dealing with violation of sepulchre so as to protect ancient cemetery areas. The law defines as criminal mischief in the third degree—an aggravated misdemeanor—any intentional and unauthorized removal of human remains from a burial site, and the intentional disinterment of "human remains that have state and national significance from an historical or scientific standpoint for the inspiration and benefit of the United States without the permission of the State Archaeologist."

Both scientists and Indians have encountered some difficulties with the new legislation. For archaeologists and physical anthropologists, two problems stand out. First, the intent of the law is to provide for investigation of only those cemetery areas threatened with destruction. Indians will not tolerate research projects that involve digging into burial grounds in a good state of preservation. In a sense, however, this is a hypothetical question in the present circumstances, since so many cemetery areas are either being destroyed or are threatened with destruction. Archaeologists and physical anthropologists, who have their hands full trying to deal adequately with emergency situations, have begun to realize that in effect the law has provided them with a cultural resource management tool, and they are developing research strategies to maximize recovery of data as it becomes available.

Their second difficulty with the law is its reburial requirements; no scientist likes to bury comparative research material. But this, too, is mitigated by practical circumstances. Between 1971 and passage of the law in 1976 it was illegal for archaeologists to excavate in Iowa cemeteries. Indian opposition was strong enough to prohibit all work indefinitely, and the general public supported the Indian position ("I wouldn't want them digging up my relatives either"). Furthermore, the publication record in Iowa had been very slim for the quarter of a century before passage of the 1976 law; very few of the many skeletons excavated—some of them highly publicized, like the "Turin Man" *(Life,* Volume 38, Number 12, 1955)—were fully reported in scientific journals. The new law at least provides for study and requires the filing of a report with the State Department of Health.

The Indians, for their part, do not want aboriginal graves disturbed at all, let alone studied, but they realize that there is no way to determine racial or cultural affiliation until a study has been made. So for them the question becomes, "How should the excavation be carried out, and who should be authorized to perform the study?" When faced with a choice between meticulous recovery and bulldozing they choose the former. Scientists generally agree with the Indians' contention that archaeologists are not the appropriate persons to study the skeletal remains from a physical standpoint, so the solution was to require that an osteologist be engaged to conduct this portion of the investigations.

In Iowa as a whole the new spirit of cooperation in the past decade between archaeologists and Indians, now formally organized in an Indian Advisory Committee, has opened the door to a number of cooperative programs and enriching activities extending well beyond concerns over ancient burial sites. The most visible of these was the preservation of over 30 ancient Indian mounds overlooking the Little Maquoketa River near Dubuque, a beautiful wooded 42-acre site threatened with bulldozing for a group of townhouses. The Iowa Department of Transportation and the Iowa Conservation Commission united to purchase the land for the state and develop it for public visitation along the Iowa segment of the "Great River Road." Indian consultants participated in the planning and design of the preserve, and Indian leaders were flown in to inspect the site during its development. Native Americans were honored guests at the public ceremony in June 1981 and at the earlier, private ceremony where medicine men consecrated the site.

The Maquoketa Indian mound site is a preserve as well. The hillsides and ridge tops have remained in a relatively natural state, with maple, basswood, oak, hickory, black cherry, walnut, and white poplar trees. The preserve harbors numerous wildflowers, a small remnant of native blufftop prairie, and many species of birds, along with deer, raccoon and other wildlife. Development of the site has been limited to what is essential for viewing from a distance. The mound area has been cleared of the underbrush that had obstructed the mounds and a protective fence encloses it.

The understanding, trust and mutual respect that developed between Iowa scientists and the Native American community were greatly enhanced by two conferences held in the early 1980s. The first, a "Planning Seminar on Ancient Burial Grounds" sponsored by the Iowa Humanities Board in 1980, focused on when and in what circumstances ancient physical remains could be disinterred. Participants from eight states expressed a variety of viewpoints, with Indian leaders calling for total avoidance of ancient graves to protect the bones and spirits of their ancestors, and scientists voicing arguments for and against the recovery, study, and aboveground storage and curation of materials. In the end, those in attendance seemed to recognize the existence of legitimate differences of opinion. All deplored needless destruction by looters and agreed that preservation of sites was the highest priority; all seemed to think that the Iowa law was a good compromise.

A strong impetus for the second conference was supplied by the uproar over a front page story in the *Des Moines Register* erroneously reporting that the physical anthropologist representing the State Archaeologist's office had found that Iowa's ancient Indians had syphilis. Although the reporter, who had no control over the untrue headline, was most apologetic, the damage had been done. To Indian leaders outside the Indian Advisory Committee it appeared that scientists were trying to demonstrate that Native Americans were the source of venereal disease; not surprisingly the Indians demanded to know just what kind of studies were being conducted and why. So the decision was made to hold another conference, one that would address the reburial question more broadly as a public policy issue.

The 1983 conference, held at Simpson College in Indianola, provided a mechanism for public participation. After expressing their various concerns about current procedures for handling ancient human skeletal remains, members of the Indian Advisory Committee, other Indian participants, archaeologists, and physical anthropologists all answered questions from the audience. Perhaps more than its predecessor the conference resulted in mutual understanding and appreciation of different points of view, and—of great significance—a strong support for both the Indian Advisory Committee and the State Archaeologist.

Another cooperative program of the early 1980s also had extensive public impact. This was the addition of a Native American farm to the interpretive program of Living History Farms, a private nonprofit educational institution in Des Moines. On the advice of the Iowa Natural Heritage Foundation, Bill Murray, the president of the Living History Farms Board, consulted the author, and the result was the formation of an interdisciplinary advisory committee including scientists, historians, naturalists, and Indian leaders. Charged with choosing an Indian culture to be exemplified at the Farms, the committee settled on the eighteenth-century Ioway people before their removal to Kansas and subsequently to Oklahoma. The Ioways' dwellings and artifacts were fairly well known, since they had lived in Iowa for centuries, and they could be depicted at a time when their culture was still aboriginal, although in contact with Euro-American traders, trappers and missionaries.

Under a grant from the Iowa Humanities Board consultants on Iowa ethnohistory and archaeology were engaged, and the author went to Kampsville, Illinois to learn about house construction and other crafts from John White as well as White's "environmental approach" to reconstruction and replication projects. The group of Ioway Indians in Oklahoma were brought into the picture through the efforts of ethnohistory consultant Martha Blaine, and the general public was invited to watch the construction of the project, which insofar as possible utilized aboriginal tools and techniques. Over 400 visitors a day enjoyed watching the flintknapping, house building, pottery making and woodworking. The Indian Village was dedicated on Labor Day, 1982, with the help of a delegation of Ioways from Oklahoma. Currently, the site draws over 100,000 visitors a year and is having a major educational impact.

Another educational enterprise carried out through the cooperation of Indians and non-Indians is the reconstruction of a portion of a Mesquakie Indian village, in the Iowa Hall exhibit gallery recently added to the Iowa Museum of Natural History. Funded in part by the National Endowment for the Humanities and facilitated by direct assistance from the Mesquakie tribe, the exhibit is a view of the past through the eyes of contemporary Mesquakies. It is based on an ancient legend about the vision of a hunter/warrior, Ke-ske-ke-kosh, to whom a beautiful woman appeared, warning him to resist the advice of another woman who would visit him in the future to urge him to move his people away from their homeland, where We-sahke-ha the creator wanted them to stay. Not surprising to contemporary Mesquakie, therefore, is the tribe's refusal to be removed to a reservation in Kansas after the treaty of 1842. Visitors to the exhibit see depictions of the series of events that followed: squads of dragoons rounded up the Indians and drove them out of the state. Also shown is the later "happy ending," when some persevering Mesquakie were granted permission to purchase land and legally reside in Iowa. In 1856 the tribe acquired 80 acres near the bend in the Iowa River where the legend locates the vision of Ke-ske-ke-kosh. And to the great pleasure of contemporary Mesquakie, the exhibit is right next to the Old Capitol where Governor James Grimes gave their ancestors permission to reclaim part of their homeland.

When Historic Fort Atkinson was being restored Indians were employed as consultants on the project. Indians serve as advisers to the Iowa Department of Transportation on matters concerning the accidental unearthing of ancient cemeteries. They participate in the presentation of public programs sponsored by state and federal humanities agencies, and they negotiate with government resource agencies for rulings favorable to the protection and presentation of ancient sites. Indians take part in the fieldwork, and they obtain help from anthropologists in preserving their tribal treasures.

All of this seems far removed from the 1976 "reburial law," and still farther from the earlier confrontations on the reburial issue. These developments in Iowa have been fortunate extensions of the decision taken by Indians, scientists and government of the state to work out a compromise on the reburial question. And they certainly supply at least a partial answer to the question, "Is reburial reasonable?"

Should reburial be practiced everywhere? Not necessarily. Archaeologists and physical anthropologists would be well advised to work on the regional or state level with the appropriate tribal officials and tailor their procedures accordingly. Such concern on the part of scientists for the human subjects with whom they interact is commonplace throughout the social, behavioral and medical sciences. Another thing to keep in mind is that times change. What may be reasonable now may not have been reasonable 20 years ago, and may not be 20 years from now. Certainly, it is not an area where a prescriptive federal law would be appropriate. Reburial is a sensitive and complex issue requiring patience, understanding, and compassion on the part of all concerned.

Duane Anderson was State Archaeologist for Iowa and is now at the School of American Research in Santa Fe, New Mexico.

DISCUSSION QUESTIONS

1. How can archaeologists determine what native group to consult before excavation of burials? How do the problems and concerns differ in different parts of the country?
2. Is reburial of skeletal remains after study better than no study at all?
3. How frequently is reburial actually demanded by affiliated Indian tribes?
4. Who should conduct the study of human remains?
5. What lessons might archaeologists learn from the experience of the social, behavioral, and medical sciences, who have long been concerned for the human subjects with whom they interact?
6. Now that NAGPRA has been enacted, what options are open to archaeologists and Native Americans on the local level?*

FURTHER RESEARCH

See also: Robert Layton, ed., *Who Needs the Past? Indigenous Values and Archaeology,* One World Archaeology, Vol. 5 (London: Unwin Hyman, 1989).

For additional references, see Chapter 19.

---

*The final rule implementing NAGPRA is available on the National Archaeological Data Base at htpp://www.cast.uark.edu/products/NADB/.

CHAPTER NINETEEN

BURYING	SHARING
AMERICAN	CONTROL
ARCHAEOLOGY	OF THE PAST
by Clement W.	by Larry J.
Meighan	Zimmerman

On November 16, 1990, Congress passed the Native American Graves Protection and Repatriation Act (NAGPRA). One controversial provision of the act requires the return, on request, of skeletal remains and burial goods to Native Americans who can prove cultural affiliation with the materials. Meighan presents a negative response to the legislation; Zimmerman defends it.

BURYING AMERICAN ARCHAEOLOGY
by Clement W. Meighan

In 1991 the West Virginia Department of Transportation and a committee of Indians and non-Indians claiming to represent Native American viewpoints signed an agreement whereby everything unearthed in advance of road construction near the 2,000-year-old Adena mound was to be given up for reburial within a year. "Everything" included not only cremated bones but artifacts such as chipping waste, food refuse, pollen samples, and soil samples. The $1.8 million rescue excavation was federally funded in the interest of science. Yet nothing of tangible archaeological evidence was to be preserved. In addition, Indian activists were paid by the state to monitor the excavation and to censor "objectionable" photographs or data appearing in the final report. The activists also insisted that, following an alleged ancient custom, human remains be covered with red flannel until reburial and that no remains, including artifacts, be touched by menstruating women.

American Indians, Australian aborigines, and ultraorthodox Jews in Israel have all attacked archaeology in recent years and continue to seek restrictions on archaeological study. In North America, the argument has been put forward that the archaeological study of ancient Native American people is a violation of the religious freedom of living Indians. Some Indian spokesmen have claimed their right, on religious grounds, to control archaeological study and specimens regardless of the age of the remains, the area from which they come, or the degree of claimed Indian ancestry.

In my view, archaeologists have a responsibility to the people they study. They are defining the culture of an extinct group and in presenting their research they are writing a chapter of human history that cannot be written except from archaeological investigation. If the archaeology is not done, the ancient people remain without a history.

A number of confusions have led to the present conflict over archaeological study of Native American remains. One is the assumption of direct genetic and cultural continuity between living persons and those long deceased. Who knows whether the Indians of 2,000 years ago believed that a corpse must be covered with red flannel and not touched by menstruating women? As if to emphasize their contempt for real ancestral relationships, the activists who demanded reburial of the remains from the Adena mound included Indians from tribes as far away as northwestern Washington, as well as non-Indians. Meanwhile, the views of a local West Virginia tribe that favored preservation of the remains were ignored.

A year before the government passed the Native American Graves Protection and Repatriation Act. According to preliminary interpretations of this law, some sort of relationship must be shown between claimants and the materials claimed. However, no line has been drawn at remains over a certain age, despite the obvious impossibility of establishing a familial relationship spanning 20 or more generations of unrecorded history. Millions of dollars have now been spent to inventory collections, including those containing items thousands of years old, and to add a corps of bureaucrats to interpret and administer the legislation. An enormous amount of scientists' time is also being diverted from research that might otherwise be done on those bones and artifacts soon to be lost to repatriation.

One wonders why museum directors are so eager to relinquish the holdings for which they are responsible. Museums house a great variety of collections and their directors are rarely trained in any of the natural sciences or have any special interest in physical anthropology. Being, for the most part, public institutions, they are dependent on good public relations, which can be undermined by activists. Like politicians, museum directors seem all too willing to satisfy activists by dissatisfying scientists. Meanwhile, in university departments of anthropology, physical anthropologists are normally outnumbered by cultural anthropologists. The latter have little interest in osteological collections; more important to them is maintaining good relations with the living tribes with whom they work. As a group, cultural anthropologists include a considerable number of politicized academics. Many of them welcome an opportunity to demonstrate their solidarity with an allegedly oppressed minority, especially when it means insisting that the latter's native religion be respected. Since their own research will not be adversely affected, they have nothing to lose. Political correctness has rarely been so all-around satisfying.

It is questionable whether Indian activists and politicized professors and curators could succeed in influencing politicians and administrators if the latter found their claims to be utterly implausible. Even the most cynical and opportunistic lawmakers would not want to be observed supporting self-evidently absurd demands. Yet the multiple laws inhibiting archaeological research, physical anthropology, and museum studies have all been instigated and justified in the name of Indian religious beliefs. This is remarkable for a number of reasons. First, no other religious group in the United States has been given the same protection. Second, most Indians no longer hold these beliefs. Third, Indian knowledge of the traditions of their ancestors is derived in large part from the collections and scholarship that the activists among them are now seeking to destroy.

That measures hostile to science have gained so much ground in this nation's legislative bodies, universities, and museums—and on so flimsy a basis—suggests that there has been a sea change in the opinions and sentiments that have hitherto guided the public in support of scientific endeavor. The New Age disposition to invoke or invent beliefs no one really holds, and to maintain that they are of a value at least equal to, if not supremely greater than, those that account for the triumph of Western civilization, is given concrete expression in the repatriation movement. Conversely, the success of this movement will further reinforce these newly fashionable doubts about the value of Western science in particular and rational thought in general.

Reasonable doubts have been raised about whether the large quantity of bones tucked away in museum drawers and cabinets are really of scientific value. In fact, these are frequently studied by physical anthropologists and their students. The techniques of statistical research require as large a sample as possible so that generalizations can be well-formulated. In addition, bones that have already been examined may be needed again when new analytic techniques are developed. Only recently has it been possible to extract antibodies and genetic material from ancient bones, making it possible to trace the evolution of specific human diseases. Future laboratory advances in dating bones and in determining the source of artifact materials will also require these objects to be available for study. Finally, the bones belonging to particular tribes are precisely those that are most valuable to historical studies of those tribes.

But even if it were true that the bones, once examined, need never be studied again, the demand that they be reburied conflicts with the scholarly requirement to preserve data. If research data are destroyed, there can be no basis on which to challenge honest but possibly erroneous conclusions. Reburying bones and artifacts is the equivalent of the historian burning documents after he has studied them. Thus, repatriation is not merely an inconvenience but makes it impossible for scientists to carry out a genuinely scientific study of American Indian prehistory. Furthermore, it negates scientific work that has already been done, since the evidence on which that work was based is now to be buried.

Repatriation also raises other issues. It is a violation of a museum's public trust to give away materials that it has held legally and at public expense. A similar violation is involved when a museum has received these materials from a private donor or at a private donor's expense. In particular, such action ignores many Indians who donated or sold materials on the understanding that these items would go into a permanent repository for the benefit of future generations of Indians.

An entire field of academic study may be put out of business. It has become impossible for a field archaeologist to conduct a large-scale excavation in the United States without violating some law or statute. The result is that archaeology students are now steered away from digs where they might actually find some American Indian remains. American archaeology is an expiring subject of study—one in which new students no longer choose to specialize. Instead, they specialize in the archaeology of other countries, where they will be allowed to conduct their research and have some assurance that their collections will be preserved.

Scientific disciplines are not immune to change, but the scientific ideal is that these changes are the consequence of new discoveries and theories driven by developments internal to science, and not imposed from without. It may therefore be questioned whether the repatriation movement is not a massive invasion of the freedom of scholarly and scientific disciplines to define their own goals and chart their own course.

What the activists know about the Indians' past depends almost entirely on the records of European explorers, missionaries, and settlers, and on the studies of past and present historians, ethnographers, anthropologists, and archaeologists. These scholars and scientists often thought of themselves as helping the American Indian to preserve his heritage. A great many Indians, past and present, shared or share that conviction. It would be interesting to know whether a majority of living persons of Indian descent actually favor reburial or the continued preservation, display, and study of Indian remains and artifacts.

SHARING CONTROL OF THE PAST
by Larry J. Zimmerman

Scholars have been slow to realize that the scientific archaeology that sprang from Euroamerican rationalist and empiricist roots may not be the only valid archaeology. Part of the rift between archaeologists and Native Americans stems from a fundamentally different conception of the past. To archaeologists, the past can be known because it has already happened and left markers—artifacts—that give clues about it. To know the past requires that it be discovered through written sources and archaeological exploration and interpretation. To Native Americans, the idea that discovery is the only way to know the past is absurd. For the Indian interested in traditional practice and belief, the past lives in the present. Indians know the past because it is spiritually and ritually a part of daily existence and is relevant only as it exists in the present. In fact, Indians object to heavy reliance on artifacts, preferring instead to focus on people and how they experienced their lives.

Archaeologists often claim to speak for past peoples, however remote. Implicit in this claim is the notion that they, as practitioners of a science, are the only ones capable of doing so. Native Americans do not accept this and challenge the very authority of archaeological knowledge. Cecil Antone of the Gila River Indian Tribes said at a conference on reburial, "My ancestors, relatives, grandmother so on down the line, they tell you about the history of our people and it's passed on . . . basically, what I'm trying to say, I guess, is that archaeology don't mean nothing." When archaeologists say that the Native American past is gone, extinct, or lost unless archaeology can find it, they send a strong message that Native Americans themselves are extinct. University of Arizona anthropologist J. Jefferson Reid believes that Native Americans see archaeological accounts of their past as a threat to traditional, Indian accounts of that same past. They fear that the archaeological version eventually will replace the traditionally constructed past and their culture, once again, will be eroded. Indians told Reid, during a recent archaeological conference, that the archaeology of the Southwest had no relevance for southwestern

Indians; in their view ". . . archaeology was only relevant to other archaeologists."

Archaeology has been slow to recognize that epistemological shifts must be made if archaeology is to have any relevance to any group other than archaeologists. We can begin by broadening archaeological ideas about the past to include an interest in how others know the past and by rejecting the view that archaeologists are somehow the only capable stewards of it. Southern Illinois University anthropologist Jonathan D. Hill has challenged the belief that historical interpretations based on written documents are necessarily more objective, reliable, or accurate than those embodied in oral tradition. In his introduction to a volume analyzing Native South American perspectives on the past, he notes that "Although oral and non-verbal formulations cannot be literally read as direct accounts of historical processes, they can show how indigenous societies have experienced history and the on-going means by which they struggle to make sense out of complex, contradictory historical processes." He concludes that history is not ever reducible to "what really happened." This suggests that the past—the very medium in which archaeologists work—is fluid; objectivity itself changes. Accepting this notion is critical if archaeology is to accommodate Native American accounts of their history.

Nowhere have these conflicting viewpoints been more visible than in the reburial issue. Some archaeologists maintain that the past is lost with reburial. Of course information from the remains is lost, but only to the archaeologist. Those who believe that American Indians or other groups are getting preferential treatment do not understand that many of these groups have been subjected to the "preferred" views of the Western world, which includes the science of archaeology.

The idea that anyone can "save" the past is a false notion. Preservation itself reveals that permanence is an illusion. As University College-London geographer David Lowenthal has written, "Saviors of the past change it no less than iconoclasts bent on its destruction." The past is always interpreted from the perspective of the present. For archaeologists, interpretations reflect changes in theoretical viewpoints, analytical techniques, and the politics of contemporary society.

New interpretations replace the old; that is, they "destroy" the past. Archaeologists construct the past, they do not reconstruct it.

Many archaeologists view the past as everyone's heritage. This implies that archaeologists, because of their special skills, are the most capable of preserving and interpreting it. Many indigenous peoples don't agree. At the 1982 meeting of the Australian Archaeological Association, Rosalind Langford, an Australian aboriginal, commented, "You . . . say that as scientists you have the right to obtain and study information of our culture. You . . . say that because you are Australians you have a right to study and explore our heritage because it is a heritage to be shared by all Australians . . . We say that it is our past, our culture and heritage, and forms part of our present life. As such it is ours to control and it is ours to share on our terms."

What steps should archaeologists who study native peoples take to insure an amicable working relationship? We should be activists in consulting groups that might be affected by our work. And we shouldn't be doing it just because it is required by law or is politically correct. Rather, we should consult Native Americans because we recognize their valid interests in the past. Working with them, they will provide us with insights into their past.

In so doing, archaeologists can share the past, rather than impose their own version of it. There are examples of archaeologists and indigenous peoples who have good working relationships. In Australia, Colin Pardoe, an osteologist studying aboriginal remains, does no excavation or analysis without intensive community involvement. He seeks permission to work on remains even if he suspects that they are not related to groups now occupying the area in which bones are found. He asks people their opinion of the research problems he is addressing. He tells them why he needs to do certain tests, and if they involve destructive techniques, he asks permission to use them. Pardoe's community reports are instructive in that they provide a mechanism for community involvement in his construction of the past. He usually has little difficulty conducting his research and he learns a great deal more in the process by sharing his study with aborigines.

216

Consider a recent reburial in Nebraska. The Pawnee Indians successfully collaborated with archaeologists to summarize the archaeological record of their tribe for a court case involving repatriation of human remains. At the same time Pawnee tribal historian Roger Echo-Hawk gathered previously recorded oral history and other materials pertaining to Pawnee origins and history. Since the case, archaeologist Steve Holen has worked with Echo-Hawk, to compare the archaeological record and the oral history to see what concordance there might be. Echo-Hawk and Holen are learning from each other. Many Pawnee narratives are reflected in the archaeological record. Others are not. Disagreements are put aside pending further consultation.

Involvement of nonarchaeologists puts some control into their hands, and most archaeologists will be reluctant to relinquish control over their research. Who is willing to do this? The World Archaeological Congress (WAC) in its ethics code has taken steps to share control with indigenous peoples. The WAC code even puts the development of research into indigenous hands. For example, WAC has eight indigenous representatives on its executive committee. Its ethics code demands that WAC members seek representation for indigenous peoples in agencies funding or authorizing research to be certain that their views are considered in setting research standards, questions, priorities, and goals. Archaeologists do not stop developing research questions—the difference is they share them with indigenous peoples, who then become more familiar with archaeological thinking.

Collaborative efforts unquestionably will limit our cherished academic freedom. Accountability to Native Americans will create a very different discipline, one that will not be scientific according to our current standards. At the same time, this new science can and will open many investigative possibilities for us, especially in areas where we wish to understand the meaning of prehistoric events or materials. We will certainly develop a better understanding of what people's lives meant to them. We may be allowed better access to areas now closed to us, particularly in the realm of the sacred. We may better learn about a commonality of human experience that is analogous to and as valuable as any we have generated using scientific theory.

Native American peoples have been extraordinarily patient with archaeologists. They recognize that some archaeology is useful to them if applied using their rules. What archaeologists must understand is that their view of the past is peculiar to their discipline and has an impact on those they study. To communicate effectively with Native American people, archaeologists will need to learn how to share control of the past.

Groups like WAC and the Society for American Archaeology have begun serious examination of what constitutes ethical practice. What is exciting about this new direction is that it does allow us the chance to become something quite different. If we don't take steps that are bold and creative in reinventing our profession, we will continue to lose access to the artifacts, sites, and people we wish to study.

Clement W. Meighan is Professor Emeritus of anthropology at UCLA and head of the American Committee for the Preservation of Archaeological Collections, a group opposed to NAGPRA.

Larry J. Zimmerman is a professor of archaeology at the University of South Dakota and executive secretary of the World Archaeological Congress, which works closely with indigenous peoples on reburial and other issues.

DISCUSSION QUESTIONS

1. How can a people whose historical memory does not rely on written records and Western science convey the essence and import of that history to a dominant community that puts primary value on written records and Western science?
2. What are some of the "different views" of Native Americans on these issues?
3. How widespread among the Native American community are the concerns about the "scientific study" of the Native American past?
4. Without archaeological study, how can anyone know to whom skeletal materials may be related or what religious beliefs were held 2,000 years ago?

5. What institutions in your area are involved in NAGPRA-related repatriation claims? How much time and money is involved? Are scientific benefits resulting from the repatriation work?

6. What role do museum directors and curators and cultural anthropologists play in this whole debate? What role should they play?

7. Do other religious groups in the United States have the same kind of protection?

8. Do most Indians still hold the ancient beliefs? Does it matter, for purposes of the present argument, whether they do or not?

9. How has the work of archaeology made a positive contribution to the lives of present-day Native Americans?

10. Historically, what have been the attitudes of various cultures about digging up graves and making some use of human skeletal remains?

11. How might the scientific needs of physical anthropologists and archaeologists be made more compelling to Native American groups?

12. Is repatriation a violation of a museum's public trust? What is a museum's "public trust"? (See also the earlier article by Rose and Acar, "Turkey's War on the Illicit Antiquities Trade.")

13. If objects now in a museum collection were acquired some time ago by purchase from an informed and consenting Indian owner, do descendants of that Indian have any right to request repatriation of the objects? (See also the earlier article by Scott, "St. Lawrence: Archaeology of a Bering Sea Island.")

14. How healthy is the discipline of archaeology in the United States? In other countries?

15. Are Indians' fears that the archaeological version of the past will replace their traditional accounts justified? (See also the earlier article by Gray, "Champion of Aboriginal Art.")

16. What are some potentially positive outcomes of accepting others as legitimate stewards of the past? What are some of the potential and actual problems and difficulties?

FURTHER RESEARCH

See also the article in Part IV by McIntosh, McIntosh, and Togola, "People Without History"; and interview local Cultural Resources Management firms.

The bibliography on reburial is vast. See, for example: Paul G. Bahn and R. W. K. Paterson, "The Last Rights: More on Archaeology and the Dead," *Oxford Journal of Archaeology* 5 (1986): 255–71; Vine Deloria Jr., "Indians, Archaeologists, and the Future," *American Antiquity* 57 (1992): 595–98; Anthony L. Klesert and Shirley Powell, "A Perspective on Ethics and the Reburial Controversy," *American Antiquity* 58 (1993): 348–54; and Robert Layton, *Conflict in the Archaeology of Living Traditions*, One World Archaeology, Vol. 8 (London: Unwin Hyman, 1989).*

---

*The final rule implementing NAGPRA is available on the National Archaeological Data Base at htpp://www.cast.uark.edu/products/NADB/.

CHAPTER TWENTY
BONES AND BUREAUCRATS: NEW YORK'S GREAT CEMETERY IMBROGLIO

By Spencer P.M. Harrington

This article presents the historical background to, and the controversies surrounding, the discovery and excavation of the Colonial African Burial Ground under a New York City parking lot. Scholarly excitement was tempered by protests from the city's black community, which felt its concerns were not being addressed in decisions about the excavation and disposition of the remains. A supplement provides information gleaned from the excavation and remains.

The bones of 420 enslaved Africans found in 1992 under a parking lot two blocks north of New York's City Hall comprise the largest and earliest collection of African-American remains, and possibly the largest and earliest collection of American colonial remains of any ethnic group. The excavation of the old Negros Burial Ground has challenged the popular belief that there was no slavery in colonial New York, and has provided unparalleled data for the Howard University scholars who will study the remains of New York's first African Americans. But as archaeologists removed the remains one by one, they dug up age-old resentment and suspicion with every trowel-full of earth. Scholarly excitement was tempered by the protest of the city's black community, which felt its concerns were not being addressed in decisions about the excavation and disposition of the remains. In the flurry of protests, negotiations, and political maneuverings, the controversy took on an undeniably racial cast. The African Burial Ground, as it is known today, became a "microcosm of the issues of racism and economic exploitation confronting New York City," says Michael L. Blakey, a Howard University anthropologist and the burial ground's scientific director.

In a national context, the controversy over the burial ground excavation became an important episode in a larger struggle of descendant communities to reclaim their heritage. But more specifically, the story was about African-American empowerment: about how a black congressman, acting on the advice of New York City's first black mayor, stopped the excavation of the burial ground; about how the African-American community chose Washington D.C.'s Howard University, the country's most prestigious black research university, as a venue for the study of the remains, thereby ensuring that black researchers and students would study and interpret the remains of their ancestors; and about how the city's black community lobbied for and received a $3 million appropriation from Congress for a memorial and commemorative museum. Equally important were the hard lessons learned by the General Services Administration, the federal agency that supervised the excavation—lessons about the importance of descendant-community involvement in salvage archaeology.

The story of the African Burial Ground begins in 1626, when the Dutch West Indies Company imported its first shipment of slaves, 11 young men from today's Congo-Angola region of Africa. Two years later, the company brought over three African women "for the comfort of the company's Negro men," according to Dutch West Indies records. Like the British who governed Manhattan after them, the Dutch encountered difficulties attracting European settlers to the new colony. Grave manpower shortages threatened the profitability of the Dutch West Indies trading enterprise, and the company was quick to import slave labor to farm its fields. In 1664, just before the Dutch ceded Manhattan to the British, enslaved Africans made up about 40 percent of the colony's total population. The British continued the slave trade, importing as many as 6,800 Africans between 1700 and 1774, many of whom had worked previously on Caribbean plantations. By the mid-eighteenth century, New York had become a thriving port town, and enslaved Africans loaded and unloaded cargo at the docks, wharves, slips, and warehouses along the East River. They also piloted boats ferrying produce from the farming villages of Long Island, repaired and expanded city streets, and worked in shipbuilding and construction. On the eve of the American Revolution, New York City had the largest number of enslaved Africans of any English colonial settlement except Charleston, South Carolina, and it had the highest proportion of slaves to Europeans of any northern settlement. Though seldom acknowledged, Africans were essential to the functioning, as well as the building of colonial New York.

In November 1697, New York City adopted a policy of mortuary apartheid, declaring lower Manhattan churchyards off-limits to blacks. Forced to look for a place to bury its dead, New York's African population, which then numbered about 700, chose unappropriated property outside city limits two blocks north of today's City Hall. There, from 1712 until 1790, in an area characterized by David Valentine, an early city historian, as "unattractive and desolate," Africans conducted last rites for their people. "So little seems to have been thought of the race that not even a dedication of their burial place was made by church authorities," wrote Valentine of what was known then as the Negros Burial Ground. Under the British, Africans were subject to a sunset curfew and city ordinances that prohibited unsupervised gatherings of more than three slaves. They were, however, allowed to gather in large numbers and with regularity at the burial ground. Some 10,000 to 20,000 people, both black and lower-class white, are believed to have been buried in the five-to-six-acre plot of land.

The growth of the city's population in the late eighteenth and early nineteenth centuries led to a northward expansion along main thoroughfares such as Broadway. Street plans were drafted, and blocks over the burial ground were divided into lots for residential and commercial development. By the end of the century, ten- and 15-story buildings with deep foundations and with vaults that were used for storage and coal delivery were going up. The Negros Burial Ground, now paved or built over, was all but forgotten, noted only in a few historical maps and documents. Meanwhile, African Americans were now burying their dead on the lower East Side, near what are now Chrystie and Delancey streets.

Nearly 200 years later a section of the burial ground lay beneath a parking lot between Duane and Reade streets. In December 1990, New York sold this property and another plot on nearby Foley Square to the General Services Administration (GSA), the federal agency charged with constructing and managing government buildings. The GSA paid $104 million for both properties, which it hoped to develop simultaneously. It planned to build a $276 million, 34-story office tower and adjoining four-story pavilion on the parking lot area. A federal courthouse was envisioned for the Foley Square property. The tower, designated 290 Broadway, would contain the offices of the United States Attorney, a regional office of the Environmental Protection Agency, and the downtown district office of the Internal Revenue Service. The pavilion would house a day-care center, an auditorium, and a pedestrian galleria.

Five months before the GSA bought the sites from the city, the agency hired Historic Conservation and Interpretation (HCI), an archaeological salvage and consulting firm, to write the archaeological portion of an environmental impact statement for the 290 Broadway site. Such statements are a legal requirement before any new construction using federal funds can begin. HCI's report identified the area as a section of the old Negros Burial Ground and included historical maps indicating its approximate location. But the impact statement predicted that nineteenth- and twentieth-century construction at the site would have destroyed any significant archaeological deposits. It read in part: "The construction of deep sub-basements would have obliterated any remains within the lots that fall within the historic bounds of the cemetery."

Still, the statement left open the possibility of some human remains being preserved under an old alley that once bisected Duane and Reade streets. That the GSA purchased the land despite this possibility suggests that the agency was betting on HCI's overall assessment that few, if any, human remains would be found there. In retrospect, GSA regional director William Diamond admits that the agency would never have bought the land if it had known it would have to remove hundreds of skeletons before sinking the office tower foundation.

In May 1991, six months after purchasing the land, the GSA hired HCI to investigate the possibility that there were undisturbed burials in the alley area. By the end of the summer the firm started to find human bones. In September a full-scale excavation was underway, and on October 8 Diamond held a press conference to announce the discovery of the remains. One year later, the last of some 420 skeletons had been removed from the site to Lehman College in the Bronx, where they were undergoing conservation before being transferred to Howard University for more detailed study.

African-American outrage over the handling of the excavation stemmed from a perception that the black community had no control over the fate of its heritage—that decisions about the burial ground were being made by white bureaucrats with little insight into African-American history and spiritual sensitivities. "Religious, Afrocentric people believe that to disturb burials in any way is the highest form of disrespect," says Gina Stahlnecker, an aide to State Senator David Patterson, who represents Harlem and the Upper West Side. "There were some people who believed the archaeologists were releasing evil." According to Peggy King Jorde, of the Mayor's Office of Construction, an early monitor of the project, the GSA initially was calling the site a "potters' field," which she felt divorced it from its African origin and diminished its importance. There were even rumors, she says, that the bones were to be removed without any archaeological study. Jorde says that GSA had only vague ideas about what to do with the remains that were coming to light.

The black community was also upset because it was not alerted at the outset to what might lie beneath the parking lot between Duane and Reade streets. While the GSA did distribute both draft and final environmental impact statements to more than 200 federal, state, and city agencies and local community groups, the agency did not alert civic groups in predominantly black neighborhoods that the buildings would be constructed on top of the old burial ground. "I spoke to hundreds and hundreds of people in the black community, and no one had ever heard about it," says Stahlnecker. While distributing environmental impact statements to descendant communities may seem like a good idea, it is not customary for private or government developers to do so. Peter Sneed, the GSN's planning staff director, argues that the distribution list was formulated in accordance with federal regulations. "We didn't include the Harlem community board because the project isn't in Harlem, it's in lower Manhattan," he says. "We felt it was incumbent upon the Mayor's office to spread the word. It's unreasonable to expect a federal agency to know every interest group in the community."

African-American fury over the excavation increased dramatically after a backhoe operator digging the tower's foundation accidentally destroyed several of the burials. The incident was reported by Dan Pagano, an archaeologist for the city's Landmarks Preservation Commission, who was photographing the site through a telephoto lens when he spotted HCI archaeologists sifting through human remains outside the excavation area, where the backhoe had scooped up earth so that a concrete footing could be poured for the tower. Pagano says jawbones and leg and arm bones were among the remains scooped up by the backhoe. The GSA blamed the accident on an out-of-date drawing that the construction crews were using to determine which part of the site was "culturally sterile." Diamond halted tower construction pending further investigation by archaeologists. The incident led State Senator David Patterson to form an oversight committee to monitor the burial ground excavation.

Miriam Francis, a member of Patterson's committee, says that the involvement of African-American anthropologists in the excavation was among the group's most pressing concerns. "If it was an African find, we wanted to make sure that it was interpreted from an African point of view," she says. But the committee soon learned that the GSA had picked physical anthropologists from the city's Metropolitan Forensic Anthropology Team (MFAT) to conduct field analyses of the remains and that the bones would be stored at the group's Lehman College facility. "We didn't know anything about MFAT, whether they were butchers, bakers, or candlestick makers," says Francis. She notes that when the committee introduced the GSA to African-American specialists like Howard University's Michael Blakey, it was either stonewalled or ignored.

Meanwhile, the GSA was having difficulty getting HCI, its archaeological salvage contractor, to produce a research design stating conservation measures and scientific study goals for the burial project. The GSA had managed to obtain extensions on the report's due date from the Advisory Council on Historic Preservation, the government agency that reviews all federal projects that might have an impact on historic sites. Still, the missing research plan sent further signals to the black community that something was wrong with the way work was progressing. "Any archaeological excavation is useless without a research design," noted Landmarks Preservation Commission Chair Laurie Beckelman at a congressional hearing on the burial ground. "It's like driving a car in a foreign country without a road map or destination."

HCI's Edward Rutsch, the project's archaeologist, says that although he was responsible for the research design, he felt too overworked to get it done properly. "They [GSA] had us working seven days a week and overtime every day," says Rutsch. "Many times it was expressed to me that millions of dollars of public money were being lost. There was terrific pressure to get the excavation done—to finish it."

In April 1992, black activists staged a one-day blockade of the site in an effort to prevent GSA from pouring concrete for the tower's foundation. Among other things, they were concerned that there was little African-American involvement in the scientific aspects of the excavation; they were visibly unhappy at the choice of Lehman College as the site for the conservation of the remains. Bones from the site had been wrapped in newspaper and placed in cardboard boxes before being shipped to Lehman. One problem, according to Dan Baer of Edwards and Kelcey, an engineering firm hired to manage the site, was that "We were digging them out faster than [storage] cases could be made." But in the African-American community there was concern that the bones were being damaged at Lehman. "They had some remains up there in boxes ten or 11 months," says Abd-Allah Adesanya, director of the Mayor's Office of African American and

Caribbean Affairs. "They were wrapped in newspaper longer than they should have been. They had to be rewrapped in acid-free paper." Baer says, "The bones were stored in newspaper, which may be scientific protocol, but it didn't appear respectful to those who visited the site. It was a mistake that was made. But the bones were in good shape and Dr. Blakey said so after touring the facility."

Blakey's tour of Lehman resulted from pressure by Senator Patterson's committee. "We kept asking them [MFAT], 'Can we go up there?' And that involved more waiting, more delays," says Miriam Francis. "It wasn't that we were against Lehman, we just wanted to see how our ancestors were being stored." Blakey's visit to the facility confirmed the community's suspicion of inadequate conservation. In a letter to *Archaeology*, Blakey wrote "We intervened in time to prevent the potential for further deterioration, such as the spread of mold in the skeletal remains due to inadequate environmental controls, and improper storage of skeletal materials on top of fragile bone."

As the excavation progressed, the GSA began briefing the public on the burial project's progress. But there was a widespread perception among African Americans that the GSA was merely paying lip-service to the public, that they were digging the bones as fast as they could so the tower foundation could be poured. "People would tell them [the GSA] their gripes, then they went off and did what they wanted," says Adesanya. "The community wanted to be let in on the decision making process, to influence the direction of the project." While descendant-community input into decisions about the course of contract excavations seems desirable when human remains are involved, consultation is not part of standard archaeological practice. Nonetheless "the [African-American] community was very unhappy," says Diamond, "and I understood that and kept saying to them, 'I wish I could help you with this but my obligations by law are contrary to your wishes, and the only way we can get this changed is by an act of Congress or an agreement from the administrator of the GSA.' And I was in consultation with them [GSA administrator Richard G. Austin and members of Congress] and they were telling me to continue the construction."

At the GSA's public meetings, African Americans also questioned the propriety of continuing with the removal of remains from the area where the pavilion would be built. They also hoped that the GSA would consider not building the pavilion, or at least modify the plans so there would be no further removals. "There were several conflicting demands," recalls Diamond. "Some wanted the exhumation to stop, others wanted nothing built on the site, and still others wanted a museum built on the site . . . But I had no authority but to continue under the law with the construction."

The GSA eventually replaced Historic Conservation and Interpretation with John Milner Associates (JMA), a West Chester, Pennsylvania, archaeological contractor. JMA had recently completed a successful excavation of an early nineteenth-century cemetery associated with the First African Baptist Church in Philadelphia that brought to light information on that city's early black history. "JMA had done this sort of job before," says Baer. "We didn't feel we had involved the community enough and we thought that JMA would improve that situation."

But reports by agencies monitoring the excavation were becoming increasingly critical. One report filed by the Advisory Council on Historic Preservation stated, in part, that: ". . . the GSA was proceeding without any clear focus on why the remains were being removed; how they were to be analyzed, how many more bodies were involved; or what the African-American community's desire was for the treatment of the burials." Mayor David Dinkins sent a letter to Diamond complaining about the lack of a research design and requesting "that the GSA suspend all excavation and construction activities in the pavilion area and bring the project into compliance with the terms outlined in the Memorandum of Agreement [a document, specifying the terms of archaeological work to be undertaken in advance of construction] . . ." There is "no basis for discontinuance of ongoing excavations" was Diamond's response a week later. "I would not be put in a position of abrogating important government contracts because of political pressure," he later recalled.

The final act in the drama was played out before the congressional committee that appropriates funds for the GSA, the House

Subcommittee on Public Buildings and Grounds. Meeting in New York, the subcommittee was chaired by former Representative Gus Savage, an Illinois Democrat, who heard testimony from the GSA, the Advisory Council, the city's landmarks Preservation Commission, and concerned citizens. At the meeting, the GSA argued that stopping the excavation would jeopardize the exposed human remains, and it estimated that relinquishing the pavilion site would cost taxpayers as much as $40 million: $5 million in interest payments, $10 million in land acquisition costs, and $25 million in initial construction costs.

Savage then subjected GSA representatives to intense questioning, during which it became apparent that at the outset the GSA was aware that a historic burial ground had once occupied the land it intended to purchase and develop, and that the agency had made no contingency plans for construction in the event that human remains were found. The meeting also revealed that the building prospectus for 290 Broadway the GSA had submitted for Congressional approval did not mention the burial ground, nor was Savage's subcommittee alerted by the agency when HCI's impact statement mentioned the possibility of intact graves. Savage ended the hearing early, noting that he would not approve any further GSA projects until he received "a more honest and respectful response" from the agency regarding its excavation of the burial ground. "And don't waste your time asking this subcommittee for anything else as long as I'm chairman, unless you can figure out a way to go around me! I am not going to be part of your disrespect," Savage said.

Three days later, Savage halted excavation on the pavilion site, and in October former President Bush signed Public Law 102–393, ordering the GSA to cease construction of the pavilion portion of the project, and approving $3 million for the construction of a museum honoring the contribution of African Americans to colonial New York City. Meanwhile, JMA removed the last of the exposed burials.

In a statement to the House Subcommittee on Public Buildings and Grounds, GSA head Richard G. Austin acknowledged that "in hindsight we could have handled some things better." Austin's statement made it clear to all parties that the GSA recognized the need for descendant-community cooperation in salvage excavations. Its office tower would be built, but African Americans would determine the course of research on the remains. The agency hired Blakey to develop a research design, which he produced in consultation with JMA and numerous black scholars. Blakey was also appointed scientific director of a five-year research program on the remains that will take place at Howard University. Sherill D. Wilson, an urban anthropologist and ethnohistorian, calls the sudden involvement of black scholars "very revolutionary." Such scholarship, she says, "is going to set a precedent for what happens to African burial grounds in the future, and how African heritage will be viewed by the public."

Meanwhile, a chastened GSA has also set up a federal advisory committee chaired by Howard Dodson of New York's Schomburg Center for Research in Black Culture that will address plans for reburial of the remains, an African Burial Ground memorial, a burial ground exhibition in the office tower, and a museum of African and African-American History in New York City. State Senator David Patterson's burial ground oversight committee seeks to create a museum that will honor African-American heritage, "a place similar to Ellis Island, something that can attest to Afro-American history." The city Landmarks Preservation Commission has also proposed that the burial ground be designated a city landmark and has requested that it be considered for National Historic Landmark status. These efforts stemmed in part from a massive petition drive spearheaded by Senator Patterson's oversight committee and jazz musician Noel Pointer that yielded more than 100,000 signatures. Among other things, the petition called for the creation of a museum and landmark status for the burial ground.

The burial ground controversy and its attendant publicity have had important repercussions nationwide. "The media exposure has created a larger, national audience for this type of research," says Theresa Singleton, an archaeologist at the Smithsonian Institution who has done pioneering research on African-American sites. "I've been called by dozens of scholars and laypeople, all of them interested in African-American archaeology, all of them curious about why they don't know more about the field. Until recently, even some black scholars considered African-American archaeology a waste of time. That's changed now."

Things have indeed changed. Public curiosity about this country's African-American past has been aroused by the New York experience. And it is probably safe to assume that in the future government and private developers will take a hard look at how to include descendant communities in their salvage excavations, especially when human remains are concerned. "Everyone could have talked more to everyone else," concludes planning staff director Peter Sneed. "There would have been a lot less heartache . . . the GSA has certainly been sensitized to archaeology."

STORIES THE BONES WILL TELL

The skeletal remains and associated artifacts from the African Burial Ground are the only concrete evidence recovered to date of the life of Africans who lived in colonial New York City. The burials were found 16 to 28 feet below street level, many coffins stacked one on top of another—an urban mortuary practice of the period. Although the majority of burials are people of African descent, about seven percent appear to be Europeans. Physical anthropologists determine racial differences by studying characteristic features of the skull, pelvis, and limb bones. The 420 skeletons found at the New York City site represent a fraction of the entire graveyard population. The condition of the remains varies considerably, from good to extremely poor. There were no grave markers or burial maps, and other than wood, coffin nails, and shroud pins, few artifacts associated with the burials were found. "These were not wealthy graves," says Howard University's Michael L. Blakey, the African Burial Ground's scientific director. "The most striking artifacts were the glass beadwork on one woman, and cowrie shells," he says. "Cowrie shells had a symbolic function in West-African funeral practice. They were symbols of the passage in death across the sea and have been variously interpreted as a return to Africa or the afterlife."

In the vast majority of the burials the deceased's head faces west, which prompted journalists to report that the bodies were arranged according to Christian burial practice so that they could sit up and see the rising sun on Judgment Day. But Blakey warns that there was considerable overlap between African and Western burial practices during this period, and it is unclear just how Christianized the Africans were. Blakey points out that a few graves facing east may indicate Moslem burials.

Spencer Turkel, an anthropologist with the Metropolitan Forensic Anthropology Team, estimates two thirds of the remains found at the site were male, and that 40 percent of the sample were children. He says that sex ratios may change after lab study because the hard physical labor demanded by slavery affected the musculoskeletal structure in such a way that some female skeletons look male. The soil in which the bodies were buried was highly acidic and corrosive to human bone, causing further complications for researchers. "One problem we've been having is trying to determine the difference between damage to the bone caused by life experience and that caused by postmortem soil exposure," says Turkel.

He notes that field examination revealed some obvious causes of death—a musket ball lodged in a rib cage, and a case of rickets, a nutritional deficiency. Diagnosis of other causes of death will have to await further study. "The major epidemics of that period were cholera and yellow fever, but here we're dealing with vague written descriptions," he says. "Many of the children would have died from diarrhea, which is a form of malnutrition. Poorly nourished children would also have been susceptible to pneumonia."

Meanwhile, Howard University scientists are contemplating the skeletal sample's research potential. Because seventeenth- and eighteenth-century historical sources tend to dismiss or ignore New York's enslaved Africans, anthropological research becomes all the more important for scholars interpreting what their life was like. "This is a unique opportunity to gain a better understanding of the biology, health, and culture of the first generation of people who would become the African-American people," says Blakey.

The primary focus of the research conducted at Howard will be the social and economic conditions affecting the health of the enslaved Africans. The interdisciplinary team studying the skeletal population will consider questions dealing with demography, epidemiology, nutrition, social history, and cultural transformation. Demographic research will attempt to provide information on the African ethnicity of the sample. "We hope to bring attention to the great variety of cultural groups that were brought over from Africa," says Blakey. "Some of these individuals may have spent time in the West Indies or South America, and we may be able to pick that up," he says. Meanwhile, epidemiologists will study the Africans' adjustment to New York's disease environment. Turkel notes that such bone-scarring diseases as tuberculosis and syphilis were relatively rare in Africa, and finding them in this population would yield interesting data on the community's acculturation to Western diseases. Research on the skeletons may also reveal information about nutrition in the colonial period, while study of mortuary practices at the site will show the extent to which African burial traditions were retained or modified.

Because the sample is large enough to account for human variation, accurate statistical analysis will be possible. And because of the age of the burial population, the sample provides baseline data against which hypotheses about the development of specific pathologies in the African-American population can be tested, such as the relatively high incidence of hypertension in today's black community. The data will also yield information on toxic-element levels in preindustrial America.

The draft research design submitted by Blakey in Fall 1992 notes that earlier studies of African-American skeletal populations tended to be descriptive of physical characteristics such as sex, age, and height rather than focused on biohistorical information such as diet, African nationality, and adaptation to disease. According to Blakey, carefully conceived, large-scale academic research plans for African-American archaeological sites are rare. "The growth of African-American archaeology reflects the randomness of the discoveries resulting from development projects," he says, adding that specialists in African-American archaeology often find themselves responding to "emergency situations," in which burial grounds or other sites are threatened by development projects. Theresa Singleton, an archaeologist at the Smithsonian Institution, says that "quick and dirty" salvage archaeology has compromised historical sites in general, and African-American sites in particular, because "you need time to study sites thoroughly, and most contractors don't have time." She adds that "many contract archaeologists don't know much about African-American archaeology." Blakey notes that contract archaeologists "have not often taken advantage of the rich literature and perspectives of Afro-American scholarship on Afro-Americans. That needs to change. And that's one of the things all the protest in New York brought about."

Spencer Harrington is an associate editor of Archaeology *and has a degree in classics from Columbia University.*

DISCUSSION QUESTIONS

1. What are the responsibilities of archaeologists to descendant communities anxious to reclaim their heritage?
2. Should scholars and students who claim descent from a culture that archaeologists are studying be given primary responsibilities for studying and interpreting those remains?
3. How can archaeologists show sensitivity to the religious beliefs of descendant communities without compromising their own scientific principles?
4. Conflicts between heritage conservation and development (in this case, with racist overtones) are increasingly common everywhere in the world. What options exist in these situations?
5. Consider the multiple roles and responsibilities of archaeological contractors.
6. What are the lessons for all parties that should be taken from this example?
7. What opportunities exist for minority group members to train in and practice archaeology in the United States? Ask a black or Native American archaeologist why she or he became an archaeologist and what the training experience was like. (If you can't locate someone to interview, think about why that is the case and try to imagine what their experience would be.)

FURTHER RESEARCH

The full reference for a detailed report by the contractors, Howard University and John Milner Associates, is included under "Further Reading" in *Archaeology*, March/April 1993: 73, along with references to current accounts of the excavation and surrounding controversies in New York newspapers.

See also: Joe Watkins et al., "Accountability: Responsibilities of Archaeologists to Other Interest Groups," in *Ethics in American Archaeology*, eds. Mark J. Lynott and Alison Wylie (Washington D.C.: Society for American Archaeology, 1995), 33–37.

PART SIX
PROFESSIONAL BEHAVIOR

The three short essays in this section zero in on the practices and training of professional archaeologists. The authors take a direct look at how the profession contributes to some of the problems addressed in the previous sections, focusing on U.S. graduate programs and academic value systems, behavior in the field, and the too-frequent failure to publish full reports on field research.

CHAPTER TWENTY-ONE
THE ARROGANT ARCHAEOLOGIST
by Brian Fagan

Enforcement of antiquities protection laws in the United States is making a dent, but only a small one. The solution to the looting problem lies in changing public perceptions about collecting antiquities. The responsibility for bringing about that huge change lies with professional archaeologists—but we may be the greatest offenders, for we "have not made conservation, ethics, and public education the core of our archaeological enterprise."

For a moment I saw red, felt sheer blinding fury. Controlling myself with an effort, I gazed in disgust and horror at the ravaged shell midden. I was hiking for pleasure along the southern California coast and looting was far from my mind. Memories of the Slack Farm affair came vividly to mind, that notorious looting event that left a late prehistoric site in Kentucky looking like a scarred battleground (see Chapter 2, "Black Day at Slack Farm"). Every time I come across instances of pot-hunting, I find them harder to rationalize, and even harder to understand. Why do people do this? For money? To satisfy a lust to own a piece of the past? Is it sheer ignorance about archaeology and the importance of the past? Or are they seeking to emulate the fictional adventures of Indiana Jones? What makes me even madder is that few people seem to care that the past is vanishing before our eyes. Many of my nonprofessional friends just shrug and change the subject. You cannot entirely blame them: most would not know an archaeological site if it was right under their feet. Even worse, some of my archaeological friends just shrug, and that's what makes me maddest of all.

John Neary (see Chapter 5, "Project Sting,") tells us that recent undercover operations have put a chill on some collecting activity in the Southwest. Clearly, these tactics, expensive as they are, work well and should be expanded. Looting statistics are daunting. According to Sherry Hutt, Elwood Jones, and Martin McAllister, authors of *Archaeological Resource Protection* (Washington, DC: Preservation Press, 1992), more than one-third of the known sites in the Four Corners region have been damaged by looters. Of the 1,720 violations reported in Park Service statistics for 1985 through 1987, only about 11 percent resulted in arrests or citations, and there were only 94 convictions.

If there is a solution to the looting problem, it is changing public attitudes toward the collecting of antiquities. This will take years, and will require a full-time commitment by hundreds, if not thousands, of professional archaeologists, not only in this country, but all over the world. It is our responsibility and cannot be left to teachers and bureaucrats. Yet, sadly, in many ways we are the greatest offenders. Our professional organizations condemn looting—they do so in uncompromising terms—but we have not made conservation, ethics, and public education the core of our archaeological enterprise.

Archaeologists live within a hierarchical value system that considers research, excavation, new discoveries, and publication the pinnacle of achievement. Anything else, for all their talk to the contrary, is secondary to these enterprises. Almost all doctoral programs in archaeology emphasize basic research. They produce narrowly focused academic researchers, future generations of professors who will themselves, in turn, train even more specialized archaeologists. The emphasis is often on high-profile research, where the chances of spectacular discoveries are higher than average, the potential for funding is considered promising, and the fieldwork will bring prestige, visibility, and, pinnacle of academic pinnacles, perhaps even a story in *The New York Times*. This is the kind of enterprise beloved of many academic deans and department heads, research that brings luster and financial resources to an institution. I am irresistibly reminded of the expedition mentality that drove so much late nineteenth-century archaeology—the University of Pennsylvania's research at Nippur in Mesopotamia is a classic example. It worked at Nippur, indeed at Ur, in an archaeological world where there were so few professionals. Today, academic archaeology is big business, turning out hundreds of Ph.D. students a year, yet the old mentality and values drive the field. Why do we persist in producing more doctoral students in specialized fields that are already overcrowded when there is so much urgent work to be done on the global threat to the past? I suspect we do because it is, well, sexier to hire a specialist in Oldowan technology or Inka urbanism than in the impact of tourism on the archaeological record.

This same skewed value system pays lip service to teaching, conservation and resource management, and the administering of the archaeological record. But, when push comes to shove, these subjects take a back seat to research. Yes, much academic research is carried out under the rubric of cultural resource management—survey, excavation, and mitigation—aimed at preserving or recording sites before they vanish under bulldozers. But very often academic research, especially excavation, proceeds without consideration of conservation issues or site management whatsoever. In fact, many academics are woefully ignorant of the extent of the damage to the archaeological record, forgetting that their own annual digs are also eroding the same human archives, often at breakneck speed. How many academics pause to think about conserving a site before they dig it? Surprisingly few . . . .

Very few archaeology graduate programs anywhere expose their students to issues of conservation, ethics, and basic archaeological values—unless they are curricula specifically addressing cultural resource management. Out of curiosity, I telephoned a random selection of archaeology graduate advisers at major universities around the country and asked them what ethics and conservation courses were taught to graduate students. Almost invariably, these topics were sidelines. "Oh, we talk about reburial in one lecture," one well-known archaeologist told me in a tired voice. "But it's very political. The Ph.D. is, after all, a research degree." What arrogant nonsense!

The looting problem is not going away. The Park Service alone reports a 40 percent increase in violations over the past few years, and you can be sure that its statistics are just the tip of the iceberg. At the same time, one learns that at least 100 archaeologists with Ph.D.s in Maya archaeology are looking for permanent employment. Unemployed classical archaeologists could almost form a professional society. These people may be excellent scholars, but they are not the kind of archaeologists we need in such large numbers today. We need people who will devote prestigious careers to conservation, to research into the fundamental problems confronting the archaeological record. Without such research, we are, both government and academics, fumbling in the dark.

Basic research is important to the vitality of our discipline. But do we need so many, ever more trivial studies when fundamental, admittedly less glamorous issues need our attention? Fascinating opportunities await the ambitious scholar, fundamental research as important, if not more so, than much of the basic inquiry that fills our journals. What is the psychology of collecting? What is it that impels people to transform their fascination with the past into a lust to own it? The last definitive work on this subject was done, I believe, in the 1920s. What do we know about the psychology and culture of professional pothunters and looters? Can such research help us develop tactics for combating looting? What about archaeological tourism? What are the effects of tens of thousands of visitors on the rich archaeological record of, say, Britain, Egypt, or Mexico? What strategies are archaeologists developing in collaboration with governments everywhere to minimize the impact on the finite archaeological record? I know of no Ph.D. program in this country that places a high priority on research of this type. Everything is theory, fieldwork, and publication. About the only organization concerned with these issues on a global basis is the Getty Conservation Institute. The Getty's efforts are invaluable, as are those of other international organizations, and of the Archaeological Conservancy closer to home.

I have been told by colleagues that research into such questions is "unimportant" or "marginal." What utter nonsense in this day and age, when the archaeological record evaporates around us daily. Surely we must now take a close look at our own value systems and priorities, at archaeological ethics and curricula. How do we, as professional scholars and practitioners of a noble art, intend to insure its survival for our grandchildren to enjoy?

Yes, this is a column written in the heat of anger, soon after walking over looters' trenches. But this anger will be channeled into a closer look at my own teaching of graduates and undergraduates, and into more columns that look at the ethical issues of archaeology and at conservation. After all, we cannot do much to steer the public's fascination with the past into benign and nondestructive directions unless we clean up our own act. Our own comfortable, sometimes arrogant attitude is much divorced from reality. It is time we took stock. We owe it to our grandchildren, if nothing else.

Brian Fagan teaches archaeology at the University of California, Santa Barbara. He is a well-known author of archaeology textbooks and a contributing editor for Archaeology.

DISCUSSION QUESTIONS

1. What external values contribute to the hierarchical value system in archaeology described by Fagan?
2. In what ways is contemporary academic archaeology a big business?
3. How could U.S. graduate (and undergraduate) programs do a better job of addressing the issues Fagan raises?
4. What career opportunities could be developed by and for archaeologists whose training includes or focuses on conservation and heritage management?
5. How could these less glamorous issues be made more glamorous?

6. What is the psychology of collecting?* How could research in this field help develop tactics for combating looting?
7. What is the impact of tourism on the archaeological record? (For one example, see Lynn A. Meisch, "Machu Picchu: Conserving an Inca Treasure," *Archaeology*, Nov/Dec 1985: 18–25.)
8. What strategies are archaeologists developing with governments to minimize the impact of tourism on the archaeological record?**

---

*For recent studies on this question, see John Elsner and Roger Cardinal, eds., *The Cultures of Collecting* (London: Reaktion Books, 1994); and Werner Muensterberger, *Collecting, An Unruly Passion: Psychological Perspectives* (Princeton: Princeton University Press, 1994).

**See K. Anne Pyburn and Richard R. Wilk, "Responsible Archaeology Is Applied Anthropology," in *Ethics in American Archaeology*, eds. Mark J. Lynott and Alison Wylie (Washington, D.C.: Society for American Archaeology, 1995), 71–76.

CHAPTER TWENTY-TWO
THE GRINGO STIGMA
by Randall H. McGuire

The local people in Trincheras, Mexico assumed the American archae-
ologists were looking for gold—and probably finding it in spite of their
denials. Why would the foreigners spend so much time and money
collecting the broken pieces of pottery and stones they claimed to be
looking for? McGuire thinks the locals' conviction that archaeologists
are treasure hunters stems, not from their ignorance of archaeology, but
from their historical experience of foreigners.

Trincheras, Mexico—People here have trouble understanding why archaeologists spend so much time and money collecting potsherds and pieces of stone. Many assume that we are looking for gold. Our protestations commonly fall on deaf ears: everyone knows that if we were recovering great treasures we wouldn't be foolish enough to admit it. I was, therefore, not surprised when a small boy confronted me on the main street of this sleepy village in the northwestern state of Sonora. "Are you from the United States?" he asked. "Yes," I replied. "Are you looking for gold and silver?" I shook my head and began to explain what archaeologists do. Before I could finish he dashed off to join his friends, obviously unconvinced.

Trincheras lies in the shadow of Cerro de Trincheras, a hill on which Native Americans built a terraced village about 500 years ago. My Mexican colleague, Maria Elisa Villalpando, and I came with support from the National Geographic Society to map and record the site. For seven weeks we studied the ancient village while the modern townspeople studied us.

During our first evening in town a shopkeeper told us about a rumored treasure in the hill. According to one account, the first rays of the morning sun fell on a cave filled with gold and silver. No one had yet found the cave because it moved each morning as the rising sun shifted position on the horizon. Another story described a bedrock throne within the hill on which rested a nugget of gold. To many of the townspeople, our presence was an affirmation of these tales. We were here to tear the hill apart, stone by stone, and spirit the gold back to the United States.

The stories were amusing, but the suspicions made us uneasy. During the first week of our project we found numerous rock piles at the site. Thinking they were remnants of railroad construction in the 1940s, we asked a local farmer about them. Two days later, one of the piles had been dug up. After that, we were guarded in our discussions of what we were finding. No doubt our reserve added to people's suspicions. During the second week we gave a talk in the town hall to explain what we were doing. The hundred or so people who came seemed convinced that we were not treasure hunters. They chuckled at the stories of treasure in the hill. But the young boy who confronted me in the street a few days later, like many others, still believed that we had come to take away something of great value. We came to realize that their conviction sprang not from ignorance of archaeology, but from their own experience and history.

Vast placer deposits lie about 12 miles south of Trincheras. These deposits played out a hundred years ago, but a few flakes and an occasional nugget can still be found. Wizened gold diggers from the United States sometimes stop in Trincheras for gas before heading off for these deposits. Treasure hunting here has not always been so benign. In 1857 Henry Crabb, a former Know-Nothing candidate for the U.S. Senate, led a private army of 100 men across the border. Crabb saw another Texas in the making, with himself as Stephen F. Austin. Sonoran troops met this bobtail army with drawn sabers and musket fire. Crabb took refuge in the old mission church at Caborca. After a seven day siege, the Mexicans produced a cannon and threatened to blow the doors off the sanctuary. The Americans surrendered, were tried, found guilty, marched out into the desert, and shot. The story of Crabb's raid is well-known to the people of Trincheras. The nearest major commercial center is Caborca Heroica, heroic because of Crabb's defeat.

After seven weeks of work we had produced a detailed map of the ancient village, and we knew that the people who had once lived there had been maize farmers and shell jewelry makers. We never found the cave filled with gold and silver, nor the stone throne with the gold nugget. Neither did we convince the people of Trincheras that we were not treasure hunters. That, after all, is what gringos do.

Randall H. McGuire is an associate professor in the department of anthropology at the State University of New York at Binghamton.

DISCUSSION QUESTIONS

1. What do the local people in areas where you have done fieldwork think you are looking for? Why? How do you know?
2. How do their perceptions affect the project's work and behavior? How do they affect the discipline as a whole?
3. Has your project done anything to inform the locals about your work? What options are available for doing so? What are the obstacles?
4. Were local leaders consulted and asked for input before the project began?
5. What benefits could follow from such consultation? What costs? Are members of your project familiar with the recent history of the area? How might that history affect interactions between project members and local people?

CHAPTER TWENTY-THREE
ARCHAEOLOGY'S
DIRTY SECRET
by Brian Fagan

The author was taught that publishing one's research before new field projects are undertaken is a sacred principle of archaeology. He finds it ironic that, in an academic culture in which publication is deemed the most noble of activities, "most archaeologists prefer to keep on digging." Preliminary reports and short articles, often derived from conference papers, and often published repeatedly in only slightly differing versions, have, too often, replaced definitive reports on sites, artifacts, and survey work. Nonarchaeological pressures may receive some of the blame, but ultimately it is up to archaeologists to meet their fundamental responsibility for publishing their research.

Some years ago, I attended a retirement party for a distinguished colleague at a prominent midwestern university. Several generations of former students were on hand to praise his many seasons of fieldwork at home and abroad. But they were tactful not to mention one problem with their beloved mentor's career: only one of his excavations had ever been published in full. Alas, the professor has now passed on, leaving behind nothing but sketchy field notes and a museum storeroom full of inadequately labeled artifacts. Even in retirement he could not find the time to publish his fieldwork. In fact he was still digging right up to the end. The loss to science is incalculable.

I was brought up to believe that publishing one's research was a sacred principle of archaeology, a task to be completed before new excavations were begun. The great British Egyptologist Flinders

Petrie was an early advocate of prompt and full publication. His reports are verbose and far from complete by modern standards, but at least they provide a body of basic information with which to work. Mortimer Wheeler was also careful to publish his excavations in full. My mentors did not always practice what they preached, but they taught us that prompt and full publication was a fundamental responsibility for any archaeologist who ventures into the field. The archaeological world has changed since Wheeler's day. A generation ago most site reports were the work of a single scholar. Today even a modest dig can involve a team of specialists and a quantity of data that may take years to study and write up. Ironically, in an academic culture that considers publication the most desirable of all scholarly activities, most archaeologists prefer to keep on digging.

The common forum for presenting field data is the academic conference, where 20-minute papers summarize new work. In recent years, publishers have printed volume after volume of such papers, often grouped under a general title, with little editorial coherence. Invariably, conference papers give a nod to current theoretical debates, present some limited original data, and end with a brief synthesis noting how the new work advances research in a particular subject area. Often, the same paper appears in several places, recast slightly to reflect a different audience or academic emphasis. In an academic world where jobs are scarce and publication of any kind is seen as the road to employment, such bibliography-padding has become commonplace, if not endemic. In one's later career the pressure to publish such papers to obtain tenure and regular promotions continues unabated. Too often definitive reports on sites, artifacts, or survey work never appear.

I know of numerous preliminary reports published a generation ago that are still the only source of basic information on excavations of first-rate importance. There are major Lower Paleolithic sites in sub-Saharan Africa excavated in the 1950s and 1960s that are still accessible only from such reports. The same can be said for many important North American and Mesoamerican excavations of the 1970s. Much of the evidence for early agriculture in Europe and the Near East is only available in the periodical literature. Kathleen

Kenyon's famous excavations at Jericho are still incompletely published. Some classical excavations have been underway for decades, with no sign that digging will stop and long-term publication begin. Some guilty parties argue that laboratory work must come first and that the whole process takes longer than it did a generation ago. But if you look closely you will find the same people hard at work in the field each year, digging up yet another site.

Clearly an overwhelming case can be made for less excavation and more analysis of previous work. Unfortunately, our scholarly culture rewards people for new and original research, sometimes defined in the narrowest terms as participation in an active fieldwork program. Grant-giving agencies contribute to the problem by funding field research while rarely giving monies for laboratory analysis or publication. Neither is a terribly sexy pursuit in a world in which museums and universities thrive on headline-catching discoveries, and, to quote a recent University of California staff document, "productive faculty publishing in refereed journals." The problem is further compounded by the exigencies of cultural resource management or salvage archaeology, whose requirements for prompt reporting result for the most part in factual accounts with limited, if not restricted, distribution. A researcher can spend days, sometimes months, tracking down what is technically published information. Meanwhile, definitive archaeological monographs, such as those on the Maya city of Tikal that appear at regular intervals, are becoming a rarity. Few outlets remain for such valuable studies. Economic realities make it ever harder for even the best endowed academic presses to produce such monographs.

Surprisingly, there is little, if any, academic discussion of these issues. Perusing the programs of several major conferences, I see no panel sessions on this issue, nor on alternative means of disseminating archaeological data. Hershel Shanks, editor of *Biblical Archaeology Review*, calls the crisis "archaeology's dirty secret." In a recent editorial, he recommended the creation of a new profession: archaeology editor/writer, "specialists who know how to publish reports."

The obligation to publish basic research is a fundamental part of archaeological ethics; some would say it is the most fundamental. It is enshrined in the Archaeological Institute of America's recently adopted Code of Professional Standards: "Archaeologists should make public the results of their research in a timely fashion, making evidence available to others if publication is not accomplished within a reasonable time. All research projects should contain specific plans for conservation, preservation, and publication from the very outset, and funds should be secured for such purposes."

Desktop publishing, CD-ROMs, and other electronic media offer fascinating opportunities for publication, and for distribution of research results and data over the Internet and other such channels. Electronics offer staggering possibilities for wide distribution of highly specialized, peer-reviewed monographs and reports. Soon, researchers will have interactive access to their colleagues' and predecessors' artifact data bases. Such access will make new demands on archaeologists to curate and analyze their data promptly. The demands of the electronic forum will make it harder to duck the responsibility of preparing one's data for scholarly use and scrutiny. In many cases, "publication" will consist of meticulously organized data bases, including graphics. The compiling of such data bases raises fascinating implications for future financing of archaeological projects. Grant-giving agencies will have to bow to the new reality and finance such far-from-spectacular activities, while cutting back on funding for more excavations.

Archaeologists have a clear obligation to publish their research promptly, and in full. After all, ours is the only science that "murders its informants," as American archaeologist Kent Flannery once put it. If we were to devote as much time to publishing as we do to excavating, we would not be accused, with some justification, of being a self-serving, special interest group that keeps its finds to itself. Some of those who make such accusations are now picking up on the publishing problem and arguing that by not producing final reports we are effectively looters ourselves. Writing final reports and monographs is far from glamorous work. But as Mortimer Wheeler and others pointed out many years ago, only the archaeologist who did the work and led the research team can write the final and definitive report that records exactly what was found and what it means. We are witnessing a sea change in the way archaeologists go about business.

I do not agree with Hershel Shanks that the solution lies in specialist report writers. It lies in archaeologists living up to their fundamental responsibilities. Fortunately, creative solutions await those bold enough to seize them.

Brian Fagan teaches archaeology at the University of California, Santa Barbara. He is a well-known author of archaeology textbooks and a contributing editor for Archaeology.

DISCUSSION QUESTIONS

1. What happens to the records and finds from a field project when the director retires or dies without publishing them?
2. Why do so many contemporary archaeologists undertake new field projects before publishing the results of an earlier project? Should something be done to prevent this practice? If so, what options exist?
3. Is there something wrong with publishing slight variations on the same paper in different places? What encourages the practice?
4. Why does it take so long to produce final reports on field projects? What could be done to improve the speed of such publications?
5. Is some form of publication in the electronic media a viable option to traditional publishing of archaeological field reports?
6. What are the expenses of publication, and who pays for the actual costs of publishing field reports?
7. Who buys field reports?
8. What are the different costs and issues of Cultural Resources Management and academic publishing?
9. Would the creation of a new category of professional, the report writer suggested by Shanks,* be a useful addition? Who would pay for the services of such professionals?
10. Given the already limited funding available for archaeological research, would you advocate that funding agencies direct more funds to publication and less to fieldwork?

---

*See: Hershel Shanks, "Archaeology's Dirty Secret," *Biblical Archaeology Review* 20 (Sept/Oct 1994): 63–64, 79.

11. What effect on the public perception of archaeology does lack of attention to publishing fieldwork have?
12. What are the problems faced, by the individuals directly involved and by the discipline as a whole, when people not originally part of a field project undertake publication of materials from an older excavation?
13. What do you think of the suggestion that unpublished materials from old excavations should be assigned as Ph.D. dissertation topics?
14. Do archaeologists give high priority to publishing articles aimed at a lay audience? Why or why not? Should they give it high priority?

APPENDIX A
STATEMENTS ON ARCHAEOLOGICAL ETHICS FROM PROFESSIONAL ORGANIZATIONS

THE SOCIETY OF PROFESSIONAL ARCHEOLOGISTS CODE OF ETHICS
(1995)

Archeology is a profession, and the privilege of professional practice requires professional morality and professional responsibility, as well as professional competence, on the part of each practitioner.

I. The Archeologist's Responsibility to the Public

  1.1 An archeologist shall:

    (a) Recognize a commitment to represent archeology and its research results to the public in a responsible manner;

    (b) Actively support conservation of the archeological resource base;

    (c) Be sensitive to, and respect the legitimate concerns of, groups whose culture histories are the subjects of archeological investigations;

    (d) Avoid and discourage exaggerated, misleading, or unwarranted statements about archeological matters that might induce others to engage in unethical or illegal activity;

    (e) Support and comply with the terms of the UNESCO Convention on the means of prohibiting and preventing the illicit import, export, and transfer of ownership of cultural property, as adopted by the General Conference, 14 November 1970, Paris.

  1.2 An archeologist shall not:

    (a) Engage in any illegal or unethical conduct involving archeological matters or knowingly permit the use of his/her name in support of any illegal or unethical activity involving archeological matters;

(b) Give a professional opinion, make a public report, or give legal testimony involving archeological matters without being as thoroughly informed as might reasonably be expected;

(c) Engage in conduct involving dishonesty, fraud, deceit or misrepresentation about archeological matters;

(d) Undertake any research that affects the archeological resource base for which she/he is not qualified.

II. The Archeologist's Responsibility to Colleagues, Employees, and Students

2.1 An archeologist shall:

(a) Give appropriate credit for work done by others;

(b) Stay informed and knowledgeable about developments in her/his field or fields of specialization;

(c) Accurately, and without undue delay, prepare and properly disseminate a description of research done and its results;

(d) Communicate and cooperate with colleagues having common professional interests;

(e) Give due respect to colleagues' interests in, and rights to, information about sites, areas, collections, or data where there is a mutual active or potentially active research concern;

(f) Know and comply with all federal, state, and local laws, ordinances, and regulations applicable to her/his archeological research and activities;

(g) Report knowledge of violations of this Code to proper authorities;

(h) Honor and comply with the spirit and letter of SOPA's Disciplinary Procedures.

2.2 An archeologist shall not:

(a) Falsely or maliciously attempt to injure the reputation of another archeologist;

(b) Commit plagiarism in oral or written communication;

(c) Undertake research that affects the archeological resource base unless reasonably prompt, appropriate analysis and reporting can be expected;

(d) Refuse a reasonable request from a qualified colleague for research data;

(e) Submit a false or misleading application for accreditation by or membership in the Society of Professional Archeologists.

III. The Archeologist's Responsibility to Employers and Clients

3.1 An archeologist shall:

(a) Respect the interests of her/his employer or client, so far as is consistent with the public welfare and this Code and Standards;

(b) Refuse to comply with any request or demand of an employer or client which conflicts with the Code and Standards;

(c) Recommend to employers or clients the employment of other archeologists or other expert consultants upon encountering archeological problems beyond her/his own competence;

(d) Exercise reasonable care to prevent her/his employees, colleagues, associates and others whose services are utilized by her/him from revealing or using confidential information. Confidential information means information of a nonarcheological nature gained in the course of employment which the employer or client has requested be held inviolate, or the disclosure of which would be embarrassing or would be likely to be detrimental to the employer or client. Information ceases to be confidential when the employer or client so indicates or when such information becomes publicly known.

3.2 An archeologist shall not:

    (a) Reveal confidential information, unless required by law;

    (b) Use confidential information to the disadvantage of the client or employer;

    (c) Use confidential information for the advantage of herself/himself or a third person, unless the client consents after full disclosure;

    (d) Accept compensation or anything of value for recommending the employment of another archeologist or other person, unless such compensation or thing of value is fully disclosed to the potential employer or client;

    (e) Recommend or participate in any research which does not comply with the requirements of the Standards of Research Performance.

Standards of Research Performance

The research archeologist has a responsibility to attempt to design and conduct projects that will add to our understanding of past cultures and/or that will develop better theories, methods, or techniques for interpreting the archeological record, while causing minimal attrition of the archeological resource base. In the conduct of a research project, the following minimum standards should be followed:

I. The archeologist has a responsibility to prepare adequately for any research project, whether or not in the field. The archeologist must:

    1.1 Assess the adequacy of her/his qualifications for the demands of the project, and minimize inadequacies by acquiring additional expertise, by bringing in associates with the needed qualifications, or by modifying the scope of the project.

    1.2 Inform herself/himself of relevant previous research.

    1.3 Develop a scientific plan of research which specifies the objectives of the project, takes into account previous relevant research, employs a suitable methodology, and provides for economical use of the resource base (whether such base consists of an excavation site or of specimens) consistent with the objectives of the project.

    1.4 Ensure the availability of adequate and competent staff and support facilities to carry the project to completion, and of adequate curatorial facilities for specimens and records.

1.5 Comply with all legal requirements, including, without limitation, obtaining all necessary governmental permits and necessary permission from landowners or other persons.

1.6 Determine whether the project is likely to interfere with the program or projects of other scholars and, if there is such a likelihood, initiate negotiations to minimize such interference.

II. In conducting research, the archeologist must follow her/his scientific plan of research, except to the extent that unforeseen circumstances warrant its modification.

III. Procedures for field survey or excavation must meet the following minimal standards:

3.1 If specimens are collected, a system for identifying and recording their proveniences must be maintained.

3.2 Uncollected entities such as environmental or cultural features, depositional strata, and the like, must be fully and accurately recorded by appropriate means, and their location recorded.

3.3 The methods employed in data collection must be fully and accurately described. Significant stratigraphic and/or associational relationships among artifacts, other specimens, and cultural and environmental features must also be fully and accurately recorded.

3.4 All records should be intelligible to other archeologists. If terms lacking commonly held referents are used, they should be clearly defined,

3.5 Insofar as possible, the interests of other researchers should be considered. For example, upper levels of a site should be scientifically excavated and recorded whenever feasible, even if the focus of the project is on underlying levels.

IV. During accessioning, analysis, and storage of specimens and records in the laboratory, the archeologist must take precautions to ensure that correlations between the specimens and the field records are maintained, so that provenience contextual relationships and the like are not confused or obscured.

V. Specimens and research records resulting from a project must be deposited at an institution with permanent curatorial facilities, unless otherwise required by law.

VI. The archeologist has responsibility for appropriate dissemination of the results of her/his research to the appropriate constituencies with reasonable dispatch.

6.1 Results reviewed as significant contributions to substantive knowledge of the past or to advancements in theory, method or technique should be disseminated to colleagues and other interested persons by appropriate means such as publications, reports at professional meetings, or letters to colleagues.

6.2 Requests from qualified colleagues for information on research results directly should be honored, if consistent with the researcher's prior rights to publication and with her/his other professional responsibilities.

6.3 Failure to complete a full scholarly report within 10 years after completion of a field project shall be construed as a waiver of an archeologist's right of primacy with respect to analysis and publication of the data. Upon expiration of such 10-year period, or at such earlier time as the archeologist shall determine not to publish the results, such data should be made fully accessible to other archeologists for analysis and publication.

6.4 While contractual obligations in reporting must be respected, archeologists should not enter into a contract which prohibits the archeologist from including her or his own interpretations or conclusions in the contractual reports, or from a continuing right to use the data after completion of the project.

6.5 Archeologists have an obligation to accede to reasonable requests for information from the news media.

Institutional Standards

Archeological research involving collection of original field data and/or acquisition of specimens requires institutional facilities and support services for its successful conduct, and for proper permanent maintenance of the resulting collections and records.

A full-scale archeological field project will require the following facilities and services, normally furnished by or through an institution:

(1) Office space and furniture.

(2) Laboratory space, furniture, and equipment for analysis of specimens and data.

(3) Special facilities such as a darkroom, drafting facilities, conservation laboratory, etc.

(4) Permanent allocation of space, facilities, and equipment for proper maintenance of collections and records equivalent to that specified in the standards of the Association of Systematic Collections.

(5) Field equipment such as vehicles, surveying instruments, etc.

(6) A research library.

(7) Administrative and fiscal control services.

(8) A security system.

(9) Technical specialists such as photographers, curators, conservators, etc.

(10) Publication services.

All the foregoing facilities and services must be adequate to the scope of the project.

Not all archeological research will require all the foregoing facilities and services, but a full-scale field project will. Likewise, all institutions engaging in archeological research will not necessarily require or be able to furnish all such facilities and services from their own resources. Institutions lacking certain facilities or services should arrange for them through cooperative agreements with other institutions.

Guidelines and Standards for Academic Archeological Field Schools

In 1974, the Society of American Archeology passed the following resolution:

Whereas each archeological site contains evidence of specific human activities and is therefore a unique source of data about past sociocultural behavior, no site can be written off in advance as unimportant or expendable. No site deserves less than professional excavation, analysis and publication, and whereas the training of students in archeological skills is an important part of an anthropological curriculum, and whereas such training is likely to be grossly inadequate and misleading to the student if it is not given in the context of a serious research commitment on the part of the instructor to the archeological resources in question.

Therefore be it resolved that the practice of excavating or collecting from archeological sites solely or primarily for "teaching" purposes is contrary to the provision against indiscriminate excavation of archeological sites contained in Article 1, Section 2 of the by-laws of the Society for American Archaeology. Such activities are to be deplored, whether conducted by anthropologists who are not adequately trained in archeological field techniques, or by trained archeologists who do not have continuing research interest in the resources in question.

Be it further resolved that such activities are unethical as defined in Article III, Section 4 of the by-laws of the Society for American Archaeology and by the guidelines of the ethics committee of the American Anthropological Association, and that members of these organizations who engage in such practices are subject to appropriate sanctions.

In accordance with these principles, and by virtue of its role in providing guidance and standards for the performance of archeological research, the Society of Professional Archeologists recommends that an academic archeological field school meet the following minimal criteria:

A. Purposes.
> 1. The primary objective of an academic field school must be the training of students; explicitly, that the field school give the initial field experience required as the first step in student career progress in her/his development as a professional (in accordance with SOPA standards) archeologist. Other goals (such as employment, contract work or salvage or threatened resources) must be secondary.

2. The field program and recovered data must be part of an explicitly designed research or cultural resource management program, which includes evidence of conservation of resources, curation, and publication of results.

3. The field program and curriculum design should include an explicit, detailed schedule of instruction and supervision, evidence of adequate facilities (see E.I.), and provision for early analysis and reporting of data generated by the program. This should be provided to all participants.

B. Personnel.

1. The Director of the field program should meet SOPA qualifications in field research, and have dominant responsibility for direct supervision in the field and in the laboratory.

2. Assistant(s)/Supervisor(s) must be qualified by completion of at least one field school which meets these guidelines or by an equivalent combination of field and laboratory experience.

3. Other specialized instructors and lectures should be used as appropriate.

C. Operational procedure should include:

1. Prefatory formal lectures on field excavation and survey observations, excavation procedures and hazards (stratigraphy, arbitrary versus "natural" levels, intrusions, reuse or rebuilding of structures), descriptive note writing, interpreting cross sections, survey, camp and dig logistics, administration, etc. Films, slides, models, and other techniques should be used as available and appropriate. At least 12 hours of lecture instruction should be devoted to this introduction prior to actual field excavation and survey.

2. Formal small group field instruction in topographic and plane table mapping, including nomenclature and terms by an experienced instructor who should be a professional topographer or an archeologist skilled in topographic mapping.

3. Formal small group field instruction by a photographer skilled in archeological field photographic techniques and problems (lighting, angles, wide angle lens, closeup, etc.).

4. Formal lectures in field or laboratory including but not limited to research plan, long-range goals, culture(s) being investigated, field problems, curation and reporting plans, etc.

5. Formal laboratory instructions and supervision in cleaning, labeling, sorting, identification of artifacts, and limited flotation exercises, mammal bone identification, etc., as appropriate. Field supervisors to alternate as lab supervisors, preferably scheduled so that field personnel process their own field data.

6. Some time devoted to reconnaissance level survey, not only to instruct in finding and recording data but also for instruction in the use of such data for defining archeological problems.

D. Field procedures/structures.

1. All students should be instructed in the use of all tools, equipment, and vehicles (as qualified), rotating as assistants with photography, grid mapping, provenience control, sketching, sampling of soils, and other specialized functions. All steps in procedures and evaluation of appropriate techniques should be repeatedly explained.

2. All students should be required to keep daily systematic notes as parts of the permanent record. All notes and records must be reviewed and critiqued daily by supervisors. Additional notebooks, photo records, etc., shall be maintained as necessary, under systematic supervision.

3. All field procedures should be guided by the concept of data and record responsibility as an integrated component of professional fieldwork, with responsibility and authority for field decisions and record keeping clearly defined.

4. All students should have access to type collections and relevant library materials (including maps, photographs, site reports and literature on the archeology and environment relevant to the fieldwork). In most cases, this will require maintenance of such resources in both field and laboratory.

E. Sponsor.

1. The institution sponsoring the field school must, by virtue of available resources, meet the minimal SOPA specifications for institutional support, including appropriate space for laboratory work, for storage, appropriate accessioning and cataloging procedures, adequate curation, and support for publication/distribution of the research results.

2. The institution sponsoring the field school must provide for the safety and health of participants.

F. A ratio of six to ten students per supervisor is optimal.

THE ARCHAEOLOGICAL INSTITUTE OF AMERICA
CODE OF ETHICS
(1990)

The Archaeological Institute of America is dedicated to the greater understanding of archaeology, to the protection and preservation of the world's archaeological resources and the information they contain, and to the encouragement and support of archaeological research and publication.

In accordance with these principles, members of the AIA should:

1. Seek to ensure that the exploration of archaeological sites be conducted according to the highest standards under the direct supervision of qualified personnel, and that the results of such research be made public;
2. Refuse to participate in the illegal trade in antiquities derived from excavation in any country after December 30, 1970, when the AIA Council endorsed the UNESCO Convention on cultural Property, and refrain from activities that enhance the commercial value of such objects;
3. Inform appropriate authorities of threats to, or plunder of archaeological sites, and illegal import of export of archaeological material.

Archaeological Institute of America
Code of Professional Standards Preamble

This Code applies to those members of the AIA who play an active, professional role in the recovery, care, study, or publication of archaeological material, including cultural resources located under water. Within the Institute they enjoy the privileges of organizing sessions and submitting papers for the Annual Meetings, of lecturing to local societies, participating in the AIA committees that shape and direct the discipline, participating in the placement service, and of being listed in the *Directory of Professionals in Archaeology.*

Along with those privileges come special responsibilities. Our members should inform themselves about and abide by the laws of the countries in which they live and work. They should treat others at home and in the field with respect and sensitivity. As primary stewards of the archaeological record, they should work actively to preserve that record in all its dimensions and for the long term; and they should give due consideration to the interests of others, both colleagues and the lay public, who are affected by the research.

The AIA recognizes that archaeology is a discipline dealing, in all its aspects, with the human condition, and that archaeological research must often balance competing ethical principles. This Code of Professional Standards does not seek to legislate all aspects of professional behavior, and it realizes the conflicts embedded in many of the issues addressed. The Code sets forth three broad areas of responsibility and provides examples of the kinds of considerations called for by each. It aims to encourage all professional archaeologists to keep ethical considerations in mind as they plan and conduct research.

ARCHAEOLOGICAL ETHICS

I. RESPONSIBILITIES TO THE ARCHAEOLOGICAL RECORD

Professional archaeologists incur responsibilities to the archaeological record—the physical remains and all the associated information about those remains, including those located under water.

1. Professional archaeologists should adhere to the Guidelines of the AIA general Code of Ethics concerning illegal antiquities in their research and publications.
2. The purposes and consequences of all archaeological research should be carefully considered before the beginning of work. Approaches and methods should be chosen that require a minimum of damage to the archaeological record. Although excavation is sometimes the appropriate means of research, archaeological survey, study of previously excavated material, and other means should be considered before resort is made to excavation.
3. The recovery and study of archaeological material from all periods should be carried out only under the supervision of qualified personnel.
4. Archaeologists should anticipate and provide for adequate and accessible long-term storage and curatorial facilities for all archaeological materials, records, and archives.
5. Archaeologists should make public the results of their research in a timely fashion, making evidence available to others if publication is not accomplished within a reasonable time.
6. All research projects should contain specific plans for conservation, preservation, and publication from the very outset, and funds should be secured for such purposes.

II. RESPONSIBILITIES TO THE PUBLIC

Because the archaeological record represents the heritage of all people, it is the responsibility of professional archaeologists to communicate with the general public about the nature of archaeological research and the importance of archaeological resources. Archaeologists also have specific responsibilities to the local communities where they carry out research and field work, as well as to their home institutions and communities.

Archaeologists should be sensitive to cultural mores and attitudes, and be aware of the impact research and field work may have on a local population, both during and after the work. Such considerations should be taken into account in designing the project's strategy.

1. Professional archaeologists should be actively engaged in public outreach through lecturing, popular writing, school programs, and other educational initiatives.
2. Plans for field work should consider the ecological impact of the project and its overall impact on the local communities.
3. Professional archaeologists should not participate in projects whose primary goal is private gain.

4. For field projects, archaeologists should consult with appropriate representatives of the local community during the planning stage, invite local participation in the project, and regularly inform the local community about the results of the research.

5. Archaeologists should respect the cultural norms and dignity of local inhabitants in areas where archaeological research is carried out.

6. The legitimate concerns of people who claim descent from, or some other connection with, cultures of the past must be balanced against the scholarly integrity of the discipline. A mutually acceptable accommodation should be sought.

III. RESPONSIBILITIES TO COLLEAGUES

Professional archaeologists owe consideration to colleagues, striving at all times to be fair, never plagiarize, and give credit where due.

1. Archaeologists involved in cooperative projects should strive for harmony and fairness; those in positions of authority should behave with consideration toward those under their authority, while all team members should strive to promote the success of the broader undertaking.

2. The principal investigators of archaeological projects should maintain acceptable standards of safety and ascertain that staff members are adequately insured.

3. Professional archaeologists should maintain confidentiality of information gleaned in reviewing grant proposals and other such privileged sources.

4. Professional archaeologists should not practice discrimination or harassment based on sex, religion, age, race, national origin, disability, or sexual orientation; project sponsors should establish the means to eliminate and/or investigate complaints of discrimination or harassment.

5. Archaeologists should honor reasonable requests from colleagues for access to materials and records, preserving existing rights to publication, but sharing information useful for the research of others. Scholars seeking access to unpublished information should not expect to receive interpretive information if that is also unpublished and in progress.

6. Before studying and/or publishing any unpublished material archaeologists should secure proper permission, normally in writing, from the appropriate project director or the appointed representative of the sponsoring institution and/or the antiquities authorities in the country of origin.

7. Scholars studying material from a particular site should keep the project director informed of their progress and intentions; project directors should return the courtesy.

8. Members of cooperative projects should prepare and evaluate reports in a timely and collegial fashion.

SOCIETY FOR AMERICAN ARCHAEOLOGY
PRINCIPLES OF ARCHAEOLOGICAL ETHICS
SAA ETHICS IN ARCHAEOLOGY COMMITTEE
(1995)

Principle No. 1:
Stewardship
The archaeological record, that is, in situ archaeological material and sites, archaeological collections, records, and reports, is a public trust. The use of the archaeological record should be for the benefit of all people. As part of the important record of the human cultural past, archaeological materials are not commodities to be exploited for personal enjoyment or profit. It is the responsibility of all archaeologists to work for the long-term preservation and protection of the archaeological record. Although archaeologists rarely have legal ownership of archaeological resources, they should practice and promote stewardship of the archaeological record. Stewards are both caretakers and advocates for the archaeological record. As they investigate and interpret the record, archaeologists should also promote its long-term conservation. Archaeologists should use their specialized knowledge to promote public understanding and support for the long-term preservation of the archaeological record.

Principle No. 2:
Accountability
Responsible archaeological research, including all levels of professional activities, requires an acknowledgment of public accountability and a commitment by the archaeologist to make every reasonable effort, in good faith, to consult actively with affected group(s), with the goal of establishing a working relationship that can be beneficial to the discipline and to all parties involved.

Principle No. 3:
Commercialization
The Society for American Archaeology has recognized that the buying and selling of objects out of archaeological context is contributing to the destruction of the archaeological record on the American continents and around the world. Commercialization of objects from the archaeological record results in these objects being unscientifically removed from sites, destroying contextual information that is essential to understanding archaeological resources. Archaeologists should abstain from any activity that enhances the commercial value of archaeological objects not curated in public institutions, or readily available for scientific study, public interpretation, and display.

Principle No. 4:
Public Education and Outreach
Archaeologists shall reach out to the public to: (1) enlist its support for the stewardship of the archaeological record, (2) explain and promote the use of methods and techniques of archaeology in understanding human behavior and culture, and (3)

explain archaeological interpretations of the past. A variety of audiences exist for these education and outreach efforts, including students, teachers, lawmakers, Native Americans, government officials, environmentalists, service organizations, retirees, reporters, and journalists. Archaeologists who are unable to undertake public education and outreach directly shall encourage and support the efforts of others in these activities. Archaeologists should participate in cooperative efforts with others interested in the archaeological record so that preservation, protection, and interpretation of the record may be improved.

Principle No. 5:
Intellectual Property

Intellectual property, as contained in knowledge and documents created through the study of archaeological resources, is part of the archaeological record and, therefore, is held in stewardship rather than as a matter of personal possession. If there is a compelling reason, and no legal restrictions, a researcher may have exclusive access to original materials and documents for a limited and reasonable time, after which these materials and documents must be made available to others. Knowledge must be made available, by publication or otherwise, within a reasonable time and documents deposited in a suitable place for permanent safekeeping. The preservation and protection of in situ archaeological sites must be considered in the publication or distribution of information about them.

Principle No. 6:
Records and Preservation

Archaeologists shall work actively for the preservation of, and long-term access to, archaeological collections, records, and reports. Archaeologists shall also promote actions by others that lead to these ends. Archaeologists shall encourage colleagues, students, and others to make responsible use of collections, records, and reports in their research as one means of preserving the in situ archaeological record, and of providing more attention and care to the portion of the archaeological record that has been removed and incorporated into archaeological collections, records, and reports.

APPENDIX B
RESOURCE GUIDE

Publications related to archaeological ethics are increasingly common in both the popular and scholarly media, but finding them can present a challenge to the newcomer. Some suggestions for pursuing questions raised by specific articles in this collection follow individual articles. This section provides additional suggestions for getting started on research in the general field. It has three sections:

1. *Basic Bibliography*—significant publications related to the subject, each of which provides extensive additional readings.

2. *Finding and Using Government Documents and Legal Citations*—suggestions for finding (a) U.S. government documents, (b) international documents, (c) legal citations, (d) titles of and additional sources for major U.S. legislation, and (e) international agreements relating to the cultural heritage.

3. *Periodicals*—listing of (a) major periodicals that frequently publish on related issues, and where to find them, and (b) the relevant publication policies of archaeological journals.

BASIC BIBLIOGRAPHY

Bator, Paul M. *The International Trade in Art.* Chicago and London: The University of Chicago Press, 1983.

Cleere, Henry, ed. *Archaeological Heritage Management in the Modern World.* One World Archaeology, Vol. 9. Cambridge: Cambridge University Press, 1992.

Coggins, Clemency. "Illicit Traffic of Pre-Columbian Antiquities," *Art Journal* (Fall 1969): 94–98.

Gerstenblith, Patty. "Identity and Cultural Property: The Protection of Cultural Property in the United States," *Boston University Law Review* 75, no. 3 (1995): 559–688.

Green, Ernestene L., ed. *Ethics and Values in Archaeology.* New York: The Free Press, 1984.

Hutt, Sherry, Elwood Jones, and Martin McAllister. *Archaeological Resource Protection.* Washington D.C.: Preservation Press, 1992.

King, Thomas F., Patricia Parker Hickman, and Gary Berg, eds. *Anthropology in Historic Preservation: Caring for Culture's Clutter.* New York: Academic Press, 1977. (Note: Appendix A, pp. 197–302, includes the texts of U.S. "Statutes, Procedures, and Associated Memoranda" from 1906 through 1977.)

Layton, Robert, ed. *Who Needs the Past? Indigenous Values and Archaeology.* One World Archaeology, Vol. 5. London: Unwin Hyman, 1989.

Lynott, Mark J. and Alison Wylie, eds. *Ethics in American Archaeology: Challenges for the 1990s.* Washington, D.C.: SAA Special Report, 1995.

McBryde, Isabel, ed. *Who Owns the Past?* Papers from the Annual Symposium of the Australian Academy of the Humanities. Melbourne: Oxford University Press, 1985.

Messenger, Phyllis Mauch, ed. *The Ethics of Collecting Cultural Property. Whose Culture? Whose Property?* Albuquerque: University of New Mexico Press, 1989.

Meyer, Karl E. *The Plundered Past: The Traffic in Art Treasures.* New York: Atheneum, 1973.

On Being a Scientist: Responsible Conduct in Research, Second Edition. Committee on Science, Engineering, and Public Policy, National Academy of Sciences, National Academy of Engineering, Institute of Medicine. Washington, D.C.: National Academy Press, 1995. (Copies available from: National Academy Press, 2101 Constitution Avenue, N.W., Washington, D.C. 20418, at $5.00 for single copies, $4.00 for 2–9 copies, and $2.50 for 10 or more. The report is also available on the National Academy of Science's Internet host. It may be accessed via WorldWideWeb at http://www.nas.edu, via Gopher at gopher.nas.edu, or via FTP at ftp.nas.edu).

Silverman, Sydel and Nancy J. Parezo, eds. *Preserving the Anthropological Record.* New York: The Wenner-Gren Foundation for Anthropological Research, 1992. (Their address is 220 Fifth Ave., New York, NY 10001.)

Smith, G. S. and J. E. Ehrenhard, eds. *Protecting the Past.* Ann Arbor: CRC Press, 1991.

Tubb, Katherine Walker, ed. *Antiquities: Trade or Betrayed: Legal, Ethical and Conservation Issues.* London: Archetype Books, 1995.

Woodall, J. Ned, ed. *Predicaments, Pragmatics, and Professionalism: Ethical Conduct in Archaeology.* Special Publication Number 1. Society of Professional Archaeologists, 1990. (Available from SOPA).

FINDING AND USING GOVERNMENT DOCUMENTS AND LEGAL CITATIONS

(a) U.S. Government Documents

Most major libraries have a Government Documents section and a librarian specially trained to help you track down and use the materials. Seek the help of those librarians. Traditional library cataloguing does not catch lots of documents, and you may emerge from a search of traditional (or on-line) catalogue files thinking your library has nothing relevant to the topic. Government documents receive extensive indexing, and even if your local library is not a repository for the specific items you need, the documents librarian can help you find them, probably somewhere nearby.

Major academic libraries will have access to the *Congressional Information Service* (CIS), which is issued every month and includes extensive indexing and abstracts of all federal legislation and hearings. The CIS also includes the numbers used to track down copies of actual texts of enacted legislation. It is a gold mine of information. An excellent way to explore the variety of issues and viewpoints behind any piece of U.S. cultural property legislation is to look at the transcripts of the testimony presented at the hearings, including statements made at the hearings and the letters written on all sides of the issues.

The *Federal Register* is published daily (in hard copy and on the Internet at http://www.access.gpo.gov/su-docs/) and includes proposed and final federal regulations, but not actual legislation. The *Code of Federal Regulations* (CFR) houses the collection of permanent regulations of the federal government.

(b) International Documents

International documents are a bit harder to acquire. The U.S. Department of State publishes an annual edition of *Treaties in Force: A List of Treaties and Other International Agreements of the United States in Force on* [month, day, year]. Any treaty that involves more than two parties is probably registered with the United Nations, but there are relatively few UN depository libraries, and it may take perseverance to get access to UN and other international documents. The **Council of Europe Publications** sales agent in the United States and Canada is Manhattan Publishing Company, 1 Croton Point Avenue, P.O. Box 650, Croton, NY 10520. The European Union maintains an office in Washington, D.C., and the staff there can provide some assistance in tracking down information on the Union.

The on-line cumulative indexing of international documents is still in its early stages. U.S. government indexing is available on-line from about 1976 on. For work with older material, you need to use the traditional paper documents and sources.

(c) Legal Citations

Patty Gerstenblith, a legal scholar who also has a Ph.D. in archaeology, describes the process of pursuing legal citations as follows:

Most legal research is now done on-line. Electronic databases include all U.S. law, and varying amounts of published legal decisions going back to ca. 1980 and earlier, for the more important courts such as the Supreme Court. These databases also contain many of the legal articles published in law reviews, as well as all statutes, most treaties, and international materials. One can search by phrase, such as "archaeology and culture," and retrieve all documents that contain the phrase. Unfortunately, unless you are a lawyer or a law student, it is difficult (and expensive) to get access to these databases, and you still need to learn how to use them.

There is also the old-fashioned method: all statutes for both the U.S. government and the states (by state) are published. Cases are published in federal reporters (for federal cases), which are separated by district court (trial level), the courts of appeal, and Supreme Court, into separate series, called, respectively, F. Supp., F., F.2d, and F.3d, and U.S. Most states publish their own decisions, at least for the state supreme court, and if there is one, the intermediate appellate court, in state reporters by state, and in regional reporters. Trial court decisions from states are not generally published. Citations include a combination of volume number, reporter abbreviation, date, court abbreviation, and page number.

Citations for all legal sources are regulated by an esoteric system called the "Blue Book," published by the University of Chicago Law School. It drives everyone nuts. Once you've gotten a citation, you have to know the system to find anything else. By the time you've more or less figured it out (no one entirely understands it), you've finished the first year of law school (pers. comm. 2/2/96).

As with using government documents, if you plan to do extensive work with legal documents, we recommend you befriend a legal librarian or a law student. Fortunately, many of the major documents of concern to archaeologists have been reprinted in accessible archaeological publications.

Some of the major documents related to archaeological cultural property and mentioned in articles in this collection are listed in the next section.

(d) Major U.S. Legislation on the Cultural Heritage

Antiquities Act of 1906. An Act for the Preservation of American Antiquities. Text in Meyer 1973: 269–70 (Appendix E). Also in King, et al., eds., Appendix A.

16 U.S.C. 460 (1974) **Archaeological and Historic Preservation Act** of 1974. Ask your government documents librarian to help find a copy.

16 U.S.C. 470aa-II (1979) **Archaeological Resources Protection Act** of 1979(ARPA). Ask your government documents librarian to help find a copy.

43 U.S.C. 2102 (1987) **Federal Abandoned Shipwreck Act (1987).** The text and excerpts of hearings on H.R. 132, an early version of what eventually became law, is printed in *Journal of Field Archaeology* 10 (1983): 105–6. *Journal of Field Archaeology* 10 (1983): 489–90 includes the text of H.R. 69, a modified version of H.R. 132, intended to meet the objections raised in the earlier hearings. *Journal of Field Archaeology* 11(1984): 79–96 provides a comprehensive, although edited, account of testimony given at hearings in both houses on H.R. 69.

16 U.S.C. 470 (1966) **National Historic Preservation Act** of 1966. Ask your government documents librarian to help find a copy.

Native American Graves Protection and Repatriation Act (NAGPRA). Public Law 101–601. (November 16, 1990), 25 U.S.C. para. 3001 et. seq. The text is published, along with the current Draft Regulations (from the *Federal Register*, Friday, May 28, 1993), in Agnes Tabah, *Native American Collections and Repatriation*. Technical Information Service's *Forum*. Occasional Papers on Museum Issues and Standards, June 1993. American Association of Museums, 1225 Eye Street, N.W., Washington, D.C. 20005 (phone: (202) 289-1818.) The final rule implementing NAGPRA and establishing procedures for determining disposition of, and repatriating, covered materials was published in the *Federal Register* on December 4, 1995, and is available on the National Archeological Data Base at http://www.cast.uark.edu/products/NADB/. The extensive preamble to the final rule addresses substantive comments received during the comment period that followed publication of the initial proposal in the *Federal Register* on May 28, 1993.

(e) International Agreements on the Cultural Heritage

The International Council on Monuments and Sites (ICOMOS), and their International Committee on Archaeological Heritage Management (ICAHM). See Ricardo J. Elia, "Icomos Adopts Archaeological Heritage Charter: Text and Commentary," *Journal of Field Archaeology* 20(1993): 97–104.

European Convention on the Protection of the Archaeological Heritage (revised). Valletta 16.1.1992. European Treaty Series 143. Council of Europe, and 3rd European Conference of Ministers responsible for the cultural heritage. Malta, 16–17 January 1992. European Convention on the Protection of the Archaeological Heritage (revised). Explanatory Report. Provisional Edition. Council of Europe. The elimination of economic borders and customs within the European Union is creating difficult and fascinating problems for cultural property.

Executive Agreement Between the Republic of Peru and the United States of America for the Recovery and Return of Stolen Archaeological, Historical and Cultural Properties, signed Sept. 14, 1981. The text is reprinted in *Journal of Field Archaeology* 9 (1982): 124–25.

Convention for the Protection of Cultural Property in the Event of Armed Conflict (the **Hague Convention**), with Regulations for the Execution of the Convention, as well as the Protocol to the Convention and the Conference Resolution. Adopted at The Hague, on May 14, 1954, by an International Conference of States convened by UNESCO. Ask your government documents librarian to help find a copy.

Law on Importation of Pre-Columbian Sculpture and Murals (1972). Meyer (1973): 274–78: Analysis of the bill by Wilbur Mills, but no text is included. Ask your government documents librarian to help find a copy.

Treaty of Cooperation Between the United States and Mexico Providing for the Recovery and Return of Stolen Archaeological, Historical and Cultural Properties. Entered into Force March, 1971. Text in Meyer (1973): 271–73 (Appendix E).

The UNESCO Convention (1970). Convention on the Means of Prohibiting and Preventing the Illicit Import, Export and Transfer of Ownership of Cultural Property. The text is reprinted in *Journal of Field Archaeology* 3 (1976): 217–20. The same issue of *Journal of Field Archaeology* includes an early draft of the U.S. implementing legislation (pp. 214–17); the text of the UNESCO Convention for the Protection of the World Cultural and Natural Heritage (pp. 220–24); and instructions for obtaining copies of various countries' antiquities laws from the UNESCO-ICOM Documentation Center (p. 225). The text of the UNESCO Convention is also reproduced in Meyer (1973): 291–301, together with President Nixon's "Message of Transmittal" of the Convention to the U.S. Senate (pp. 279–80), and the State Department Summary of the Convention (pp. 281–91).

U.S. Cultural Property Implementation Act. The U.S. law that implements the UNESCO Convention in this country is Public Law 97-446: Title III—Implementation of Convention on Cultural Property. The text, signed into law on January 11, 1983, is published in *Journal of Field Archaeology* 10 (1983): 351–60. Many issues of the *Journal of Field Archaeology* from 1976 through 1983 include, in the "Antiquities Market" section, some discussion of UNESCO and the process of U.S. implementation. *Looting, Theft and Smuggling: A Report to the President and the Congress.* The Cultural Property Advisory Committee, 1983–1993, U.S. Information Agency, Washington, D.C. is the 10-year progress report of CPAC, the committee created by the Cultural Property Act.

The UNIDROIT Convention on Stolen or Illegally Exported Cultural Objects. The International Institute for the Unification of Private Law, Committee of Governmental Experts on the International Protection of Cultural Property. The final version was signed in Rome on June 25, 1995. The text will be published, with commentary by John Merryman, early in 1996 in the *International Journal of Cultural Property,* and in the *Journal of Field Archaeology,* with comments by Patty Gerstenblith.

PERIODICALS

(a) Major Periodicals Featuring Cultural Heritage Issues

American Antiquity. Published by the Society for American Archaeology. Subscriptions: by membership in the society.

Antiquity. Published by Antiquity Publications Ltd., 85 Hills Road, Cambridge CB2 1PG, England. Subscriptions: Oxford Journals, Oxford University Press, Walton Street, Oxford OX2 6DP, England. Fax: 1 (865) 267-773.

Journal of European Archaeology. Published by the European Association of Archaeologists, EAA Secretariat, c/o Riksantikvaren, Postboks 8196 Dep., N-0034, Oslo, Norway. Fax:+44-2294-0404. See: Henry Cleere, "The European Association of Archaeologists," *Journal of Field Archaeology* 22 (1995): 253 for information about this relatively new society and its journal.

International Journal of Cultural Property. Published for the International Cultural Property Society. Subscription information from Walter de Gruyter & Co., Postfach 30 34 21 D-10728, Berlin, Fax: 30-26005-251. Editorial policy: "The Journal is an organ of communication among people throughout the world who are interested in questions of cultural property policy, ethics, economics, and law. In addition to referred articles, it publishes documents, judicial decisions, correspondence, bibliography, and information about meetings and events. Its pages are open to all responsibly held and courteously presented points of view."

The Art Newspaper. Published monthly, except August. The international edition of *Il Giornale dell 'Arte*, 8 via Mancini, 10131 Torino, Italy. U.S. subscriptions: $69 from P.O. Box 3000, Denville, NJ 007834-9776. Fax: (201) 627-5872. Provides frequent articles and news accounts related to ancient art and antiquities.

ARCHAEOLOGICAL ETHICS

The Journal of Field Archaeology. Published by Boston University, 675 Common-wealth Ave., Boston MA 02215. Publishes regular features on the antiquities market and other public issues in archaeology.

Public Archaeology Review. Published by the Center for Archaeology in the Public Interest, Dept. of Anthropology, 425 University Blvd., IUPUI, Indianapolis, IN 46202-5140. Fax: (317) 274-2347. *PAR* "provides a forum for discussing the interface between archaeologists and the people who are affected when archaeology is done."

The popular publications, *National Geographic, Smithsonian, Vanity Fair,* and *Connoisseur* often have articles of relevance to the international art market in antiquities.

(b) Publication Policies of Professional Journals

The *American Journal of Archaeology* presents its policy on publishing undocumented antiquities on the reverse of each issue's title page: "*AJA* will not serve for the announcement or initial scholarly presentation of any object in a private or public collection acquired after December 30, 1973, unless the object was part of a previously existing collection or has been legally exported from the country of origin (see *AJA* 94 [1990]: 525–27)."

The 1990 reference fills in the background of this policy, quoting the AIA Council's 1970 resolution in support of the UNESCO Convention; two 1973 Council resolutions, one calling on museums to refuse to collect materials exported in violation of their country of origin's export laws; the other refusing to allow presentation at the Institute's Annual Meetings of papers that serve for the announcement or initial scholarly presentation of objects in conflict with the 1970 resolution.

"*Latin American Antiquity* will not knowingly publish articles that rely on archaeological, ethnographic, or historic objects that have been exported in violation of the national laws of their country of origin, or that have been recovered in such a manner as to cause unscientific or intentional destruction of sites or monuments." This policy now applies also to *American Antiquity.*

See also: Alison Wylie, "Archaeology and the Antiquities Market: The Use of 'Looted' Data," pp. 17–21; and Christopher Chippindale and David M. Pendergast, "Intellectual Property: Ethics, Knowledge, and Publication," pp. 45–49 in *Ethics in American Archaeology: Challenges for the 1990s,* eds. Mark J. Lynott and Alison Wylie (Washington, D.C.: SAA Special Report, 1995).